The

EVERYTHING®
Guide to Writing a Novel

Dear Reader:

We began this book because so many people ask us about different elements of novel writing. In every workshop we give, there are different questions that all deserve good answers. We've collected a great deal of knowledge through the course of writing more than forty books. The problem was finding a way to put all of those answers together.

There are plenty of workshops and seminars for writers that break down many of the answers. But small chunks of information gathered from hundreds of different sources are sometimes confusing and difficult to remember. We wanted to put as much as we could in one place.

We hope the information contained here will be easy to use. Writing and publishing can be a strange and mysterious world. Our goal here was to take away some of the mystery with clean, straightforward answers. Hopefully, we've accomplished some part of de-mystifying the process for everyone who reads this book.

Joyce and Jim Lavene

Welcome to the EVERYTHING Series!

These handy, accessible books give you all you need to tackle a difficult project, gain a new hobby, comprehend a fascinating topic, prepare for an exam, or even brush up on something you learned back in school but have since forgotten.

You can choose to read an *Everything*® book from cover to cover or just pick out the information you want from our four useful boxes: e-questions, e-facts, e-alerts, and e-ssentials.

We give you everything you need to know on the subject, but throw in a lot of fun stuff along the way, too.

We now have more than 400 *Everything*® books in print, spanning such wide-ranging categories as weddings, pregnancy, cooking, music instruction, foreign language, crafts, pets, New Age, and so much more. When you're done reading them all, you can finally say you know *Everything*®!

QUESTIONS?
Answers to
common questions

FACTS
Important snippets
of information

ALERTS!
Urgent
warnings

Quick
handy tips

PUBLISHER Karen Cooper

DIRECTOR OF ACQUISITIONS AND INNOVATION Paula Munier

MANAGING EDITOR, EVERYTHING SERIES Lisa Laing

COPY CHIEF Casey Ebert

ACQUISITIONS EDITOR Lisa Laing

DEVELOPMENT EDITOR Elizabeth Kassab

EDITORIAL ASSISTANT Hillary Thompson

Visit the entire Everything® series at *www.everything.com*

THE
EVERYTHING®
GUIDE TO
WRITING A NOVEL

From completing the first draft
to landing a book contract—
all you need to fulfill your dreams

Joyce and Jim Lavene

Adams Media
Avon, Massachusetts

For Sandi Starrette; a great writer, artist, and friend.

An Everything® Series Book.
Everything® and everything.com® are registered trademarks of F+W Media, Inc.

Published by Adams Media, a divsion of F+W Media, Inc.
57 Littlefield Street, Avon, MA 02322 U.S.A.
www.adamsmedia.com

ISBN 10: 1-59337-132-2
ISBN 13: 978-1-59337-132-6
Printed in the United States of America.

10   9   8   7   6

Library of Congress Cataloging-in-Publication Data
Lavene, Joyce.
The everything guide to writing a novel / Joyce and Jim Lavene.
p.   cm.
(An everything series book)
ISBN 1-59337-132-2
1. Fiction–Authorship. I. Lavene, James. II. Title. III. Series.
PN3365 .L38   2004
808.3–dc22   2004005403

This book is available at quantity discounts for bulk purchases.
For information, call 1-800-289-0963.

Contents

Acknowledgments

Our appreciation to our agent, Jacky Sach, whose help and guidance were essential in creating this work; our editor, Kate Burgo, without whose helpful suggestions we would have been lost; and the wonderful writers who paved the way for today's authors with their timeless works of novel-length fiction.

Top Ten Reasons
to Write a Novel

1. You have a story to tell. You have to write it or you just might explode.

2. You have a passion for words and you love to write.

3. You've experienced something you feel the world should know.

4. You're dissatisfied with the books you read. You believe you can write better.

5. The story you want to tell is too detailed and involved to fit into a short-story format.

6. You want to have the satisfaction of knowing you've completed a manuscript.

7. You want to try your hand at getting a novel published.

8. You're looking for a career that you never have to retire from.

9. You're looking for a career that can travel with you, no matter where you go.

10. You want to see if you can capture a piece of the fame, wealth, and glory that a successful novelist can enjoy.

Introduction

▶WHEN THE FIRST NOVEL WRITER sat down with his parchment and a quill in hand, the entire world shifted. It was 1605. Miguel de Cervantes had written *Don Quixote*. Nothing would ever be the same again.

In the seventeenth century, epic poems and lengthy short stories were already in vogue. There were plays and sonnets galore. But no one knew what to expect from this new art form. What could a longer, more complex story offer a reader?

As it turns out, novels have offered millions of readers around the world a means of escape from their familiar, sometimes humdrum lives. Even though over 100 years passed before the next great literary novel would appear, the concept eventually flourished. Writers like Daniel Defoe, Jonathan Swift, and Henry Fielding kept scribbling away, creating works like *Robinson Crusoe* (1719), *Gulliver's Travels* (1726), and *Tom Jones* (1749). Imaginations took flight and publishers soon learned there was money to be made from the prose of these talented masters.

Readers have gone to the ends of the earth with daring explorers like Phineas T. Fogg and Allan Quartermaine. They have witnessed the colonizing of Mars before it ever seemed technologically possible. A reader was onboard the first manned space station years before the human race ever went into space. Readers have fought in the foxholes with soldiers and have been present at the coronation of kings—and all without leaving the comfort of their armchairs.

Millions of novels have been published since the idea for one first crossed a writer's mind. Thousands of writers have made their mark on the wall of literature. Many of them spend their entire lives working on their masterpieces. Many more don't get started until they're past the responsibilities of family and job. Other writers of all ages give up before they ever see the end of their first novel.

This is understandable: Writing isn't always easy. Long hours in a solitary dream world can wreak havoc on a person's life. Creating just the right form, character, and plot can be as hard as trekking up the side of a mountain. But like any other good climb, it's the view from the summit that takes your breath away. When you've seen the sun rise at the top of the world, nothing else will do. There is an unbelievable exhilaration that accompanies the completion of every new book.

In essence, novel writers have the power to give birth to people, worlds, and ideas. They can ask the most daring questions and propose the unthinkable. Novel writers make all of us take a hard look at who we are and the stuff we're made of. They challenge the bounds of society and the boundaries of the imagination. Novels stretch our minds and quicken our pulses.

Looking back at Jules Verne's submarines and E. E. 'Doc' Smith's Skylark and Lensman space sagas, the question comes to mind, Did the art of novel writing create the reality that we know today? If so, what are today's novelists forecasting and creating for our future? Mary Shelley's *Frankenstein* seemed farfetched almost 200 years ago, but it's not so impossible today. How far away are we from Michael Crichton's *Jurassic Park*? As a novelist, you'll have the power to create entire worlds or change the thoughts of thousands of people. As clichéd as it sounds, the pen is mightier than the sword. Something that you have to say could affect how people view the world in another generation. Ⓔ

Chapter 1
Novel Writing

Novels have taken readers to the jungles of Africa with Tarzan and to living on the planet Pern with dragons. They have illuminated minds and evoked visions of terror. A good novel can quicken the pulse or get a chuckle. Where would we be without Captain Nemo or Peter Pan? Novels are book-length works that have changed over the years but continue to entertain, mystify, and inspire their readers.

History of the Genre

Most scholars consider *Don Quixote,* written by Miguel de Cervantes in seventeenth-century Spain, as the first modern novel. *Don Quixote* follows the exploits of an old man who envisions himself as a knight errant fighting dragons and rescuing damsels in distress. *Robinson Crusoe,* written by Daniel Defoe in 1719, is considered by many to be the first novel in English. Prior to these books, there were lengthy epic poems and short stories.

The sixteenth century was just the beginning. It wasn't until the nineteenth century that the ability to print many books cheaply expanded the genre to the popular market.

The Pulp Novels

The birth of mass-market paperbacks is attributed to American publisher Beadle and Adams. In July of 1860, the company released *Malaeska,* a romance novel that sold for one-tenth of the price of other books—all it cost was a dime! Dime novels, as they became known, were 4½ by 6⅝ inches. They were made from less-expensive paper than their more refined counterparts and were cheaply bound. They were also enormously popular. With the advent of dime novels came the first attempts at marketing books to draw in potential readers, such as through the creation of colorful covers.

The late 1800s and early 1900s were the heyday of the pulp paperback. Writers like H. G. Wells, Jules Verne, William (Buffalo Bill) Cody, and Ann Stephens began their careers in this new format. Stories of heroes, mystery, science fiction, and romance began appearing around the world. No one had ever seen anything like them. Ellery Queen, Sam Spade, and John Carter of Mars were born between the pages of these "trashy" fiction novels.

Novel Genres Today

The early novel genres like mystery, romance, adventure, and science fiction are still striving and serve as the basis for all novel writing today. All those heroes and heroines who astounded and surprised readers years ago are still around. Plot lines may be a little more complex but the basic story at their heart remains the same. Heroes like James Bond continue to save the world, and villains like Hannibal Lector continue to threaten them. Men and women still fall in love and get their hearts broken. Wonderful places on distant planets continue to appear on the horizon. For all of the changes that novels have gone through, they remain very much the same as those from 200 years ago.

From Leather-Bound Tomes to E-Books

Many things have changed since the first novel was published. The size and shape of the novel has gone through many incarnations. Leather-bound books became hardbacks that in turn became paperbacks. Today, a book may be published in one of the following formats:

- **Hardbacks:** This format is the top of the line and a goal of many writers. The price of the hardbacks puts them out of the reach of most publishers, unless the author is well known or the publisher specializes in a hardback market, like library sales.
- **Mass-market paperbacks:** These are the smaller paperback novels that have been popular since the 1930s. Mass-market paperbacks are cheaper, easier to carry, and more likely to be on bookstore shelves.
- **Trade paperbacks:** These are larger paperbacks, as expensive to buy as most hardbacks, but easier to produce than mass-market traditional paperbacks. Trade paperbacks have recently become the darlings of small presses.
- **Electronic books (E-books):** The new kids on the block—electronic books are sent from computer to computer or E-book reader, and they are rarely seen in print. They are simple to produce and cost-effective because there's no paper involved. E-books are growing in

popularity, especially with travelers and teenagers. They're usually much less expensive than a traditional print novel.

- **Audio books:** Once used by the blind, books on tape and CD are popular among busy "readers" who listen to them on the go.

Electronic and audio books both call for special formatting of the manuscript. Writers need to be aware of which publishers are involved in working in these formats and how to prepare and submit these works for publication.

Changes in the Publishing Industry

Publishers have changed too. Many small publishers with one or two authors have merged into megaconglomerates that support hundreds of authors. Sales are so important that the novelists must be involved in selling their books. Writers must worry more about the "hook" that will keep the reader going than the beautiful scenery or back-story that would have been included in a Victorian novel. The dime novels of yesterday are now $10 and $20 apiece. Publishers carefully orchestrate their promotion and marketing. Book covers are competitive, vying for space and attention on crowded store shelves.

What Stayed the Same

Despite all the changes, there's one thing that has stayed the same—to be successful, a novel must be a great story. No one can argue with a wonderful tale, masterfully told. Ask any agent or editor and they'll say the same thing. They're looking for the stories that thrill them, scare them, or make them believe in love again. That single fact hasn't changed since *Don Quixote* was published. Readers still want to be entertained. And if the writer manages to educate or challenge the readers at the same time, so much the better.

Novelists Yesterday and Today

Throughout time, fortune and fame smiled on many novelists. In the nineteenth century, they were celebrated and copied, and some even had statues built of them. Edgar Rice Burroughs's Tarzan novels, wildly popular in his own time, are still made into movies today. Sir Arthur Conan Doyle was mobbed whenever he appeared in public.

On the other end of the spectrum were authors like Robert E. Howard, who committed suicide before his Conan the Barbarian novels became popular. Many other writers achieved literary heights after their deaths. No doubt, countless more wrote in obscurity and we will never know their works or their names.

Many female authors like sci-fi writer Andre Norton (Alice Mary Norton) and George Eliot (Mary Ann Evans) chose male pseudonyms. Only since the 1960s has it become "acceptable" for women to write in genres other than romance.

Even today, authors write under pseudonyms for various reasons. Several male romance writers write under female names—Harold Lowry writes under the pseudonym Leigh Greenwood. Many times, two people writing together will publish under a single name. For example, John Muncie and Jody Jaffe write together as John Jaffe.

Contemporary Novelists

Today, thousands of manuscripts cross an ever-shrinking number of editorial desks. The numbers of novels being sold is not diminishing, but corporate mergers have made the number of novel markets smaller. At the same time, there seems to be an ever-increasing group of people who want to write.

At one end of the novelist spectrum are the giants: Stephen King, Danielle Steele, and John Grisham. These writers churn out bestsellers year after year. In the middle are the authors who are not household names but manage to be no less viable: Leigh Greenwood, Jean Lorrah, and Kenneth

Flint. The last category includes hundreds of authors who are known only to a few readers: Mary Taffs, Daniel Bailey, and Richard Helms.

Despite dire predictions, the contemporary novel market is alive and well. J. K. Rowling's Harry Potter books have shown all writers the possibilities. She's proven that every major literary market is still open to a good story told in an engaging manner.

FACT

Book sales in the United States alone totaled over $26 billion in 2002. This represents a 5.5 percent increase in sales over the previous year. For the first time, these statistics included not only the traditional forms of publishing but also electronically published books.

What They Have in Common

In looking at profiles of the better-known novelists of yesterday, it's easy to see that they have a great deal in common with today's novelists. Beyond working hard to get their writing published, there are other characteristics that seem to define successful novelists:

- Focused enough to finish an entire book but restless and unhappy in other work
- Strongly creative, usually in more than one art form, despite childhood admonitions to be more practical
- Tend to have many different jobs in their lifetime. (Others interpret this as lack of commitment, but writers see it as research.)
- Have problems with being labeled "dreamers"
- Have a burning desire to tell a story and can see their story played out before them like a movie

As you may have noticed, these traits aren't always desirable, particularly outside of the writing world. In fact, they usually cause heartache and disappointment to the would-be writer.

There's a Novel in Everyone

Many readers finish a book and declare, "Anybody could write that!" The power of the imagination takes over and the important question—what if?—comes into play. This single question has spurred thousands of people to take inspiration from a novel they read, or from an incident that happened to them in their life, and turn it into a 100,000-word novel.

The Allure of the Craft

What is it about writing a novel that people find so attractive? It takes real effort to put together 100,000 words, whether it's on a word processor or an old-fashioned typewriter. Yet people have been writing novels for the past 400 years! In today's busy lifestyle, you'll find writers getting up at dawn or slouched over a keyboard at midnight. They'll mortgage their homes for a chance to meet with an editor. They get fired for working on their manuscript during work hours. The burning desire to create a literary masterpiece must rank high with other forms of madness.

Being a novelist comes with its own special charm. It's more than just the joy of seeing your name in print or the potential for appearing on *The Oprah Winfrey Show*. Writing a novel is a statement of accomplishment. It means that you are in the company of the masters. As you type away at your keyboard, Papa Hemingway is beside you pounding at his typewriter. The spirits of Victor Hugo and Mark Twain are smiling down at you.

When a writer types "The End" and holds a completed manuscript, it's nothing less than the birth of a child. Of course, there's always the possibility that your baby is going to be brilliant. The *New York Times* bestseller list is full of dreamers who were willing to work hard at their creations. But there are also lots of writers who have worked for years and never came closer to being published than a polite rejection. There is never any guarantee of success.

Finding Your Story

Whether your idea for a novel comes from real life or a good imagination, pulling all the pieces together to create a masterpiece requires initiative and commitment. One of the first things the writer must accomplish is making the story real to him or herself. Only then can the writer convince readers to suspend their disbelief and enter his or her fictional world.

Your story should haunt you. It should wake you in the morning and keep you up at night. It should make you wish you could quit your job just so that you could get the whole story out of your head. Finding an idea that has power over you creates its own magic. Once you find your story, the trick is to be able to tell it to everyone else in such a way that leaves them gasping for more.

ALERT!

Hundreds of would-be writers, desperate to get published, are taken in by scam artists every year. Look out for unscrupulous agents and publishers who promise to help you—for a fee. Always check credentials and never pay anything up-front unless you know what you're getting into.

The Realities of Being a Novelist

Jim Rohn, a motivational speaker, once said, "It takes what it takes." He was referring to finding the right place to live your life. For most writers, working at a manuscript is the right place to live their lives. It's a dream that can become reality, but not without some hard work.

Finding the Time

It takes a long time to write a novel. Everyone is different. Some writers are like Monet, able to finish a project quickly and easily. Some writers are like Michelangelo; it takes years to complete what others do in months. The one thing every novelist has to do is realize that writing 60,000 to 100,000 words is a difficult process. There is always something to be revised or edited. Telling a lengthy, complex tale requires time and patience.

The realization of what it takes to finish a novel is enough to dissuade many people from beginning to write one. If you can't imagine yourself sitting at a computer or word processor for extended periods of time, it might be better to contemplate another dream.

It Takes Commitment

Committing to any project is difficult, especially a project that requires learning a whole new skill set just to get started. Most beginning novelists have a family, work other jobs, and have many responsibilities. They have demanding spouses who don't understand their compulsion to write and well-meaning friends who remind them that they will probably never get published.

Putting your butt in the chair is what most struggling authors call commitment. It means finding time for character analysis and revamping your plot when you'd rather be at a ball game or shopping with friends. It can mean staying up late, getting up early on Sundays and holidays, or giving up afternoon naps.

There is also a financial commitment. A good writing course can cost anywhere from $100 to $1,000. Buying marketing books or attending marketing seminars can set you back $30 to $500. Sending out manuscripts to be critiqued or joining writing groups can get expensive. That's not to mention trying to get your work published. Starting a novel can be daunting if you truly realize what you're letting yourself in for. But the better prepared you are for the task, the better the chances are that you'll be able to complete it. Thousands of writers start writing a novel every day. Only a few finish.

Good Material

Is your story a novel? That's an important question to ask yourself. Do you have enough material to create 400 to 600 pages of text? Many would-be novelists find as they start writing that their novel is really only a short story. There is no hard and fast rule for trying to decide if you have a novel in you. But by taking the time to carefully examine what you want to write, you can save yourself the heartbreak of beginning a manuscript that is never completed.

Clubs and Organizations

Many writers find it useful and comforting to be part of a writing group. A group of sympathetic ears and hearts that are all going through the same thing can be a great motivation to keep going.

> Watch out for clubs, organizations, and societies that charge large amounts of money to join but offer nothing of real value in return. Know what benefit you're getting for your dollar.

ALERT!

Mystery Writers of America (MWA)

For mystery and suspense writers, that group is the Mystery Writers of America. It is a national group of about 3,500 writers, agents, and editors that has regional chapters. The group has programs and information useful to the aspiring mystery writer. Once a year MWA gives the Edgar Award to the best mystery novels, which are nominated by publishers. They have annual dues and a quarterly publication sent out to all members as well as insurance benefits and a fund set up to help struggling writers. Writers don't have to be published to join the group, but only published members are allowed to vote for officers and on other group issues.

Romance Writers of America (RWA)

The Romance Writers of America is an aggressive group dedicated to the romance genre. They are 8,000 strong in the United States and several other countries. Local chapters in many different cities hold monthly meetings.

At their annual convention, they give out awards for the best romance novels published that year (the RITA) and for the best unpublished work (the Golden Heart). RWA has many programs set up to help the aspiring romance writer, including critique groups, agent and editor meetings, and workshops on the craft of romance writing.

Writers don't need to be published to be a member of this group and all members are eligible to vote on group issues. They charge annual dues at both the local and national level. RWA sends out a monthly magazine and local chapters usually send out a newsletter.

Science Fiction and Fantasy Writers of America (SFWA)

The Science Fiction and Fantasy Writers of America is one of the oldest writing groups in the United States. SFWA is a national group that produces a quarterly newsletter for its members. There are no local groups, but SFWA has a great deal of useful information for writers, including the best reports on scams by disreputable agents and publishers. Writers must be published in book length or magazine sci-fi or fantasy to join the group. There is an annual fee to be a member.

Despite the wonderful camaraderie found in groups of writers, keep a close eye on your time. Too much time spent at groups talking about writing can deter or destroy your writing efforts.

Author's Guild

Probably the oldest generic author's group in the United States, the Author's Guild promotes its members through publications and their Web site. The group was founded in 1912 to fight for author's rights. The guild also helps with legal issues such as copyright infringement and plagiarism. You must be published in novel format by an established American publisher to join the guild. They charge yearly dues that include their publications. There are no meetings for this group.

Local Writer's Groups

Most big cities, small towns, and rural counties have local writer's groups. These groups support and help find ways to promote their members. Usually anyone with an active interest in writing is eligible to join. Activities include anthologies, participation in literacy campaigns, and just getting together to share one another's woes and successes. These organizations are usually a diverse group of writers. There are groups for every type of writer, from poets to novelists. The goal can be publication or fellowship.

These groups meet at libraries, art councils, and restaurants on a weekly or monthly basis. They are a good source of beginning networking for writers. One way to locate a writer's group near you is to go online to a local arts council or city/county government page. You can also find them listed in the arts/books section of your local paper.

Chapter 2

Defining the Novel

The novel is a work of fiction written to a certain length. There are quite a few novel genres, but the differences are minor, and quite a few "rules" apply to all novel formats. Publishers around the world generally acknowledge and expect to have these rules followed. Writers who want to be novelists should take heed and follow guidelines carefully. Even beyond editorial directions, readers have certain expectations. Part of the challenge of being a professional writer is to create a fictional world within these boundaries.

Fact Versus Fiction

There's a fine line between reporting the facts and creating fiction. Sometimes, this line tends to get a little smudged. It's easy to emboss fact with just a little fiction to keep it interesting. And it's equally easy to get caught up in the facts and forget that your work is supposed to entertain. The distinction between fact and fiction is there for a reason.

ALERT!

Spend enough time checking out a prospective publisher. Don't get involved with someone who is only trying to make money from writers unhappy with rejections. Understand the difference between paying a publisher to publish your book and a publisher paying you.

Journalism

It's important that fact is kept clear of embellishments. As a society, we depend heavily on our newspapers and other forms of nonfiction to keep us informed. Newspaper reporters and nonfiction book authors should get detailed accounts of every situation. Nothing should be left to the imagination or added on to make the truth easier to swallow. Every fact should be validated.

Fiction writing has no role in this media. All writers should understand the difference between creating a world and telling people about the real world. Reporters who manufacture stories from their own imaginations are not likely to be in this field for long. And novelists who only list the facts won't sell many books.

Fictional Accounts

Novel writers many times start with a grain of truth or even an entire real-life event and turn it into a fictional novel. It may be as simple as a nurse who witnesses a doctor being less than professional. Using her imagination, the nurse/writer begins to think about the rest of the doctor's life, or perhaps she extends his lack of regard for his patient into murder. Anything is possible. From the tiniest bit of reality, whole other worlds may be constructed. The writer can move away from any incident to go in any direction she chooses.

Some novelists have used real people as their characters and included accurate accounts of their lives. In most cases, this is a bad idea. Many writers have been sued despite the disclaimer at the beginning of every novel that says that all characters and events are fictional. If a book contains a story about your next-door neighbor murdering his wife and it has his real name, address, and other statistics, expect trouble. No one wants that kind of attention, even if the charge is false.

To avoid problems, convert fact into fiction. If someone takes you into his confidence about something that happened to him, you can write an entirely fictional account with different names and different locations. Being a successful novelist means having the ability to take real-life events and change them into exciting fiction.

Separating the Field

The writing world is full of rules and regulations. Many of these rules can be bent; some novelists even change grammar rules to suit their story. Nevertheless, many of the rules are so stringently followed, it's like they're engraved in stone.

Word Count and Number of Pages

Today's novel is classified by word count and the number of pages. Word count begins for most novelists at 50,000 words for a complete manuscript. Publishers and agents maintain that this is the bare minimum standard for works of novel length.

At the other extreme, most commercial manuscripts won't exceed 100,000 words without being broken up into more than one book. Some lengthy tomes can go as high as 150,000 words, such as Diana Gabaldon's time travel romances. But by today's standards, that would be a difficult length for the beginning novelist to sell. Since most novel writers are hoping to have their work published, it's best to keep your manuscript between 85,000 and 100,000 words. If you have a story that simply can't be told in less than 300,000 words, it would be better to consider it as a trilogy of books.

Most writers use the word-counting function located in the Tool section of their word-processing software program to keep track of how many words they've written. Some writers still use the old-fashioned method of counting their pages. Until the advent of personal computers, when novelists didn't have the luxury of a machine that counted the words for them, they estimated that the average typewritten page contains about 250 words with proper spacing and margins.

QUESTION?

What is the best word processor for writers?
Many writers prefer using a Macintosh computer over an IBM PC compatible. While the Mac users claim greater artistic flexibility PC users claim greater compatibility. In short, the best one is what works for you.

Novellas and Short Stories

By comparison, the smaller version of the novel is the novella or novelette. This format is frequently sold in pairs to make one book. Ace Publishing coined the phrase "Ace Doubles" for these books back in the 1960s. Harlequin Romances markets a pair of novellas as "Duets."

The novella contains all of the basics of the novel: plot, characters, dialogue, and setting, as well as a beginning, middle, and end. But its length is usually between 20,000 and 40,000 words. Some writers set out to create these mini-masterpieces, but many would-be novelists end up with a novella instead of a novel because of a lack of planning. There's a big difference between writing 20,000 words and 100,000 words!

By today's standards, some of the best-known authors of the pulp fiction novel era, such as Robert Heinlein, actually wrote novellas. Length requirements began to change in the late 1960s and early 1970s. As the price of novels began to climb, readers expected more for their money. The shorter novels became novellas and writers began to look for longer, more complicated plots and characters.

Anything below 20,000 words is usually classified as a short story. This format can go down as low as 100 words, known today as flash fiction. For the reader who doesn't have time for full-length novels, this is a way to get their fiction fix. Again, the short story has all the makings of its bigger brothers and sisters but without the fat. Short stories are frequently published in groups of anthologies, either by one author or multiple authors. They are the stuff of magazines and sometimes form the backbone of larger works, such as Anne McCaffrey's Dragon Rider series. Author Stephen King has had remarkable luck having the briefest of short stories made into complete movies. But the majority of short-story writers write for the pleasure of the experience rather than financial rewards.

Novelistic Genres

There are many Internet experts, books, and workshops set up to help the beginning novelist understand what a novel is and how to write one. One of the most important things any writer will ever learn is that professionalism is important. Go to any bookstore and pick up a copy of your favorite author's work. Compare it to any other author in the same field. Notice the similarities. These are your boundaries.

What Is a Genre?

This defining word for category fiction literature comes to us from the French. It is a hodgepodge of styles, which includes as many worlds as there are readers. As with every other aspect of writing, there are certain guidelines that make a book one of the many genre types of fiction. Each category—whether it's mystery, sci-fi, or romance—has its own rules.

Author E. D. Hirsch defines *genre* as a set of relationships: "The best way to define a genre—if one decides that he wants to—is to describe the common elements in a narrow group of texts which have direct historical relationships." That says it all.

Each genre has its own characteristics; for example, a traditional romance novel always has a happy ending. Different genres also have their own plot devices and elements that readers have come to expect. A good science fiction story must contain elements of understandable science even when they are strained to the ultimate limits of imagination.

Genres have become so diverse as to create subgenres within the market. In mystery, we've got the hard-boiled private eye stories of Mickey Spillane and the techno-thrillers of Tom Clancy. Every genre now has its own smaller niches that make up the bulk of what's written and published today.

Understanding these pockets and learning to write within them can be a daunting task for the beginning fiction writer. Yet, it's the key to becoming a successful author. Is your mystery novel a cozy or a police procedural? Is your sci-fi a space opera or is it psychological? Is your romance a contemporary or a paranormal? Or both? It's easy to get confused. A good look at the market and plenty of objective homework categorizing your novel should set you straight.

Some writers are rebels, defying classification with their work. Anne Rice's vampire novels are difficult to confine in one genre. Are they horror? Or are they romance? Readers have their own opinions. It's not against the rules to write a book in more than one genre, so long as you understand the combination.

FACT

The large writing groups such as Romance Writers of America and Mystery Writers of America maintain good information on understanding the various pockets in their genre. This information can be found both online and in their publications.

Mainstream Novels

Categorizing mainstream novels is harder than genre novels. Mainstream work can include everything from romance to sci-fi. It can be several different genres and subgenres all in one book. These works tend to be more eclectic, less simple to identify. They are the heart and soul of the publishing industry, while genre and nonfiction are the backbone.

So, what defines the mainstream novel and separates it from the genre novel? That can be a difficult question to answer. Sometimes the understanding lies more in what the mainstream novel lacks. For instance, *Message in a Bottle* by Nicholas Sparks is a romance that ends in tragedy—it's romantic fiction but it doesn't really fall within the romance genre. It doesn't follow the formula set out for romance novels because the boy doesn't get the girl.

There's a fine line between the two categories, but that's where the differences become apparent. Mainstream authors don't follow any rules beyond the basics of double spacing and using white paper. They are free to follow their instincts and truly write what their hearts dictate, without the comfort of being able to rely on a genre formula. This is why it's harder for mainstream authors to be successful. Sometimes the very nature of their work puts them outside established themes and pushes them into obscurity. For every author on the bestseller list, there are 100 authors whose books will barely be reviewed, and hundreds more whose work will never be published.

Telling the Story

The writer is the artist. He creates emotions and characters. He paints a background and introduces the reader to his world. Everything here begins in the mind and ends up on the paper. The reader becomes part of everything that's going on in the book. The reader can be a master spy or a lowlife scum. She can fall in love or find herself alone.

The Beginning

Everything has a starting point. It's where the fire begins and the river has its source. For writers, starting is the hardest part. Those first few words, sentences, and paragraphs will be written and rewritten during the course of the manuscript; then they'll be rethought and rewritten again when the manuscript is finished.

The first words of any manuscript are the most important. They set the mood and lure the reader into the story, making him want to know what happens next. If the beginning fails, the reader will put down the book and never read it again.

The beginning can be powerful, violent, or passionate. It can be subtle like a gathering storm. It can be dialogue or narrative. But however you choose to begin your story, it must be exceptional.

ESSENTIAL

One of the best ways to get a feel for what the beginning of a book should be like is to go to a bookstore and look at the books you think you would enjoy reading. Compare authors and see what qualities their beginnings share.

The Middle

While the beginning of the book must drag readers away from their everyday life, the middle must catch fire and hold them. It's not an easy task with so much competition for time and entertainment. The book that an author has pored over and rewritten a hundred times now faces its true test. Will it make the reader stay up late and shiver in the shadows around her? Will it transport the reader to an incredible world that she has never seen before? Can the reader imagine herself falling in love with the hero?

The main bulk of the text has to be powerful. A book is said to have a "sagging middle" if the bulk of the middle is badly written. This is no man's land, which no writer wants to visit. It exists somewhere between the margins of 50,000 and 75,000 words in a 100,000-word book. This is the place where it's too soon to end but the manuscript has lost the glory of the beginning. It's as though the writer gets bored or can't figure out what to do next, so he kills time by not doing anything important with the characters or plot.

A good middle is like a series of surprise birthday parties. Readers shouldn't know what's coming next—but they can't wait to get there.

The End

Not every book has a surprise ending, and it doesn't have to be amazing either. The end can be subtle, like a good wine, and it should linger with the reader for a while. It should make the reader want to go out and buy everything else the author has ever written.

In the end, everything comes together. All the loose strings should be tied up neatly. Don't end too quickly, so that the reader is sent scampering back through the book trying to figure out what happened. Remember that you and the reader are on a journey of discovery together. Don't leave him out in the cold when it comes to understanding what happened and why it happened.

Every writer wants to create a novel that ends with the reader sighing, wiping away a tear, or turning on all the lights in the house. The words that end a book should always come from the reader and they should be, "That was the best book I've ever read." That is ultimately what everyone writes for. That is the true power behind every story. Most writers will never know how many people their work touched. Fortunately, most will never know how many threw the book away either.

Recognizable Content

No matter what its genre, each novel must tell its story in a way that readers recognize. To accomplish this, every writer must learn a few ground rules about plot, characters, setting, and dialogue.

Story Line or Plot

Every fiction novel must have a plot, and most books have more than one. The plot is the story line: What happens, who it happens to, and why. While it may not be the most important part of the story, it is the part that moves the reader from one place to another. The more cohesive the plot, the more likely the reader will make it from beginning to end.

Though the characters and dialogue sustain the plot, it must be able to stand on its own. Think of it as the art of storytelling. The first tales told by humans were by word of mouth, and their heroes were larger than life, but it was the plot that captured the imagination and passed the stories along.

What is a subplot?
A subplot is an offshoot of the main plot. It can add to the main plot or be a catalyst for other action in the book.

Characters

The simpering sister-in-law. The evil stepfather. The goodhearted prostitute. The wise waitress. The strong and silent hero. The beautiful heroine who steals your heart. These characters are clichés, but all of them represent the writer's search for a great presence to dominate his or her book. Who can forget Captain Ahab and his obsession with killing the white whale? Plot takes the back seat to such a powerful character.

Fictional characters are frequently modeled after real-life people. Most are a composite of several individuals the author has met or heard of in the past. Good or bad, all characters strive to impress the reader. If plot is the vehicle that moves the story, character is the driver. A lackluster character can destroy the most brilliant plot, but a dull plot can be given new life by a brilliant character performance.

Backdrop or Setting

The backdrop of the story is like a tapestry. It must be carefully woven so that all of the colors and patterns blend together. Settings like the sleepy little beach town or the great city that never sleeps create the mood of the novel.

The setting should never overpower the plot or the characters. Even when the setting becomes part of the plot—like when an avalanche in the Rockies traps a group of people or a hurricane in the Atlantic Ocean dooms a wealthy family—it's essential that the backdrop stay in the background.

In the past, writers took up entire paragraphs with description of the setting, letting the reader know what a beautiful house looked like or what a gloomy forest felt like. Today's writers use more of the five senses to explore the settings for their novels. Readers skip through long pages of narrative that describe a place or a thing. Setting can be captured in fewer words, even within dialogue, to give a full picture of where the hero or heroine is at any given moment.

The Power of Conversation

Dialogue is every novelist's best friend. It can spice up a dull story line, enhance a character's image, and tell a story all on its own. A friendly Southern diner wouldn't be the same without a few pieces of essential dialogue. "Y'all come back!" and "Bless her heart." Just these words alone identify a place and its characters. Most people would know where they are in this story without being told.

Slang and cliché can be powerful tools for the fiction writer. Taut conversation can put the reader on the edge of his seat the same way that the parting scene between two doomed lovers can draw tears. Emotions are conveyed within quotation marks. Nuances and subtle hints of character are evident in what people say. Writers today are more likely to use dialogue than narrative as a means of advancing the plot. Authors are told again and again: Show, don't tell. Dialogue shows the reader what's going on.

Breaking It Down

Every book has certain similarities no matter how different the content. The structural units that hold the novel together follow certain rules and regulations, allowing the writer to fly free with her imagination while keeping her feet firmly planted on the ground.

ALERT!

If you're interested in publishing your work, check the guidelines set up by the publishers most likely to accept what you're writing. These are available either online or by request from the publisher with an SASE (self-addressed stamped envelope) enclosed.

Chapter Divisions

Not every novel is broken down into chapters. Some experimental mainstream work comes in a kind of free flow of words. Not using chapters to organize a novel is the exception, though, and not one that most beginning novelists will want to make. This would be particularly risky for genre writers.

The chapter is basically a unit of measurement that keeps a novel in order. Chapter lengths may vary. Some authors prefer to write a few longer chapters; others write very small chapters and put more of them in the book. Many authors stagger the amount of text in a chapter, using it to emphasize a particular happening. For instance, a mystery author might use a chapter just long enough to contain a heinous murder scene. There is no hard and fast rule about the number of chapters required to make a novel.

In our tightly wound, competitive society, chapter beginnings and endings have become crucial moments. The writer must learn to "hook" the reader's interest at these moments. There are no long moments of contemplation or reminiscing at these critical junctures. And the hero and heroine never start out asleep or end up asleep. Too much sleeping might just put the reader to sleep and he might never pick up the book again.

A good story and even a great character can get lost in the pages of prose. Paragraphs should make sense to the reader. They should begin and end with the same thought.

Paragraphs

A smaller unit of literary measurement is the paragraph. It can be of any length, from a single sentence to an entire page. In dialogue, even one word of speech is a paragraph by itself. A paragraph is set apart by use of punctuation and indentation. The paragraph supports changes in mood or concept as well as dialogue and narrative.

Short paragraphs are frequently used to denote excitement, anger, or fear. Longer paragraphs are used for explaining background to the reader.

Most writers today don't write paragraphs that are more than ten sentences. Editors believe the reading public gets bored easily when trying to wade through long paragraphs. Breaking up text into paragraphs makes it easier to read.

Sentences

Most people know what sentence structure is. They know that the subject should agree with the verb: "Writing is an art," not "Writing are an art." They know that a sentence is our smallest unit of writing and is fairly easy to construct.

Many English teachers who want to be novelists have to forget all they have learned about sentence structure. Writers use clipped, choppy sentence fragments to convey heavy emotion or frantic movement. It's perfectly correct in the fiction-writing world, even though it can make an English teacher's hair go white! Writers begin sentences with conjunctions and frequently don't use enough commas. They are known for taking liberties with style, structure, and grammar.

The sentence is the writer's playground. With it, she creates a world filled with light, color, sound, and people. Just a few words can linger in the reader's mind for a long time, or even give him nightmares. The way the writer chooses to say these words within the structure of the sentence has a lot to do with their effect.

FACT

The best thing to do before playing with style, structure, or grammar is to have a sound understanding of them. Two of the most concise books ever written on this subject are *The Elements of Style* by William Strunk, Jr. and E. B. White and *The Elements of Grammar* by Margaret Shertzer.

Publishing Format

New York is the center of the traditional publishing world. Multimillion-dollar deals are made there every day. Thousands of writers have started there, some going from door to door with a manuscript under their arm. It's been that way since the 1800s. New York is the universe of senior acquiring editors, editors, associate editors, and line editors. It's a jungle of hardbacks, paperbacks, subrights, and clauses. Hundreds of persistent writers become authors every year. Thousands more get their hearts broken.

Traditional Publishing

What makes the traditional publishing world traditional is the way business is done. A manuscript comes into a publisher's office, either from an agent, a friend of the editor, or an unknown writer (in the business, the unsolicited submissions are known as the slush pile). Most manuscripts never make it past the intern, who opens the envelopes and scans the manuscript for name recognition, hooks, or other possible items of interest. The majority of manuscript submissions are shuffled back into return envelopes with form rejection letters. Another, much smaller group makes it upstairs to an associate editor's desk. These manuscripts are carefully scrutinized again for the same criteria. Another batch, possibly 1 out of 1,000, makes it in to the senior editor, where the process begins again. One in about 10,000 manuscripts will actually see publication through this process.

Out of the manuscripts that are published, only a handful will attain the recognition most authors crave. Even more to the point, the average published author only makes about $3,500 a year. While this fact can be disappointing, there are many midlist authors who will never see the *New York Times* bestseller list, but make enough (more than $20,000 a year) to continue with their dream.

Consider the Alternatives

The small press publishers around the world are thriving despite predictions of doom. Because of consolidations within the New York City publishing world, many talented editors lost their jobs and decided to create their own publishing houses. These alternative publishers are springing up like weeds in June. And they're taking a bite out of the Big Apple's literary profits.

ALERT!

A good literary agent can be the writer's best friend, but a bad agent can be his or her worst nightmare. The Association of Authors' Representatives (AAR) maintains a Web site (*www.aar-online.org*) that contains information about what you should expect from a reputable agent.

A day in the life of a small press publisher is very different. Most small presses are run by only one or two people. Many times the person who opens the envelope and makes the first evaluation is the publisher herself. She doesn't have a staff of editors to convince of a story's worthiness. Like so many other people with small businesses, the publisher makes those decisions herself. She likes to buy what she likes to read. She likes to find writers she can work with for a long time and whose books are profitable. A small press publisher doesn't have the overhead of the bigger, traditional publishers because many times her office is in her basement.

Thousands of new writers from Maine to New Mexico will get their start with this type of publisher. Unfortunately, when the author's books truly become profitable, the author will jump ship and desert the small press that published him for the larger New York City publishing house with the big advance and better distribution. Then the cycle begins again for the small press publisher. It's a cycle that allows room for more writers to be published even though it can be disastrous for the alternative publisher. ⒠

Chapter 3

The Right Genre for You

One of the hardest things any writer has to do is to be objective with his or her work. This process probably begins with deciding where to put your words. Understanding the various genres and subgenres of fiction could actually be a book in itself. Fortunately, you don't have to learn everything about every fiction classification. The best thing to do is to figure out where you belong, then learn about the rest as you go along.

Love and Romance

Romance is the crowning jewel of all novelistic genres. It outsells all of its competitors and has the greatest number of books published each year. Romance readers are loyal and dedicated. It's not unusual for a person who reads romance to go through three to five books a week! The only prerequisite to writing romance is that every book has to end up with the man and woman living happily ever after.

FACT

The Romance Writers of America keep up with sales records for their genre. In 2002, romance sales topped $1.52 billion world-wide. Despite their critics' nickname of "bodice rippers," a term used to describe some of their graphic covers, the genre continues to grow and draw new readers every year.

Contemporary Romances

As the name implies, contemporary romances feature boy meets girl in today's world. Dialogue is usually witty and occupies a large portion of the book. Today's men and women are looking for love both seriously and humorously. These books are the lighter side of the genre. Length is anywhere from 50,000 to 100,000 words. They range from "sweet," where the couple exchanges only a few kisses, to "erotic" where sexual encounters are hot and heavy. The stories take place in every country in the world. But background and plot take a backseat to the basic concept of the hero and heroine and how they come together.

Historical Romances

Real history was never the way romance novels portray it. But this sub-genre flourishes on an idealized vision of history. In these books, pirate captains bathe frequently and are always tall and handsome. They are bad, but in a good way. They might do terrible things to other people, but when they meet the heroine, it changes their lives forever. The heroine is usually a feisty but demure virgin. And usually, we find at the end of the book that the pirate captain is really a duke or the prince of a small country in Europe.

These books can be funny or serious. They range between 60,000 to 100,000 words. Sexual encounters are usually mandatory; most are erotic, although a few publishers have "sweet" lines.

Paranormal Romances

Witches (both good and bad), demons, and werewolves inhabit the pages of this subgenre. Anything can happen. Paranormal romance goes from handsome ghosts who beckon to hapless young women to futuristic worlds where couples are not of the same species. It's difficult to put any specifics to these books. But if the romance doesn't fall into one of the other subgenres, it probably belongs here.

Paranormal romances may be funny or serious. They range from 85,000 to 100,000 words. Sexual encounters vary from book to book. The only important thing to remember is that the romance takes precedence over the story, whether it takes place on Saturn or in a castle ruled by a vampire.

Suspense Novels

The only thing that really separates suspense from mystery is the romance. In these books, there might be a bad guy on every page. But the hero and heroine must still be working on their relationship. Despite everything that happens, they must end up together. Word count ranges from 85,000 to 100,000. Sexual encounters are usually erotic.

Suspense can cross other subgenres:

- It might take place in ancient Britain (historical).
- It might involve a beautiful ghost (paranormal).
- It might be about a woman looking for the man who killed her sister (mystery).

Mystery Novels

Today's mystery novels are a colorful quilt of ideas, time frames, and settings—everything from vampires who solve crimes in 1920s Chicago to

Ellis Peters's Cadfael series set in medieval England. There are detectives who solve crimes in the future and thrilling car chases set on the streets of contemporary Los Angeles.

FACT

The Mystery Writers of America began to give out their coveted award for best first mystery novel in 1946. The award is named for Edgar Allen Poe, who is credited with writing the first detective story. The winner of the first award was *Watchful at Night* by Julius Fast.

Thrillers

Put together a desperate man with a dose of high-end technology, toss in some evil drug lords and sophisticated weaponry, mix in some explosions and a high body count, and you have the recipe for writing a thriller. The thriller usually takes place in present time and ranges from 85,000 to 110,000 words. It can include some romance but mostly the reader wants to see the bad guy get killed in some terrible way and the good guy get out alive.

Cozy Mysteries

This popular subgenre has been taken to many different places in the past few years. What began in England with Agatha Christie's Miss Marple books has evolved into a variety of such story lines. There are candy store owners who stumble across dead people. There are witches who solve murders with incantations and innkeepers who can't keep murderers out. All of these books have one important thing in common: a quirky, nonprofessional sleuth who manages to solve the crime. They can have virtually any setting, any time, and range between 60,000 and 100,000 words. They normally contain some light romance but have very little sex or vulgarity.

Police Procedurals

This subgenre includes the popular police mysteries. In this case, one police detective or a group of police officers solve the crime. They might be unorthodox and may not always follow the rules, but they go step by step, following the clues, and end up with a suspect in custody. They have complete access to records, search warrants, and sophisticated surveillance. These books are usually contemporary and have between 60,000 to 100,000 words. They can be graphic in detail and may contain profanity.

ALERT!

Because of the amount of realism connected to the police procedural mysteries, writers are advised to obtain as much real-life information as possible. Police and sheriff's departments maintain Web sites and will answer questions about their jobs.

Historical Mysteries

To qualify as a historical mystery, the story must be set in the past. The crime must be solved by means available to the sleuth in that time period. Most historical mysteries are also cozies, but there is the occasional book that is a historical thriller or police procedural. Details of the time and place must be accurate. Because this subgenre can cross other subgenres in the field, word count, sexual encounters, graphic content, and profanity can vary.

Paranormal Mysteries

Mystery writers call this part of the genre "woo-woo." It can include everything from deadly witch doctors to futuristic crime solvers like the character of J. D. Robb's mysteries. There are ghosts who solve crimes and shape-shifting entities who commit them.

The sleuth doesn't have to use paranormal means to solve the crime. All that matters is the touch of otherworld menace that permeates the book. Word count can be between 85,000 and 100,000 words. Sexual content is usually strong. Graphic violence and profanity can vary.

Hard-Boiled Mysteries

Detective mysteries were one of the first types of pulp novels published. Everyone is familiar with the depressed, independent detective who has a dark past and needs a shave. He inhabits movies and television shows as well as the pages of hundreds of books. His weasel-faced informants and sexy clients are legendary. He solves the case by threatening whoever gets in his way and staying away from the cops. The police never like this man and frequently harass him. But he is the beginning of cool. He exudes male dominance and keen animal instincts.

The hard-boiled noir is as popular today as it was fifty years ago. These books usually don't cross other subgenres. Their word count is 85,000 to 100,000 words. Violence, sexuality, and profanity are usually appropriate here.

Science Fiction

All science fiction novels are grounded in some principle of scientific fact. It may be the smallest germ of truth—for instance, that we can travel in space and that Venus exists. Science fiction is always at the cutting edge of what's possible. Authors create realistic worlds that readers come to love and share. They introduced us to space travel, journeys into the center of the earth, and the inner workings of the human mind.

Space Operas

This term describes a vast number of science fiction books, like H. Beam Piper's *Space Viking* and Edmond Hamilton's *Captain Future and the Space Emperor*. The possibilities for this subgenre are as limitless as the stars. The important thing is that the books take place in space. Their length can be from 85,000 to 150,000 words. Graphic violence, sex, and profanity are all possible but not necessary.

FACT

The space opera has fallen on hard times in recent years. It was king in the 1940s and 1950s, when sci-fi readers were amazed by the notion that aliens might exist. Somehow, humankind's own explorations of space have driven many of these books from bookstore shelves.

Psychological Sci-Fi

Talk of recurring dreams and telepathy brought about a new wave in sci-fi. When Duke University coined the phrase ESP (extrasensory perception), it became fashionable to write stories that borrowed this concept and others like it. Of course, for years before this, sci-fi writers were already exploring the capabilities of the mind. Alan E. Nourse with *PSI High and Others*, Andre Norton's *The Sioux Spaceman,* and Jean Lorrah's Savage Empire series are all good examples of this subgenre.

In recent years, psychological sci-fi became characters facing terrible personal difficulties. It has also come to include futuristic politics like Frank Herbert's Dune series and Piers Anthony's Space Tyrant series. Where the main characters in early sci-fi were heroes and heroines, these books are more likely to have tortured souls who are capable of terrible deeds. The average length of this subgenre is 85,000 to 100,000 words. And like their earlier counterparts, they can be graphic, sexual, and contain profanity.

Fantasy Novels

Fantasy and science fiction are often grouped together, but these two genres are more like cousins. They both rely on the author's imagination. Fantasy books are as likely as sci-fi to be in space, underwater, or in another dimension, but that's where their similarities end. While sci-fi is rooted in science fact, fantasy has no roots. There doesn't have to be even the smallest possible reality in a fantasy novel. This genre is the writer's amusement park where anything and everything becomes possible.

A new combination of fantasy and romance is emerging today. Most of these books are a fifty-fifty combination of relationships and magic. This is different from the pure romance or fantasy of the past because it allows more character and plot development.

Sword and Sorcery

This subgenre can take place in any time and in any world. Usually, the books have an almost mythological feeling to them and are peopled with gods and goddesses, demons and angels, mighty heroes and heroines. They perform larger than life deeds that frequently save the world or what's left of it. What began with updated tales of Hercules and Ulysses became Conan and Elric.

Beautiful sorceresses accompany heavily muscled sword wielders. Magical creatures abound. These books ebb and wane in popularity but their universal appeal seems to create a new market for them every few years. They are usually between 85,000 and 150,000 words and can be graphic in sex, violence, and profanity.

Magic Users

Just like the sword and sorcery novels, books in this subgenre include the use of magic, but this is where the similarities end. A magic user is a kinder, gentler breed of novel. There may be a sword or two, but today's magic user would be more likely to drop it on their toes than use it. They are repressed souls who resort to magic to keep themselves sane or, like Harry Potter, they are born unwittingly into it.

There have been many magic users of this nature throughout fantasy. Barbara Hambly's Windrose Chronicles and Ursula K. Le Guin's Earthsea series are only two of these unique groups of books. It's not unusual to have magic users in modern-day settings. They hide in the shadows until the world needs them. Then they come forward with trembling hands to save the world. The word count for this subgenre is between 85,000 and 100,000 words. Graphic sex, violence, and profanity are still likely even though the heroes and heroines are less prone to fighting than their muscle-bound counterparts.

Horror Genre

Today's horror novels are usually so gruesome that it's hard to believe they began with *Frankenstein* and *Dracula*. The transformation is just another example of how times change, as does the taste of the reading public. What was once considered unthinkable to mention in a novel is now passé.

A good horror story should scare the socks off of the late-night reader. Mystery and suspense can be this book's companions but ultimately, what has to come across in the author's words is sheer throat-tightening terror. Everyone knows that awful moment when you hear a footstep in the hall when you thought that you were alone in the house. That is horror.

FACT

A 1992 Harris poll found that 35 percent of adults in America today believe in ghosts. An astounding 42 percent believe they have spoken with or seen dead relatives.

Psychological Novels

Most horror novels today are included in this subgenre. Authors like Dean Koontz and V. C. Andrews have been torturing readers for years, keeping them up at night and making them question their own sanity. Readers must love them for it, because they keep buying their books.

Psychological horror is the product of the mind. Or is it? That's the basic thrust of all nightmare realities. These books cause people to wander through the dark recesses of the human soul. The pathways are torturous and never safe. It seems like the authors of these novels must be demented souls to be able to write them. The stories can be slow and creeping or pulsing and vibrating like a livewire.

Most psycho-horror is set in contemporary times to get the best effect. The books range between 85,000 and over 100,000 words. They are likely to contain graphic images, sex, and profanity.

Slasher Novels

The blood-and-guts horror novel has almost faded away from today's bookshelves, but authors like Richard Matheson and Douglas Clegg keep it alive. These books are extremely gruesome and graphic, full of blood, sex, and violence—and many readers wouldn't have them any other way. From terrible creatures waiting to devour innocent travelers to knife-wielding maniacs, the slasher novel doesn't care about what the killer is thinking so much as what he's doing. Only a few publishers sell these books. Their word count is usually at least 100,000 words.

Paranormal Horror Novels

Nothing can scare a reader like a good ghost story. Since the beginning of time, human beings have probably sat around campfires giving themselves nightmares by telling scary stories. It's no wonder that many authors incorporated this idea and some have taken it to the extreme. From Peter Straub's *Ghost Story* to H. P. Lovecraft's *Dunwich Horror*, readers have delighted in ghoulies and creatures of the night.

Tales of the supernatural still sell books. They can sometimes seem to cross with slasher horror, particularly in the modern-day vampire and werewolf horror novels. But they don't have to be bloody to be frightening. For most people, just the idea of the dead returning in any form is terrifying. The concept of waking up in the middle of the night to see a ghostly presence standing beside their bed can keep most people awake.

Paranormal horror novels are at least 100,000 words. They can contain graphic sex, violence, and profanity. They are just as likely to be set in the past and are just as effective without any extra trappings.

Mainstream Fiction

This is what many purists call "real" fiction. Some examples are Alice Sebold's *The Lovely Bones* and Robert James Waller's *The Bridges of Madison County*. This gives you an idea of the broad spectrum of ideas that is mainstream fiction. These are the books high school teachers give out as reading assignments.

We tend to think of classics like *Moby Dick* and *David Copperfield* as mainstream fiction, but many of the respected classics are actually genre literature. The important aspect of mainstream is that it tells a classic story: the eternal struggle between good and evil in every human or the rise and fall of power and politics. These books are difficult to categorize. They can be written in many different ways and include many different ideas.

Contemporary Fiction

Authors like Pat Conroy, John Irving, and Toni Morrison make up the backbone of the contemporary mainstream market. In this case, contemporary doesn't necessarily pertain to present day. Anything set since World War II can be included in this group of books. Like all mainstream novels, these are family sagas, stories of relationships and personal tragedy, and "coming of age" tales. The word count for mainstream fiction novels usually starts at 100,000 words. Graphic violence and sex as well as profanity may or may not be appropriate.

Historical Fiction

This subgenre is full of books about ancient Greece, the Spanish Inquisition, and the French Revolution. They can be far-reaching, many beginning with real-life people who are put into fictional settings. Examples of this type of mainstream novel include Gillian Bradshaw's *Cleopatra's Heir* and Richard Sapir's *The Far Arena*.

QUESTION?

Do some periods of history work best in historical novels?
It would be difficult to say what time frames or civilization work best for these novels. They must be epic in proportion but deal with personal relationships between characters. The background can be as sweeping as the fall of the Roman Empire, as long as it's seen through the eyes of a young servant boy who kills his master, for example.

Historical mainstream novels frequently cross over into different types of genre, including romance, fantasy, and mystery. The word count for these books begins at 100,000 words and can contain graphic violence, sex, and profanity.

Romantic Fiction

Just as genre romance is the most popular category of novel, romantic fiction is the most popular subcategory of mainstream fiction. There is a very fine but distinct line between genre romance and romantic mainstream fiction. This line is observed mostly by genre romance readers who expect happy endings from any book that calls itself a romance. Romantic mainstream novels are about romance, but they are likely to end up with one or more of the romantic couple leaving or dead. Such is the case in Nicholas Sparks's *Message in a Bottle*.

Authors like Sparks, Danielle Steele, and Channing Hayden write in this subgenre. The stories are closely woven with the romance but never actually fulfill the genre reader's fantasy. These books frequently dominate the *New York Times* bestseller list and have a growing audience. The word count for them starts at 100,000. They can contain graphic violence, sex, and profanity.

Young Adult Novels

The young adult (YA) novel market includes books for children between the ages of twelve and eighteen. They frequently mimic adult fiction, except that the heroes and heroines are teenagers. They are sometimes angst-ridden stories about coping with real-life problems or they can be about two kids who save the world from aliens.

This is a growing market right now but it had been in a slump since the 1960s. Publisher's guidelines vary greatly in this market. For the most part, you won't see graphic violence, sex, or profanity in a young adult book. But the story line can't make kids feel like it is being told by an adult talking down to them, either. To write in this field, it takes a good imagination and an understanding of what kids like.

Historical YA Novels

This subgenre contains thrilling tales of yesteryear that also give children a feeling for history. These novels are fictional stories about real-life heroes and heroines. These can include stories about soldiers, like Alan

N. Kay's *Nowhere to Turn* or Bette Greene's *Summer of My German Soldier*, or stories of the Depression era in the Deep South, like Mildred Taylor's *Roll of Thunder, Hear My Cry*.

Historical settings for these books include anything that isn't happening today. They are meant to be wonderful teaching tools that make learning fun. They offer glimpses into the past through the eyes of someone who doesn't seem all that different from today's young adult reader. These books are usually from 40,000 to 60,000 words.

Contemporary YA Novels

Like their historical cousins, contemporary young adult fiction wants to teach children important lessons. But while the previous subgenre wants to make history fun, this part of the field wants to relate to young people's lives today. These stories deal with sometimes gritty, real-life issues that face all teenagers today. Subjects can include teenage pregnancy and abortion, street gang and drugs, as well as problem relationships. Authors like Louise Plummer (*The Unlikely Romance of Kate Bjorkman*), Cynthia Rylant (*A Kindness*), and David Carkeet (*The Silent Treatment*) all take a hard look at these important issues. They try to speak to the problems and events that make up every teenager's life. These books can be realistic and difficult. The word count is between 40,000 and 60,000 words.

FACT

Young adult horror is one of the fastest-growing parts of genre writing. With authors R. L. Stine and Philip Pullman leading the way, monsters and witches walk the streets of suburban neighborhoods today.

Genre YA Novels

This is the place where kids just have fun. It's the world of J. K. Rowling's Harry Potter and Robert Heinlein's *Podkayne of Mars*. These books can be one of any genre including romance, mystery, sci-fi, fantasy, and horror. They include not only the works of J. K. Rowling but also

Andre Norton's Witch World series. This is the domain that made the Hardy Boys and Nancy Drew mysteries household words for generations.

There is probably some learning going on here as well. Friendship, working with others, even honesty comes into play in these books. But their primary goal is to entertain. While contemporary young adult fiction wants to give their readers examples of how to cope with real life, genre wants to take them away from it all. These books can deal with real life, but they do so in a fun way. They range in word length from 40,000 to 60,000.

Novels for Men

This genre is dedicated to the male reader ages eighteen to thirty-five and focuses on subjects of particular interest to men. Whether it's a mystery, sci-fi, fantasy, or horror, you won't find flowery language or effeminate wizards here! These books exemplify the true sense of how far men will go to test themselves against the elements and society.

Adventure Novels

Spies lurking around every corner. Beautiful, sexy, sometimes deadly, women. Fast cars. Exciting gadgets. All of these are in the territory of the men's adventure genre. They can happen in contemporary times, in the past or the future. The adventures can take place on this planet or any other. The only prerequisite is that they meet the excitement quotient—that is, they take their readers out of their armchairs and into an unbelievable action fantasy.

It's possible that the first author of these books was Ernest Hemingway. While today he is considered a writer of the classics, his work reads more like men's adventure.

Today's writers aren't much different, but they tend to be far more graphic. Warren Murphy, Richard Sapir (the Destroyer series), James Axler (the Deathlands series), and Don Pendleton (the Executioner series) are all prime examples of this genre. These books range from 85,000 to 100,000 words. They contain graphic violence, sex, and profanity.

Western Novels

The men's Western subgenre has had its ups and downs through the years. Immensely popular at times and difficult to find at others, it is still around today, and some of these books have graduated into the classics. Authors like Zane Grey and Louis L'Amour don't ride the range anymore, but their tough breed of hero continues to delight a hard-core fan audience.

Today's Westerns aren't much different than they were fifty years ago. The possible exception to this is that more women are writing in this field and more gun-toting heroines have appeared in novels. Lauran Paine's *Open Range* and David Thompson's *Wilderness* are two good examples of present-day Western novels. Their books tend to be a little more Native American and woman friendly than their predecessors, but the Western genre largely remains man's territory.

Westerns range from 60,000 to 100,000 words. They can be violent and sexually explicit, but the street profanity from a contemporary book wouldn't apply.

The market for Western novels today is not a thriving business. The Western Writer's Association acknowledges that only a few major publishers still accept submissions in this subgenre. Most writers are using Westerns as a crossover, changing the name to Western historical.

Erotic Novels

In the past, only certain underground publishers accepted erotica, but this genre has gained some respectability in recent years. Today, erotica is a genre that's not quite pornography and not quite literature, with softer edges and some plot beyond simple sexual encounters.

Erotica's rebirth into the regular adult market has made this field extremely lucrative for writers. In many cases, they use the profits from these books to subsidize their more "legitimate" writing.

Women's Erotica

Also known as *romantica,* this category is basically a hybrid between erotica and romance. It means that the novel is a romance with all of the genre trappings including the happy ending. The only difference is that there are more sex scenes between the hero and heroine, and the sex is more graphic. Women who read these books want all the juicy details. They want the couple to have a relationship, but they want them to spend a great deal of time consummating it. Various positions and unusual locations are possible and encouraged.

These books range from 85,000 to 100,000 words. While descriptions of sex are graphic and some profanity is expected, there's rarely any violence.

ALERT!

Even though romantica has made erotic material for women more acceptable, most authors who write these novels still write under pseudonyms. They don't want their reputation as a writer of erotica to affect their other writing.

Men's Erotica

Men's erotica remains pretty much the same as it was fifty years ago. Many of these novels have developed genre plots that usually don't include relationships but do look for action/adventure, sci-fi/fantasy, or horror/mystery. These hybrids give their readers the combinations they crave.

These books tend to be graphic in sex and violence and liberally sprinkled with profanity. They tend to be shorter than other genre novels, ranging from 50,000 to 85,000 words.

Chapter 4

E Brainstorming Your Idea

You have an idea for a novel. You think it's a good idea. You've thought about it for a while and decided it's something you'd like to do. What's the next step? For most people, it's brainstorming. Coming up with an entire novel full of people, places, and plot is difficult. It's nothing less than having a storm in your brain. The question is, how do you take a mass of random ideas and make it into a coherent story?

Finding Story Ideas

Most writers don't have a problem coming up with ideas for novels. The problem usually involves too many ideas. You have to pick and choose between them. It's very much like having five children who all need shoes. You don't have much money, so you have to decide which child needs a pair of shoes first. In the case of story ideas, you have to decide which story won't wait to be written.

Choose the one idea that makes you feel like you could drag yourself out of bed at five in the morning to write it. It's the one that's burning a hole in your brain. The others will wait. Put them on the back burner for now and go with the story that's most important to you.

Use Your Imagination

A good imagination can get you started. A great imagination can take you to the moon. Tap into the wellspring of your imagination—if you've been neglecting it with grown-up beliefs and too much reality, you'll have to work on it. Give yourself time to dream every day. Find a quiet corner and allow yourself to imagine all the possibilities around you.

A story idea that comes completely from your imagination can be brilliant. Like the goddess Athena springing forth from Zeus's head, it can emerge fully formed. Or it may be just the germ of an idea. For instance, it could simply be an idea to write a story about a woman from another world who uses her incredible musical voice to mine crystals for interplanetary communication. Taking that basic concept, author Anne McCaffrey created her Crystal Singer books. The wealth of imaginary detail that accompanies the idea is what makes these novels so enjoyable. The author allowed her imagination to invent a strong, believable character who triumphs over her difficulties.

Reality as Inspiration

Many fiction authors create their work from something that really happened to them. Still others watch the news and scan the newspapers for events. They write down scraps of ideas that strike them as story possibilities. Creating fiction from real life is nothing new. Even writers with fantastic imaginations sometimes need a jump-start.

Of course, some fiction genres really depend on reality. Police mysteries rely on some grain of truth to appeal to their experienced readers. In a few cases, entire true incidents are recorded as fiction, but for the most part, you'll find authors using their life experiences in fiction. For example, a small-town newspaper reporter might write about a big-city journalist who uncovers evidence and becomes a target of the mob. Such a person would know enough about the journalistic field to give her work a sense of realism, even though her imagination takes it from there.

FACT

A Virginia family sued Patricia Cornwell in 1992 for releasing true information in her book, *All That Remains*. The information was privileged and part of a murder investigation. Cornwell worked on the real-life case in her job at the medical examiner's office.

Other Fiction

It may seem odd or even unethical to take ideas from other people's fiction to create your own. Taking the exact text from someone else's work is illegal, but getting ideas from the books you read happens to everyone. Some people even go so far as to get permission from other authors to mention their fictional characters or places in their own book.

Some books are actually written from one basic idea, place, or character and are meant to be shared between authors. Robert Lynn Asprin's Thieves' World series was created to showcase various authors. This isn't the same thing as books written by contracted authors who continue a series after the original author's death. The James Bond/007 novels that have been published since Ian Fleming's death are written and published by agreement with the author's estate.

Building a Novel

The very definition of a novel-length work creates certain expectations. To expand a single story idea into 100,000 words requires in-depth thought into the elements that make up the plot, characters, and setting that drive the work. A writer must be able to take everything she sees in her mind, magnify it, and create a microcosm of this world. Her words are the building blocks. The scope of her novel is the depth of her imagination and creativity.

There are certain things that every reader expects to find when he or she buys a copy of a book. These concepts are elemental and honored worldwide. They include:

- Characters—the people or other beings who inhabit your novel
- Plot—the roadmap that takes your characters from one place to another
- Setting—the world, real or imagined, where your ideas take place
- Dialogue and narrative—the way you express all the aspects of the story

There are themes to every book that revolve around the concepts you create. Is your hero looking for himself by exploring his past? Is your heroine trying to get over a terrible love affair? Will your story deal with the hard issues of life in a humorous or serious manner? All of these things must be decided before a writer ever prints up a rough draft.

Every writer has to understand the concepts that he wants to include in his novel, the concepts that are important to him. In understanding what he wants to say, the writer begins to understand his characters and his goals.

Story Line—the Story's Timeline

What happens in your story? How do you go about presenting it? Many novels begin with an introduction of the main character. They give the reader reasons to like or dislike this character. Then they begin to introduce the plot. During this process, the writer weaves in information about other characters who contribute to the story. The tapestry takes on life as the writer creates a mood and background for the story.

The story line has to engage the reader from the beginning. He or she has to care about this character and want to know what makes the character tick and what will happen to this character next. The reader must feel empathy with the story and the character.

Bringing in excessive details about the past or the setting will throw the reader away from your true goal. You can always connect the reader to other details once he or she has established some feeling for the characters. Even the most fascinating alien world or terrible anguished past will be boring to the reader without some emotional empathy with the characters.

Characters and Plot

Give equal attention to both characters and plot, but keep your details about what's going to happen from getting mixed up with your character sketches. Understanding these two aspects of your novel, how they mesh and how they don't, will give you the creative power to write thought-provoking yet exciting novels.

FACT

The main character from every book carries the weight of success or failure on his shoulders. If the reader doesn't relate to the main character, it doesn't matter how great the writer feels about him.

Many writers feel that their plot is so exciting and so involving that it doesn't matter what character they put into it. If this were true, Tom Clancy's character Jack Ryan could be Barney Fife. The plots and settings of Clancy's books are always exciting. But Jack Ryan is who we care about. Conversely, you could take the same character and put him on an Arkansas farm and the book would still be interesting. Yet, even this dynamic character couldn't take Barney's place in Mayberry, because Deputy Fife's character is what helps define the sleepy little Southern town.

Character will always overshadow plot and setting. Characters need depth and background to help us understand them. They need to be as real and frail as we are. Creating them can be difficult. It may start with an idea of what they'll be like in the book, what you want them to accomplish. Maybe you want your male character to look like Keanu Reeves but have the muscles of Sylvester Stallone. Maybe he can solve crimes like Sherlock Holmes and he can dance like Fred Astaire.

But don't think you can shortchange the plot because you have a great character. Your wonderful character won't be much fun sitting in a rocking chair on his front porch watching the world go by. Your plot must pick him up, give him a first-class vehicle to ride in, and send him down the road. It must let the reader see all of his strengths and weaknesses. If the character sat around just thinking about how wonderful he was, the reader would be bored and the book would be in the garbage.

Consider your characters separately from your plot. Separating the characters from the plot is like separating whites and colors before doing your laundry. If you throw the dark purple shirt in with your white underwear, everything will come out lavender.

Thinking It Through

Some writers prefer to contemplate their creation at a bar, a coffee shop, or at the beach. Others feel that it is necessary to be wherever their story takes place, whether it's Athens, the Himalayas, or Amazonian jungle. The reality, of course, is that many writers have full-time jobs, families, and many other responsibilities. They find the time to work out the bugs in their plot while they're taking a bath or riding to and from work.

However you choose to find your muse, the important thing is that you can see the entire story in your mind. Before the plot thickens, the writer has to see how it all fits together. Like an evolving jigsaw puzzle, all of the aspects come together only to fall apart and come together again in a different way.

Telling Yourself the Story

You can do it in the car. You can do it on your lunch hour. You can do it during your vacation. Despite anything else that comes to mind, this "it" is telling yourself the story of your novel. It's an effective way to understand what you want to say and how you want to say it. But unless you have someone with a sympathetic ear, this will have to be a solitary excursion.

Many writers tell themselves the story the way a parent tells a child a bedtime story. They go to sleep at night repeating their ideas in an almost once-upon-a-time format. This gives their subconscious the chance to work on the story as well. Writers are a strange and unique group of people because they are always living at least two lives—their real-time life and a virtual life for one of their characters.

Looking for the Weak Spots

A sure way to find the holes in your story is to hear it read or told aloud. Maybe that's why so many writers would rather avoid this step and go right to the word processor. Once you've seen the hole, you feel obligated to patch it; if you never see the hole, you can let yourself believe it isn't there.

Every plot and every character has weak spots. These aren't the necessary flaws to make the whole thing seem more realistic. These are unintentional mistakes that can destroy a book, like unexplained knowledge of a sleuth, the romantic hero's unromantic behavior, or the lack of progression in the plot.

It's important that the writer knows the explanations behind everything, even if she hasn't shared it with the reader *just yet*. Obviously, most mystery writers know who the killer is. Telling the reader in the first page (unless the book isn't a whodunit) will ruin the story. But leaving readers out in the cold and suddenly revealing the killer to be a character they've never heard of before just won't work. It's the writer's job as the master architect of her novel to make sure the plot and the story make sense and build up the action so that everything is revealed at the right time and the reader is prepared for the revelations.

FACT

Here's one sure way to test if a character or plot point is essential to the story: Take it out of the story. If the story collapses, the character or idea is important. If not, you may need to weed it out to strengthen the manuscript.

Write It Down

How do you know when you've found the right idea? Writers have asked this question a thousand times. The right idea is always the strongest one, the one that won't let you go. It moves your heart and fills your head when you should be thinking about other things.

Is the right idea always the big idea? Unfortunately not. Writing is a craft. Not everything you write is going to be marketable. Even if your feelings for the book are passionate, there may never be an editor who shares your passion. So, what's a writer to do?

Write the book. If the idea you have in mind works for you, write it down. All writers learn by writing. No workshop and no book can teach you more than sitting down and writing. Your idea may never sell, but you learn something new with each book. You grow as a writer.

Keeping Track of Your Ideas

Most writers have a collection of odd mementoes scattered around their homes and offices. These include matchbook covers, napkins, business cards, and old envelopes. Some writers even manage to keep notebooks. What are they keeping? Ideas.

Ideas can come at the most inopportune times. You may be having lunch with an old school friend that you haven't seen for twenty years.

Suddenly, there it is. An idea that solves part of a plot problem that's bugged you for a week. You know you need to write it down because your brain is like a sieve. Your friend is going on and on about her life. What's a writer to do? Grab the nearest scrap of paper and write down the idea before it burns a hole in your brain. Then you can go back and converse like a normal person.

Some writers have learned to say, "Excuse me." They casually reach into their pocket or purse and pull out an idea notebook. They've managed to get beyond the stage of caring that their friends think they're weird.

The most important thing is to write down the idea. Snippets of conversation, questions about characters, all of these things will be useful when you finally have an hour at your computer to work on your manuscript. If you're the notebook type, so much the better. If not, find some way to organize those drink coasters and stray receipts that you've written on.

ALERT!

If you don't want to pay to have information copyrighted, you can use the poor man's copyright system. Put your information into a sealed envelope and mail it back to yourself. Put it in a safe place and don't open it.

Stay Organized

It would be wonderful if everyone were organized. The sad truth is that most people aren't. If you are one of the latter variety, how will you ever get organized?

Organization is a skill anyone can learn. Because writers are essentially small business people, it's important for them to learn this skill as early on in their careers as possible. If you ever manage to sell a book, you'll be glad you kept those receipts, letters, and notes. They prove to the IRS that you're serious about your career. Even if you're not published, they can be useful documents.

The computer is a wonderful organizational tool. It can keep track of appointments, phone numbers, and other time-related information. But for letters and other miscellaneous paper, there's nothing like a file cabinet. Make a file folder for receipts, another one for correspondence, and a third one for all of your random notes. Keeping your ideas and other writing-related information close at hand can keep you from hours of searching through old suit coats and the glove compartment in your car, and that gives you more time to write.

ESSENTIAL

You'll probably find that once you've begun to organize, everything else in your life seems to be a mess. If you get the urge to organize your entire life, check out Organized-mom.com's free monthly newsletter (✍ *www.organized-mom.com*). They have some fun ideas to organize everyone.

How to Stay Flexible

You've come up with the greatest idea for a book. It's slightly different than anything you've ever read. Not only is it an idea that keeps you up at night, it's a big idea. You might be able to sell this manuscript to a big-name publisher in New York.

But when you write the query letter for it, the editor tells you that romances that are set in the 1890s don't work for them. They love the character sketch you sent of the hero and heroine. Can you change the basic setting and time period?

Change the idea? But it's a winner. And you love Paris in the 1890s. Your story revolves around this time and place. You can't possibly change your idea. It's not fair for them to ask you. Characters are more important than time and place anyway. If this is your reaction, you need to learn some flexibility.

What If—Play with It

A writer should always be asking, "What if?" What if the hero suddenly loses his way? What if the heroine doesn't want to go home? Every writer asks these questions to learn about his or her plot, characters, and setting.

While it seems impossible to alter an idea already in place, these same questions work for that as well. Using the concept previously mentioned, you could start by asking, "What if my setting changed? What if my story takes place in London instead of Paris? What if the time frame was changed from the 1890s to 1901?"

QUESTION?

How can I rework my idea?
The best way to rework an idea is to look at it from a different angle. Change your approach to the problem and you can probably change your idea.

This means doing some research, of course. It means rethinking a lot of ideas that you felt were concrete. But while you lose those ideas, you always gain new ones. You can play with your ideas in the same way that children play with building blocks. They might cry for a while when their masterpiece is destroyed, but they move right on to building a new one. All writers have to learn to be flexible with their work, and not just for the sake of getting published. Many ideas that you start out with won't hold up under the pressure of 100,000 words. Even if you're writing for the simple pleasure of saying you've written a novel, you'll still want it to make sense.

Don't Be Afraid to Make Changes

Sometimes, the only way to move forward is by tearing down your old ideas. This allows you to make room for new ones. It can be frightening to make these changes. After all, you're happy with what you have. But if you find yourself wrestling with the plot, characters, or setting, something just isn't working. Changing an idea, especially a large idea that might mean ripping up half of your work, isn't easy. It's not something that any writer looks forward to. But it happens. The trick is not to fall in love with any one idea. Realize that everything can be torn down and put back together. It will be different. But it can be better.

The writer's job is not just to write; it's also to rewrite, and rethink, and revamp. There are millions of ideas and thousands of words to choose from, and no one is ever the only perfect option.

Be Honest with Yourself

Should you make changes just because someone else tells you something would be better if you changed the hero or the plot? You're the only one who can make that decision. But try to look at it with the objectivity of a surgeon rather than a parent. Would your manuscript benefit from these changes? Would it make the characters or plot stronger or smarter? Look at your work critically. Is this what you want to say and how you want to say it? If not, make it different. Throw in a little something extra. Make it better.

ALERT!

Critique groups can be a wonderful way to get feedback on your work, but they can also be a disaster. Be sure you are in sync with the people who will be helping you shape your work. It's not true that a bad critique is better than no critique at all.

It's Time to Research

All writers need to learn how to do research. Not only will you have to research some ideas for your novels but you'll also want to research publishers, agents, and other people who can help you with your writing.

Probably the greatest research tool ever made is the Internet. Thousands of sites, both personal and professional, are available at your fingertips. You can learn anything from how to repair a toilet to how to make cheese. You can certainly research any ideas you'd ever want to put into your book.

Do Some Reading

There is no substitute for reading books in the genre that you've chosen to write in. Every professional involved in the writing world—editors, agents, and critics—will give you this same advice. It is next to impossible to write a good romance without ever reading a single romance novel. It would be like buying a car without test-driving it first. Sure, the engine would probably run and the transmission would shift smoothly. Unfortunately, because you never tried to drive a sports car before, you didn't realize how small it was, or how difficult to control.

If you're dying to write a thriller mystery, read one. Better yet, read Clancy and Grisham. Then read a few of the lesser-known authors. This will give you the perspective of both the successful author and the up-and-coming author. Even if you think your book is nothing like anything out there, this is still the most practical and successful way to learn about what you want to write.

Find Out What the Guidelines Are

Publishers create guidelines for their books because they know what they want to see. They also know what they don't want to see. Even the best idea and the greatest writing won't work if it's in the wrong format.

If a romance publisher wants to see romances that don't include violence or graphic sex and you want to write for that publisher, take the violence and sex out of your agenda. They won't fall in love with your ideas if they don't mesh with theirs. A detective mystery without a detective isn't going to be well received. A mainstream fiction novel primarily about racecars and the size of their engines isn't going to get published.

Of course, if you are one of those rare writers who doesn't care about ever getting published, you can write your novel any way you want. But mostly, fiction writers don't write personal memoirs that they want to give their children. They write stories about things they imagine. And mostly, they want those stories to get published.

Go to any bookstore site and take a look at the books that are being published. If your idea is close to something already being done, with a twist you can make it original. If your idea is exactly what someone else is doing, you might want to rethink it.

Chapter 5

Developing Your Idea

Once you've finished brainstorming, it's time to take that great idea and begin developing it into a detailed story. The development process might be more difficult than you think. Many writers have no trouble coming up with ideas, but they don't always know what to do with them once they get them. The tools and techniques described in this chapter can help you make progress from a great idea to a great story.

The Virtues of Being Organized

Everyone knows the value of being organized. If you organize your sock drawer, you'll never be caught wearing mismatched socks. If you take the time to write down your credit card information and file it away, you'll be prepared if your wallet gets stolen.

And everyone knows what it's like when you're not organized. You're late for work on the day of the important presentation. Then, you realize that you left important papers scattered around your desk at home. You meant to send your suit to the cleaners but you forgot and there's ketchup on your lapel. If only you'd been more organized.

Good organization can do more than just keep your writing going smoothly. It can help you if you are audited by the Internal Revenue Service. It can also protect you if any of your work is ever plagiarized by providing the background proof that your work is truly your own.

Being an organized writer means never misplacing an idea that you loved six months ago but didn't have time to include in your novel. It means you always know what chapter you're working on and where you sent your last manuscript—and if your manuscript is rejected, you'll remember not to send a similar submission to the same publisher.

The writer is a head of a small business and needs to wear many hats—agent, editor, publicist, and creator. He or she can't afford not to be organized.

So Many Ideas

Author Isaac Asimov (1920–1992) was one of the most prolific authors ever published. He wrote over 500 books in his lifetime, and that doesn't include his 400 essays. Using a basic ratio for what happens to most writers, that meant that he had thousands of ideas for books that didn't work.

How many ideas do *you* have? Probably too many to ever turn into novels. Very few writers are lacking for things to write about. Finding the time to do it is the problem. That's why you can only write the big ideas. If you want to get anything accomplished, you'll have to pick and choose.

But what do you do with all of those ideas? You'll have to be objective. Try not to think of them in the same category as your children or other cherished items. Write down at least a paragraph for the really good ones and file them away. Write down at least a sentence for the ones you might consider but aren't sure about and file them away. Everything else—just discard. There is only so much of you to go around.

Try not to force too many ideas into one book. This will only confuse the reader. Stay clear and focused on what you want to say. Let those extra ideas stayed filed away until the time is right for them. More is not always better.

Keeping It Straight

With so many ideas buzzing around, how do you keep from getting confused while you're writing? One old standard is the file cabinet. It doesn't have to be big. All you really need are some file boxes available for a few dollars at a discount store. Different stories you're working on, even if they're only ideas for stories, can be put in color-coded file folders. That way if you have a handful of notes that go with a synopsis, you can put them all in one file together.

Keeping those ideas inside the box and out of your brain while you're writing isn't easy. Many beginning writers go from story idea to story idea, never quite finishing any of them. They begin writing one great idea only to be sidetracked by another. Finally, they get disgusted and give up writing altogether.

The discipline to keep yourself in one story line comes with time and effort. If you can begin to forget the ideas you put into your file box until you want to use them, you'll be on your way to developing that mindset.

Writing as You Think

Some people think that a novelist sits down at the computer and the words just start coming out in complete and perfect sentences. Everything is always spelled right and makes perfect sense. These people are wrong: writing is rarely that easy.

Most novelists write, edit, and revise a manuscript many times. Everyone knows the first draft is not the last draft. Even if the plot, characters, and setting are as fresh to you as Aunt Mary's birthday party last Sunday, putting it down on paper that way can be difficult. For some reason, the brain sometimes slips into a coma state while the fingers are still typing. The result isn't always what you want to send to an editor.

The Seat of Your Pants

Human beings tend to value originality. Everyone loves new inventions and their inventors. They like to think that what they're doing is new and unique. And they like to think they can do it without a lot of fuss or bother. The stories about the man in his basement workshop who creates something wonderful using aluminum cans and coat hangers are the stuff of legend. We all want to be this way, and writers are no different.

Many writers will deny any allegation that they outlined, organized, created a timeline, or otherwise decided how their book was going to be written. The basic reasoning behind this is that characters must "find" themselves. The story must "evolve" without the writer's awareness or consent. If a writer knows where the story is going, he or she risks losing the ability to be fresh or spontaneous.

FACT

English novelist Barbara Cartland, the queen of romance, was probably the most prolific author who ever lived. She began as a reporter in Fleet Street then went on to publish more than 700 novels that were translated into forty-six languages. She died in 2000 after a long writing career.

This method of writing works for many people. But many more, especially beginning writers, get confused and frustrated. Knowing that you want to drive from Boston to Chicago isn't enough—if you get in your car without a roadmap, you'll have a very difficult time getting there. Maybe it's not as artistic to know what you want to do and how you want to do it—but if you're trying to get to Chicago and you end up in St. Louis, you're going to wish you looked at a map.

Losing Your Idea

The loss of a good idea is like the loss of a valued friend. It doesn't matter whether you lose the idea because you weren't organized and threw it away or because you forgot to write it down in the first place. The idea is gone and it will be difficult to replace.

You can lose an idea without misplacing it. Maybe the idea that seemed so fresh and exciting when you first came up with it suddenly seems stale and boring. In a way, you might wish it was as simple as throwing it away.

Keeping your ideas from getting old while you're working on them is important. Enthusiasm is one of the writer's greatest weapons. If you can't stay focused on an idea, what makes you think it'll draw in your readers and impress your editors? That doesn't always mean that the original idea is bad. It may simply be that you've become distracted by another idea or that something in the story isn't working the way you imagined.

When you feel your concentration slipping and wish that character you created would just go away, back down for a while. Give yourself some time to get a fresh perspective. Is it really the idea that's tired or is it your perception of the idea that's worn out? Take a break. Don't come back or start anything new until you've cleared your mind and refocused your thoughts.

Learn to Take Notes

Taking good notes is an important skill. A writer's life is full of odd ideas and concepts. Keeping good notes will help you organize your ideas and save them for one day in the future, when you can finally use your idea in your writing.

Everyone keeps notes differently. All that you might need to remember an idea is just a few words jotted down on a piece of scrap paper. Or, you might need to write up a small synopsis of a story idea. One strategy is to write lots of small notes about individual characters, plots, or settings. Then, when you're ready to start writing, reread all your ideas and pick out the ones that still work for you.

Many writers will revisit an idea months or years after first considering it. They have stacks of notes ready for the time when the story seems ripe. It gives them a reason to forget about their creative ideas and focus on their present work.

Novel writers who base their fiction on real-life events will want to be especially careful with their notes. It's important to keep the facts straight. Even though the fictional account will have different names or places, understanding what happened and why it happened is important to the overall quality of your writing.

Keeping a Notebook for Your Notes

Many authors begin a new notebook for each novel, so that every note can be found in one place. If you try to cram all your ideas into one notebook, you're bound to get yourself confused.

If you get an idea and your idea notebook isn't around, write it down on anything else—a napkin, bar tab, or any other piece of paper—then staple or tape it to your notebook when you get home.

Or You May Prefer Index Cards

Another way of keeping notes on a project is to use index cards. Some authors keep all of their notes for each novel in individual boxes. They keep receipts and stray ideas that all pertain to the same book in the box. Because the boxes are self-contained, very little information can get away. The one drawback to this theory is trying to save larger pieces of paper. An index card box can quickly fill up that way.

Many writers use this method because they like to lay out their notes, then move them around until they find an order they're happy with for their novel. Each card represents each character. There are cards for particular aspects of the setting and plot points. Cards can also be used for bits and pieces of defining dialogue. This would be a sentence or way of speaking that you want to capture.

Talking It Out

Writers love to talk about their work. They like to talk about it over coffee, over lunch, over drinks in the bar. They'll go to conferences to talk to other writers about it. They'll pay an editor to listen to them. They will spend long hours on the phone with their agents and editors just to be able to hear themselves tell the story out loud.

Editors and writers understand the need of writers to tell and retell their story. Maybe that's why it's not unusual to see a successful author divorce her architect husband to marry her editor. Writing is powerful and personal work, and writers don't want to stay quiet about it. But most friends and family members are worn out from listening to them long before a single novel is finished. That may be why so many writers have learned to talk to themselves!

Tape Recording

As silly as it may seem, a tape recorder can be a wonderful listening device. It keeps track of everything you say and then plays it back for you. As long as you keep up with the tapes, you can save all of your thoughts on a project without having to write them down and keep the papers organized.

It may not be a perfect sounding board like a good friend or critique partner, but it can be very helpful when you're arguing with yourself over a character flaw or plot device. Sometimes just listening to yourself saying it aloud can be enough to move you forward. And unlike late-night drinks in a bar, a tape recorder doesn't cost much money. You can take it with you in your car. There are waterproof tape recorders you can use in the shower. You can take them on vacation to help you avoid irritating your spouse, who probably complains that you can't leave your work at home.

ALERT!

> If you use a tape recorder to record an interview with a subject, be sure to get his or her permission. Even though you are writing fiction, if you are using real-life accounts, you may need to verify your interview.

Find a Writing Group

Most writers join writer's groups to talk about writing. It gives them a chance to socialize with other writers and empathize with their situations. Writer's problems are unique in some ways, and sharing them with people who aren't writers can be difficult, but a fellow writer might understand what you're going through—whether you have writer's block or a problem with your spouse, who just doesn't understand why you need to devote so much time to your writing.

Most importantly, participating in a writer's group can help you formulate your story ideas. Imagine the following scenario: You come up with a brilliant new character that's going to save your plot. You get all excited and tell your best friend all about it. He looks at you and asks you why you're spending so much time on this book when you could be improving your golf swing. A writer would never ask you that question.

Sharing ideas, getting feedback to create new ideas, and understanding why you're having a problem with a particular chapter are all part of getting your mind organized about what you're writing. Critique groups and partners can be very helpful in setting you on the right road. Your relationships in writing groups are essential tools in your writing career. They can make the difference between success and failure.

Remember to be a good listener as well. Another writer's success could depend on your understanding, commiseration, or helping her find the answers to her questions. Treat your writing friends with the grace and respect you'd like for yourself.

Who knows—paying attention to a fellow writer's stories could make you famous. Just look at the dedication in Ray Bradbury's *The Martian Chronicles*: "For it was my friend Norman Corwin who first listened to me tell my Martian stories. . . ."

Try Visualization

Most writers see their books played out in their minds like a movie. This is because a great deal of creative processing in the brain is done through visualization. When you can visualize an idea, you can achieve it. You can also use this technique to create the book itself. Visualize your characters as people you know, or imagine watching them in a movie. Settings are also easier to create when you have pictures of them in your mind.

To inspire visualization, you can post pictures on the wall in your workspace, listen to music that is in tune with the story you're writing, and keep trying to imagine what it is you're writing about. Don't be afraid to play with these ideas. Your imagination can really help you take your writing to the next level.

Photographs

Who hasn't felt stirred by a beautiful sunset or a quiet lake? Alternately, a picture of a destitute child can move you to tears. Newspapers know that good pictures sell lots of copies. This is why good photographers are always in demand.

You can use pictures to organize and highlight your ideas. For example, if your plot takes you to an abandoned warehouse, you can prowl around until you find a real-life warehouse that strikes your creative brain. A picture of that warehouse will serve as a reminder of where you are in your book.

Writers who use this technique sometimes keep these pictures on the wall beside their writing space. Or you may choose to keep them in a box with your ideas, or in a photo album devoted to one novel. In any case, keep these pictures handy, and they'll help you focus on any important aspects of your novel.

Drawings and Doodles

Some authors are also brilliant painters or sketchers. If this is true for you, you can definitely use your visual creativity for inspiration. Let your doodling help you visualize what you're writing. Even if these pictures won't make it into your book, they'll certainly help you make the writing more vivid.

Even if you don't think you're much of an artist, that's okay. Whatever works for you is what helps you through the process. If a stick figure with curly hair reminds you of a curly-haired character in your novel, that's all that matters. Drawing diagrams can help you figure out the lay of the land, the layout of a castle, or the topography of a planet where the action of your novel takes place. You don't have to be a genius with a paintbrush to find inspiration in drawing and sketching.

Charts and Graphs

A graph is a visual aid that newspapers and technical writers use to express various ideas. Sometimes these can be mathematical—for instance, a graph that shows the population growth in a town. Charts and graphs help give people a better idea of what the numbers mean by providing a visual.

Fiction writers can use graphs to give themselves ideas on change or growth within their story line. Writers who use this technique have large pieces of paper and markers to create their images. It doesn't matter if you use graphing paper or not. The graph you create simply needs to express your concepts. You don't have to be a physics professor to understand them. Make your graph in such a way that it appeals to you.

If you want to make a chart, visit the National Center for Education Statistics Web site (✍ *http://nces.ed.gov*). You can find information there that will help you create simple or intricate charts. Remember that your chart is what will guide you from one place to another in your novel. It doesn't have to be anything more than a map that helps you when you're stuck and not sure where to go next.

The Power of Storyboarding

Telling a story using a picture on a board is one of the oldest ways of communicating. Storyboarding is a simple way of taking pictures or drawings and putting them in order to create a narrative. This approach is popular among screenwriters, and cartoonists have used this method for years.

Novelists can use storyboards to organize ideas and invoke a kind of creative trance. This allows them to dream up their characters or settings. It's a fun way to look at your story from different angles. It changes as you manipulate your visual aids.

Dry Erase Boards

Any type of storyboarding material may be used, from felt to cork and slate, but probably the most popular among writers is the dry erase board. It doesn't allow for images to be posted on it but it does have a great deal of flexibility. Felt tip markers are cheap and colorful. You don't have to be a great sketch artist to use one. Just create images that you understand. You can erase and re-create or move these images from one place to another.

Even if you don't feel up to the task of drawing images, you can use words or word groups to identify your place in the story. Don't be afraid to include character descriptions, dialogue, or specific geography. Some mystery writers use the entire board to represent a house or hotel where a murder took place. They divide up the board into sections of the house with small notes about what took place in each area. As they write, it becomes an ever-changing map of where they are in the novel.

Puzzle Making

This is probably one of the most creative and time-consuming ways of keeping track of your story. You write down the story line on paper, then cut it into pieces with scissors. The sequence of events is shuffled around until it looks the way you want it to look. You can use this (dis)order of events to present your story.

Another way of using puzzle making in your idea development is to write down character names on pieces of paper and then arrange them in a certain hierarchy (like a family tree) so that you can visualize their relationships with each other and where they are in the story. Romance writers use this device to see which couples will end up together and who will break up with whom. Mystery writers use this to see who died and who killed them. But any fiction writer can use puzzle making as a way of tracking their ideas.

Computer Software You'll Find Useful

While computers weren't invented for writers, they are the best thing that ever happened to us. Anyone who can remember using a manual typewriter for their novels can tell you how much easier it is to use the computer. The days of whiteout and retyping pages that have more than three errors are gone, at least for most people. There are only a few purists left who claim they can't work on a computer.

The computer age has made everything easier for writers. Research on the Internet and conducting online interviews make what was once a time-consuming process fast and simple. Many publishers and agents have begun to appreciate how computers can save them time and money. It's been a slow process but finally, editors are accepting work sent via e-mail. What takes three to five days and $6 to send through the U.S. Mail can now be e-mailed for free in a matter of seconds.

StoryCraft Story Development Software

Many people feel that using writing software that helps develop your book is a sophisticated form of cheating. But many writers do find software programs like StoryCraft immensely helpful and they don't see it as cheating at all.

Writer John Jarvis, who developed StoryCraft, says he created the program "to give people the latest thinking in story/screenwriting construction without all the heartaches and making all the mistakes I did." This is the only major software that uses author Joseph Campbell's approach to writing, as described in his book *The Hero's Journey*.

This software does it all, from conception to organization to putting you in touch with other writers. It tries to make novel writing a no-brainer, and all for just $99.

Storybook Weaver

This software was created to help young children ages six through twelve develop their writing skills, but is now widely used by beginning adult writers. Although it may be too basic for some adults, others do appreciate its playful approach and colorful images. Storybook Weaver Deluxe takes this software one step further to help children think creatively as well.

Before purchasing any software, check to be sure that it is compatible with your computer. For instance, a Mac program will not run on a PC unless it's specially designed for both systems.

Spreadsheet Software

These software packages were developed for offices to keep track of all kinds of information, but writers soon learned the value of keeping track of their own information with them. Series writers (writers who create books with the same characters and/or places) find them especially invaluable. These office packages range in price from $150 to $700 and can be purchased online or at office supply stores, but you might already have one in your computer. These software packages include:

- Microsoft Office (Excel) created by Microsoft
- WordPerfect Office Suite (Quattro Pro) created by Corel
- SmartSuite Office (Lotus 123 spreadsheet) created by Lotus (IBM)
- StarOffice created by Sun Microsystems
- ThinkFree Office created by ThinkFree Corporation
- Mariner Pack by Mariner

Electronic Organizers (PDAs)

A PDA (personal digital assistant) is a tiny hand-held computer that is small enough to fit into your pocket. Its size makes it an excellent way to keep track of writing notes on the road or while waiting in a doctor's office.

FACT

Hand-held devices have infiltrated so far into the writing world that today's editors are using them to edit books. Awe-Struck publisher Dick Claassen says he "wouldn't be without one." Even though you can only see a paragraph at a time, some editors like the portability and convenience.

Despite their small size, these devices are capable of holding large amounts of information that can be shared with your computer. Probably the best known of these is the Palm Pilot. They have many different models in different price ranges and even color schemes. The least expensive is the Zire, which retails for under $100. Other companies sell various other hand-held organizers as well. You can check them out at your local office store or shop online.

Chapter 6

(E) **Creating Your Characters**

Characters make the book. A great character can inspire a series of novels; a less than great one can sink your novel. It's worth repeating that your characters are your first priority. If you want your novel to work, create characters that will make the reader care what happens to them. If you want all that research you did to matter, be sure that it matters to your characters. The people in your novel must be as real as the people you see and deal with every day.

The Main Characters

You love him or you hate him. He makes you want to keep reading or compels you to put the book away and never look at it again. You will remember him for a long time and you'll feel like you knew him intimately—or he'll make no sense and sound completely contrived. He is the novel's main character, the center of the story around whom everything revolves.

ESSENTIAL

> If you've got several characters in mind, and you can't quite figure out which ones are the main characters, let your feelings dictate whom to put in the leading role. The character that interests you most and whose fate you care most about is probably the best one to choose as your main character.

It's really impossible to say what makes a character unforgettable. What is it about James Bond that has kept him alive and spying for so long? In sharp contrast, yet no less unforgettable, what keeps Count Dracula appearing in new stories? These characters just won't go away. Dracula has been revamped so many times that Bram Stoker would hardly recognize his creation.

Wouldn't you love to create characters so real, so intriguing that they will be used in countless books and movies? Every writer longs to accomplish that feat. You may not understand what makes a character like Bond or Dracula come to life, but you can certainly strive to emulate their success.

Most novels have at least two main characters: the protagonist, who is the hero of the story, and the antagonist—the bad guy, the one the readers will love to hate.

Protagonist: The Story's Hero

Everyone loves the hero, especially if it's a well-written character. Readers don't mind if he's a little rough around the edges or even if he's his own worst enemy. He can be quirky, downright crazy, loving, or uncaring. All the reader wants is a personality so strong, so fascinating, that she can't look away.

In romance, the hero must sweep the heroine off her feet, and the readers must be swept along with her. He must be cool but passionate, loving and tender but strong, a take-charge guy. In short, everything most women are looking for all rolled up in one gorgeous six-foot, athletic package. In mystery novels, heroes vary. They can be short or tall, male or female. They can be strong or weak. The one thing they all have in common is solving the mystery and getting the bad guy.

Heroes and heroines must be unforgettable. Readers have to believe that they're capable of dealing with the antagonist and coming out on top. They have to be able to empathize with the protagonist and to imagine themselves doing all of those remarkable things. A good hero can save the world many times over. A bad hero might save the world but no one will remember his name.

QUESTION?

What is an anti-hero?
He's the good guy who's done a few bad things but always comes through in the end. He's Han Solo or Harry Paget Flashman. The hero we share a love-hate relationship with.

Antagonist: The Hero's Nemesis

This is the character your readers should love to hate. Think about all the bad guys you can remember reading about or seeing in movies. What did they have in common? Besides the fact that some of them are brilliant and some of them fall flat, they all serve to antagonize the hero/heroine.

This doesn't mean that the antagonist has to be evil—it's simply a main character that just happens to work against the story's hero. How many books have you read where you wished the antagonist was the good guy? Sometimes the distinction is so unclear, it's difficult to say which character is the antagonist in the story.

The best kind of antagonist is one that the hero can stand up to but not easily overpower. In *Silence of the Lambs,* by Thomas Harris, Hannibal is an unforgettable protagonist, but Agent Starling is his match. He is never really able to overpower her. Harris's supervillain protagonist is almost in awe of Starling. In turn, the reader becomes fascinated with her as well, and the result is a strong antagonist character.

What Makes Them Tick

Have you ever wondered what makes people do the things they do? What makes a runner get up at four in the morning and run five miles? What makes a teenager leave so many dirty socks and empty Pepsi bottles on the floor that he can barely make his way around the room? Why does your boss insist on passing you over for promotion when you work harder than anyone else?

You may never have the answers to these questions, but asking them is the first step in trying to understand the people around you. You have to take some time to analyze those people if you want to analyze the characters you plan to write. They are all motivated and driven by the same things in life.

ALERT!

While your analysis of the people you know may not be perfect, it can serve as a guideline for creating realistic characters for your novel. You may not understand everything about your creations either. In fact, there will always be something new that you learn about them.

Everyone Has Goals

We use goals to keep track of what we've done and what we plan to do. Some people may ignore their goals, but it doesn't mean these goals aren't there. Goal setting helps people be productive, so long as they can accept that they may not always achieve every goal they set for themselves.

Well-developed characters are the same in this regard. They have dreams and ambitions. They may set goals for themselves consciously, or maybe their goals aren't clear to them. They can be impatient or frustrated because they can't reach their goals. Understanding your characters' goals can help you understand them as people.

All characters will have more than one goal. Your main character might be a mystery sleuth who is a genius at solving most cases, but this one has him baffled. He obsesses over it day and night. But he's also worried about losing enough weight to pass his police physical. Soon, after thinking so much about these other aspects of his life, he begins having trouble with his marriage. Another goal is added: to save his relationship.

Character Motivation

What gets you out of bed early on a Saturday morning when you know you can sleep late? Is it the thrill of being out at the lake for the first catch of the day? Or of hunting for bargains at yard sales? Or is it your eight-year-old soccer player who needs a ride to the playing field?

All of these are motivations. You are motivated by something inside of you that wants to write a novel, so you're willing to find the time and energy to accomplish this feat. Your characters should have motivations as well.

Motivation doesn't have to be complicated; a character may be motivated by greed, anger, frustration, love, fear, or the need to have power. Not everyone is set on world domination or other extraordinary things. Readers will more easily identify with characters that share their motivations.

ESSENTIAL

Author Debra Dixon's book *Goal, Motivation and Conflict* is an excellent resource for any writer to understand the importance of proper motivation for their characters. Dixon wrote her guide primarily for romance writers, but any writer can apply this information to their work.

What Stands in Their Way

Conflict is what keeps you and your characters on your toes. It keeps your plot moving forward even as it creates obstacles for your characters to overcome. It shows the reader what your character is made of. Is the character strong enough to overcome the obstacles? Can he overcome the problem and still get the girl or figure out who the killer is?

Conflict can be as subtle as a woman fighting herself and other obstacles in her quest for love and power, as in Barbara Taylor Bradford's *A Woman of Substance*. Or it can be as mind-boggling as the sorceress' quest to defeat a mad sorcerer, as in Tanith Lee's *Volkhavaar*. No matter how great or how small, the obstacles must engage the reader. They must seem real and important to the character, so that the reader can empathize with the character's struggles.

Look around you for events that keep people from getting what they want and how people have overcome them to reach their goals. What you see might inspire you in your writing.

Internal Conflicts

Fear. Anger. Love. Hate. Readers face these barriers every day. Emotions can keep people from getting what they want from life. And the same is true for your characters.

Internal conflict is inside the mind. Is your character unable to chase the bad guy on the roof because she's afraid of heights? Fear can be a powerful internal conflict. The fear of rejection can keep a woman from asking a man at her office out for coffee. She thinks about it for so long, it achieves epic proportions in her mind. Finally, that fear causes her to stalk him. Another plot hatches!

External Conflicts

While internal conflict is like a character flaw that makes the readers sympathetic to the character's struggles, external conflict shows how she handles the world around her. External conflicts don't have to be huge; there is no need for an earthquake or plane crash in every novel. Some external conflicts are smaller, but this doesn't mean that they don't affect the character. As long as the conflict keeps the character from getting what she wants, even a thunderstorm at the wrong moment can be conflict.

A Mix of Conflicts

Most genre books require both external and internal conflict. In romances, the internal conflict is the heroine's changing feelings, while the external conflict may be that her house is being torn down (contemporary), or that her father wishes her to marry one of her suitors (historical). In mystery, conflict is balanced between the sleuth's inner workings or personal feelings and the terrible events going on around him.

ALERT!

> What your character wants and needs from her life has to be dictated by the character development you do. It can't be thrown in randomly to achieve conflict. It has to be part of the character.

For some novels such as men's adventure, external conflict is more important than internal. These books don't require the hero to go through a great deal of soul searching, because they thrive on action.

Their Strengths

Is your hero a superhero who can pick up cars in one hand and save a busload of children with the other? Maybe not. Maybe your hero is just an ordinary mom who manages to raise a crippled son and a rebellious teenage daughter. Or maybe it's a down-on-his-luck private detective who finds out that the mob is trying to take over Venus. Character strengths vary from character to character. Even bad guys have certain strengths that make them believable and challenging to the hero.

Every character is endowed with certain character strengths. Even though Frodo in Tolkien's *Lord of the Rings* trilogy has no great physical or mental prowess, his strength is his inner goodness. It's enough to carry him to victory against the forces of darkness. A character's strengths can make an ordinary person into a hero and a nickel-and-dime villain into a supervillain.

Skills and Abilities

What does your character know how to do? What are her skills? What does she excel at? It doesn't have to be something dramatic. She might only be the best cherry pie maker in the county. Or she might be the family storyteller. It doesn't take a great deal of thought to consider what makes people special to other people.

What can be difficult is showing that "specialness" to the reader. How do you tell the reader what a wonderful or terrible person this character is without having it sound like a shopping list of traits? One way is to allow the characters to be seen by other characters. The pie-baking mother is seen through the eyes of her daughter (who resents her being so wonderful at such a menial task) and her best friend (who envies her because she wants to be the best cherry pie maker in the county).

It may take some time for you to ferret out your characters' abilities. They should be essential qualities that will help solve problems or create them; you should add skills that you consider essential to your story line. You might pattern some of them after people you know in real life.

> **ESSENTIAL**
>
> Making skills and abilities an important part of a character's life requires either experience or research on the part of the writer. Learn to do it yourself or find someone who can teach you about it.

The Importance of Charisma

By definition, charisma is extraordinary personal magnetism. This is the kind of thing that can get a person elected as president and keeps him in office despite scandals and strong opposition. Han Solo personified charisma in *Star Wars*. It didn't matter that he was a bad boy who lived on the edge of right and wrong. Everyone wanted to be him.

A charismatic character is irresistible. Every woman wants him and every man wants to be his friend. Another good example is Robin Hood, a character that has been around for a long time, probably thanks to his charisma. Even a villain can have charisma. Long John Silver in Robert Louis Stevenson's *Treasure Island* is a black-hearted rascal, but every reader loves him.

Creating a charismatic character takes a great love and a willingness to work with the idea. The writer must have empathy with the character, and the readers will too.

Their Weaknesses

Every character has a few character flaws. Without them, the character will turn out perfect—and unrealistic. Imagine a perfect character that never had any doubts or had anything go wrong. Such a character would not only be boring but readers would find themselves unable to sympathize with this perfect persona. It's difficult to get emotionally involved with a character that has no flaws.

Weaknesses are like strengths. They can be large or small. They can cause conflict or help the character take care of problems that arise. A weakness should make the character feel more "human"—this still applies even if the character is an animal or an alien being.

A good example of a character flaw is a quick temper, like Ken Kesey's character R. P. McMurphy in *One Flew over the Cuckoo's Nest*. The character flaw may be employed to set off the story's conflict, thus moving the plot forward. In Stephen R. Donaldson's *Lord Foul's Bane*, the main character, Thomas Covenant, is a leper who is transported into another dimension. Because this character's flaw is stubbornness, he refuses to believe that what he sees is real, creating all manner of conflict that sees him through the novel.

Fear: An Inner Weakness

Everyone is afraid of something. Your character may be afraid of heights, or she may experience fear when she is caught in the middle of an earthquake. Some fears are very internal—purely in the mind of the character. Fears are so much a part of human nature that everyone can relate to them. Who hasn't been afraid of something at some point in their lives?

Deciding how a character deals with his fear can be a major part of how you portray the character. What the fear causes him to do and how he overcomes it are important to the development of your character and your plot. Even if the character never overcomes his fear, it becomes a part of him and affects the story line.

Here's one scenario: Your character is a young boy whose family have always been trapeze artists in the circus. His parents have put him on the trapeze since he could walk, but it still terrifies him. Unfortunately, he must start performing in order to pay for his mother's surgery. How does he overcome his fear and save his mother's life? This is just one example of how fear influences character and plot.

ALERT!

Be careful that your character's disabilities aren't too great to overcome within the context of your plot. It would be unrealistic to have a woman in a wheelchair who has to climb a mountain to solve a mystery or catch a killer. Disabilities have to work with the story line, not against it.

Physical Disabilities

Whereas fear is a good example of an inner weakness, a physical disability is external. For instance, in the romance *The Hardest Step* by Jane Bierce, the heroine has been in a terrible accident that leaves her crippled. She is afflicted both mentally and physically by the trauma. She doesn't believe anyone can love her because of her disability.

Novelists have used physical limitations in many genres. In Anne McCaffrey's *The Ship Who Sang*, the heroine was born deformed. Rather than live life that way, she is integrated into the control functions of a starship. Because of this conflict, she moves forward with adventures that she wouldn't have had without her disability.

A disability can be used to create empathy for the villain as well. Most people sympathize with physical limitations, and this response can draw in readers, only to be even more appalled by the terrible things the antagonist does.

What Makes Them Unique

You've thought about your characters. You understand what motivates them and who they are. You've given them strengths and weaknesses. But can they play the piano?

What makes everyone unique is a combination of many different characteristics. The past haunts or enriches your characters. They move forward with confidence or despite terrible fears. Your hero is tall and strong. Your heroine is always fighting with her best friend because her cherry pies are better.

But just like you, your characters are more than just their fears and desires. They have lives. They work or go to school. Their grandparents taught them to fish when they were children. They used to sneak out and cruise around the neighborhood when they were sixteen. They are not real people, but they should be realistic. Now it's time to have some fun with them!

Hobbies and Interests

Bearing in mind that the things that make us unique can be helpful or a hindrance, what does your character do when she isn't busy going after the bad guys or flying to Mars? Not all hobbies will necessarily make it into your novel. Sometimes it's enough that you know what your characters do in their spare time. Sometimes you may mention it in passing but it may never be a significant part of the plot.

Your cozy mystery sleuth can be a closet romance reader. Your tough-as-nails thriller agent may like to play the saxophone when he isn't saving the world. Your villain who eats good guys for breakfast may love to watercolor. Anything is possible and serves to make the characters more realistic to you and the reader.

Personality Quirks

Your space federation hero won't wear a spacesuit. Your mystery sleuth is afraid of the dark. Your mainstream novel protagonist makes jelly when she gets upset. Your strong, intelligent romance heroine is fascinated by antique wallpaper.

What do all of these things have in common? They're all quirks or ticks in a person's makeup. Our personalities tend to develop little offshoots of our natures—biting your nails, playing with your hair, even only chewing a certain type of gum. These traits can endear your characters to your reader. Everyone has a favorite aunt who knits backwards or likes to stand on her head. Show your reader that your characters can be quirky. This applies to secondary characters as well as main characters.

Be sure that your characters' quirks don't get out of hand. Make them believable and natural for the character, but don't let them overpower the story. Read them to yourself and check to see if you feel confident that these personality glitches enhance the character and make her more interesting rather than annoying or unrealistic.

Likes and Dislikes

Not everyone likes ice cream. Not everyone dislikes anchovies. Part of who your characters are includes the things they like. Consider what your characters like to eat and drink. Do they like to wear blue shirts or green sweaters? Do they like to walk in the rain? Do they like hockey or basketball?

Again, these likes aren't necessarily something that enhances plot. They don't even need to make it into the story. They are there to give your characters more depth. It doesn't mean that you have to list your main character's favorite foods in every paragraph. But you could mention that your hero looks into his closet as he's getting dressed and there are twenty-five blue shirts. Seems he really likes blue shirts. That shows us what he likes (and that he's a little quirky).

Moreover, another look into his closet will show your reader that there are ten pairs of sandals. Your character hates any shoe except a sandal. He's tried boots and moccasins, but he won't wear anything but a sandal.

What your character dislikes can be as telling about him as what he likes. It can represent part of something he fears. Or it can just be something he can't get over. Maybe he doesn't like to eat popcorn because he dislikes food that sticks in his teeth. His dislikes create another aspect of him as a unique individual. While this may not help him solve the crime or firmly put his Aunt Zelda in her place, it helps your reader relate to him. Maybe your reader doesn't like popcorn either.

Naming Your Characters

William Shakespeare may have been the first writer to note that not everything is contained in a name. And it's true: There are many things that aren't done justice by their names.

However, since you're the creator of your world, you have the power to give characters names that do fit them. You should have a reason for giving a character a particular name. And place names should fit their purpose in the story too.

Many writers say that their characters come with names, while others take weeks to come up with just the right name. However your characters and places come to you, be sure their names fit.

QUESTION?

I need help looking for the perfect name for my characters. What should I do?
BabyNames.com (☞ www.babynames.com) is a good source of names online. The site has millions of names and what they mean. Or you might like to purchase a book of baby names, like *20,001 Names for Baby* by Carol McD. Wallace or *The Everything® Baby Names Book* by Lisa Shaw.

Finding the Perfect Name

Is your romance heroine named Sarah after her late aunt? Is the evil alien slave trader named Gronk because he likes to hit people on the head? And what about great Uncle Jefferson who was named for the president?

Parents want to find the perfect name for their baby. There are countless books ready to help them with this auspicious task. After all, your child will probably live with this name for the rest of his or her life. Some people legally change their names because they feel that the name their parents gave them doesn't fit, but characters can't change their names. So, as their "parent" you have an obligation to make their names fit their roles in your story.

You may think the world of your grandmother whose name is Sherazadhey, but giving this name to your character may not work. Carefully consider the impact of your character's name on your reader. You don't have to use stereotypical names (every prostitute doesn't have to be named Desiree) but a name should say something about the character and be memorable to the readers.

Making Up Names

The name Mary rarely appears in most alien worlds. Science fiction writers want to make other worlds less mundane. They want the reader to feel that they're in another place where no female would ever have an ordinary Earth name. Science fiction names tend to be more like Six or T'Poli; they sound alien when you read them.

Fantasy writers also use exotic names for places and people. Their reasoning is the same. Names are important in helping the reader escape to alternate dimensions. But the right name for your earthbound rancher who lives in the wilds of Australia might be equally exotic. There are no rules that say that names have to come from name books. Writers have named characters everything from Shorty to Tomahawk. If the right name for your character is something you created, it doesn't matter. As long as it portrays the person the way you see them and communicates that to the reader, anything is possible.

Common Mistakes

When you create characters for your novel, there are very few things you actually need to avoid. With the exception of misplaced flaws or exaggerated strengths, most readers will forgive an interesting character anything. If your character is a complete package, with all the attributes of an individual, you can make him the most heinous killer of the greatest hero.

However, there are some things that you'd do best to avoid. Be careful about being overzealous and trying to impress the reader with how beautiful the heroine is or how terribly shy Aunt Sally has become in her old age. Any character trait can be overdone. This can be as bad as a character that lacks in basic personality.

To avoid these mistakes, allow your characters to unfold before the reader. Don't try to tell them what each person is like. Let them get to know them through other characters and their actions.

FACT

The phrase "one man's trash is another man's treasure" comes to mind here. As surely as you avoid writing something that seems wrong or misplaced, another writer is going to come along and get published doing the same thing. There are no real guidelines on what you should avoid. Let your good judgment be your final guide.

Skip the Stereotypes

In comedy, using a representation of a person or group can be amusing. If you're writing comedy, you can use this device carefully to make your point. But if you're writing a serious novel, back away from using stereotypical characters like these:

- The dumb blond bombshell
- The prostitute with a heart of gold
- The fast-talking, in-your-face reporter
- The slow-as-molasses Southern sheriff
- The ethnic convenience store clerk
- The heartless greedy lawyer

It's not that you can't find these types of people in real life. And it's not that some well-known writers don't have them in their novels. But as a beginner, it's best to create a fresh approach to your characters. Consider making your blond bombshell an intelligent pianist. Or maybe your reporter has a lisp. By staying away from stereotypes, you give your characters room to grow. They are free to be extraordinary, charismatic people who will surprise and enchant your readers.

ALERT!

Be careful if you decide to use stereotypes. Maybe you think that a character in your book just has to be written in this fashion, but try to find some way to take a fresh approach. You can accomplish this with an unusual quirk or hobby that makes him less of a caricature.

Unsympathetic People

This is the character everyone dreads. You wrote him at three in the morning when you were half asleep. When you read him the next day, you want to believe it is okay. But you know in your heart he is wrong. When your sister reads him the next day and proclaims him to be a dead fish, you know you don't have any choice but to rewrite.

Yes, it's the unsympathetic character. He's taking up space on the page but that's about all. He adds nothing to the work or, even worse, detracts from the story. This can be a main character or a secondary character. Maybe he's supposed to carry the plot or maybe he's just comic relief. Whatever he's supposed to be doing, he misses the mark.

The only thing you can do when you create an unlikable character is to admit the mistake and change him. It's not always easy to figure out what makes one character so lovable and another unremarkable. Be brutally honest with yourself and your work. Did you try hard to make him three-dimensional, with likes and dislikes, fears and strengths? Did you give him interesting hobbies? Is he someone you'd like to work with, fall in love with, or worry about meeting in a dark alley? If the answer is "no," it's time to get back to character development. Ⓔ

Chapter 7

Getting Characters to Talk

One of the most important resources that a writer has is dialogue. It's long been known that how you speak is a reflection of who you are. If you speak intelligently, people believe that you are intelligent and well educated. If your speech is sloppy and full of slang, people tend to believe the opposite. It may not always be true, but in writing, authors use speech patterns to create impressions—to make readers believe something about their character.

Creating Realistic Dialogue

Because dialogue is so important to creating your character's personality, make sure your dialogue is up for the task. So, what can you do to create realistic dialogue? Start by listening to your character's voice in your head. What does he or she sound like?

FACT

Writing Dialogue by Tom Chiarella is a good book for any writer interested in writing great dialogue. It takes you through the process of how to write dialogue, explains the differences between good and bad dialogue, and shows you how to listen to the speech around you for clues about how to write the way people talk.

Everyone recognizes the voices of their loved ones and friends on the phone. What features do we use to distinguish between different voices? What makes a person's voice distinctive or even memorable? Whatever these traits are, you can also use them to make your character's speech memorable for your readers. Make sure your characters are special and that something of their voice lingers in the minds of your readers. Like a song from the radio that you can't get out of your head, your characters will live on long after the reader puts down your book.

Listening to People Speak

The next time you're at a party, listen to the people around you. You'll find a myriad of speech patterns that accompany the conversations. There's Joe, who's from Chicago, who says "dese" and "dose" instead of "these" and "those." He's a bartender who relates everything he hears to the people who frequent his bar. He knows the names of every mixed drink and manages to tell his listeners about a new one whenever they see him. You can hear Georgette above any noisy crowd. She's an investment banker. Her conversations are full of what's happening on Wall Street and how surplus goods are affecting the economy.

There is a big difference between real and realistic dialogue. Real dialogue can be about the weather or the economy. But unless the weather or the economy directly relate to your character and plot, stay away from mundane subject matter.

Mary whispers all of her words. She's a trauma nurse who frets over any injury, no matter how old, and remembers to ask if you've had your flu shot. And Arthur whines when he speaks. His whining voice always centers on what he knows: How to tell one sickness from another and how many rare diseases he's had so far this year. Don't get caught in a conversation between Mary and Arthur!

Reading Aloud

You've listened to the people around you and applied some of the things you've heard to your characters. You've written a scene that has important dialogue between your two main characters. The words just don't seem right but you can't tell what's wrong. Everything looks fine. But something's bothering you.

The best way to make corrections in dialogue is to read it out loud. Don't forget that people are supposed to be saying these things. If the words don't sound right as you speak them, you should be able to tell why and make corrections.

For instance: "Susan, what is that that you are looking at?" Obviously, this is a bad piece of dialogue for more than one reason. Try saying it aloud. You'll find that it's stilted and the double *that* makes it sound like a Martian has taken over your mouth.

It could be changed to read this way: "What are you looking at, Susan?" By repairing the dialogue, it sounds more natural. You eliminate the *thats* and streamline the sentence. It has the same meaning; it's just more effective.

Dialogue That Fits

Your tough cowboy walks into a crowded saloon and says, "Could you please give me a small glass of whiskey?" This line just won't work. What's wrong with it? Try this scene again. Your tough cowboy walks into a crowded saloon and says, "If I don't get some whiskey soon, I'm just going to die of thirst." Still not right? That's because this dialogue doesn't match the character. Tough cowboys talk tough. If he walked into a saloon, he'd demand whiskey, not sound like he was at the malt shop.

It's important that dialogue reflects the character's role and personality. Your reader will be reading the dialogue you write and hearing the voices in his or her head. The voices have to ring true or you've lost one of the most powerful tools you have for showing who your character is. Many characters are remembered for their clever speech patterns or unique way of speaking. You'll lose a reader completely if your characters don't respond as the reader expects them to.

What's Said about the Character

Dialogue is an excellent way to tell your reader about your character. You might have characters say something about another character you're trying to describe. A good friend of your romance heroine could be thinking that she's too nice or that she's too good for the hero. She could be considering that the heroine could lose a few pounds or that she has always been too worried about everything being neat and orderly.

Even if you're only telling the story from the heroine's point of view, you can have her overhear people talking about her. Or she could get some strong advice from her relatives about the way she lives her life. This way, the reader comes to know something about the character that doesn't have to come out in narrative or while the character is looking in the mirror.

What They Say about Themselves

So, when can you let your characters speak for themselves? While you can have them reflect on their lives or their appearance, keep it brief. Remember that you wouldn't want to spend much time with someone who constantly talked about his hair or the minute details of his life. You want your characters to be the kind of people your reader will want to spend time with and come back to visit.

Dialogue also says something about the people who are talking. How they say things and what they choose to leave out is just as important here. Using conversation with another character is a good way of handling character development. Let the character talk to a friend or relative about her concerns. The reader will get to know the character by listening in on these conversations. By understanding the concerns of family and friends, even by using a police background check, the reader begins to empathize with the character.

If you listen closely, much of real-life conversation is repetitive and unnecessary. That's fine for real life. But in a novel, dialogue should never be meaningless conversation. It should always help advance the plot or tell the reader something about the character.

Masculine Voice

Is there a certain way of speaking that can be defined as "masculine"? When you pick up the phone, how do you decide if a man or a woman is speaking? Generally, most people decide by the sound of the voice. Is there something else that gives away gender? If so, what is it and how do you write it?

There are writers who are considered the epitome of male voice. Ernest Hemingway, Mickey Spillane, and Erle Stanley Gardner are known for their masculine writings. There are many others who write in particularly male-dominated genres. Authors like Margaret Mitchell, Barbara Cartland, and Agatha Christie wrote books that establish the feminine voice in writing as well as in dialogue.

What He Said

"I saw her run down the street after the dog. She was wearing tight shorts and a low-neck sweater." Without any context for this dialogue, can you tell if a man or a woman is speaking? If you guessed a man, the dialogue did its job. The description of the woman was from a male point of view, what a man would notice and describe to someone else. This is a subtle way of creating gender in your character's words.

"I saw that little lady run down the street after that dog. Looked like she was almost wearing nothing." This is a far less subtle way of engendering dialogue. It's very obvious that the speaker is a man. Of course, this kind of dialogue would only work for some characters. Most male characters are subtler in their speech.

The Way He Said It

"I saw her run down the street after the dog," he said with a broad grin of appreciation on his face. "She was wearing tight shorts and a low-neck sweater."

Adding a dialogue tag that tells the reader what's going on around the words will contribute to the overall feel of gender. The man obviously enjoyed seeing the woman run after the dog. When dialogue and narrative work together, it gives the reader a better sense of the character that's speaking.

Even without a specific addition to the dialogue, you can enhance the text with the action that accompanies it. For example: "The cop turned to the first man he saw in the crowd and asked him what happened. 'I saw her run down the street after the dog. She was wearing tight shorts and a low-neck sweater.'" Here the story line and the dialogue become one in order to explain what's happening.

Not all characters are distinctly male or female. If you're writing a science fiction novel, you may have a genderless character. Decide early on how you want to refer to this character and stick to it.

Feminine Voice

One of the biggest complaints about feminine voice comes from romance readers. They claim to be able to tell when a man is writing a woman's character. The discussion always centers on dialogue. But is there really a way to define feminine voice? Women express themselves differently than men, and writers need to make sure the difference is in the writing.

What She Said

Looking at the scene that served as our example in the previous section, how would a writer need to change the dialogue to express what a woman saw? "I saw her run down the street after the dog. She was wearing bright red shorts and a pink cashmere sweater." Even without dialogue tags that identify the speaker or specific context to continue the story line, the reader probably knows a woman is explaining what she saw.

A less subtle way to create the effect of gender would be: "I saw her run down the street after the dog. She was wearing bright red shorts and a white shirt. I saw that same shirt on sale at Bergman's last week." Adding the last sentence tends to prop up the reader's view that a woman is speaking.

There could be other telltale hints that could give it away. The witness might add the color of the woman's lipstick or something about her jewelry, anything that a woman might think to mention.

The Way She Said It

"There was something about him," she said with a smile as she twisted her finger in her hair. "He was good looking, but it was more than that. He really looked at me. You know what I mean?"

Male and female characters also require different ways of describing how they act and speak. Aunt Sophie's voice might be described as sweet or shrill. If she has a deep voice, it would be husky or even manly. While society looks for ways to make men and women equal, writers look for ways to tell them apart.

Dialogue tags for women must denote the speaker as they do for men. To use action with your dialogue, think about the physical differences between men and women. The two genders tend to have similar habits, but women usually gesture, walk, and carry themselves differently than men. They have different ways of laughing and expressing themselves. Keep your eyes open in a crowd of men and women to observe the differences.

E ALERT!

If you are writing the new type of tough female character that is popping up in many genres, be careful to allow her to sound feminine without being wimpy. These characters are equal to or better than the men around them. They never back down and neither should their dialogue.

Using Slang in Your Writing

Language is fluid. It changes with the times or it dies. No doubt this is why dictionaries began accepting slang words into their hallowed pages. Because of this, there is an ever-growing realm of words that make teachers wince and kids applaud.

Everyone uses slang. Your characters will use it too. It creates another bond with the reader. For the writer, understanding and using slang effectively is what matters.

Proper Slang

For the purpose of classification, there are two forms of slang, proper and improper. You might wonder how any slang can be considered "proper." Proper slang in this case is slang that you can find in the dictionary. Such words make it into the dictionary after several generations of use. They include words like *ain't*, *gonna*, *bye-bye*, and *cabby*. These may not be words that English teachers encourage their students to use, but you're a novelist, not an English teacher. Don't be afraid to use these "legal" slang words in your character's vocabulary.

Improper Slang

Some genres require using words that aren't found in the dictionary, at least not yet. These include profanity and what society calls "street talk." When it comes to words, fads change quickly, and using words that'll fade out of existence might date your book. But they can speak more eloquently to some people than all of Shakespeare's sonnets.

You should only use profanity or trendy slang words if it makes your character seem more alive and it fits the way he or she would speak. If you're using the words just to make an editor raise her eyebrows or because it will look "cool," then don't waste your time. It takes a lot to surprise an editor. And what's cool today is old stuff tomorrow.

QUESTION?

Does a writer have to use slang?
Writers are free to decide if they want to use slang. But in most novels, including historical and science fiction, characters that come alive for the readers use some slang.

Contemporary or Historical

Slang has definitely changed in the last hundred years. If you write in any historical genre, you have to know what the slang was for that time. Beware of using contemporary slang that wasn't in use during the time of your novel. For example, the contemporary use of the word *gay* has changed dramatically just in the last fifty years. Keeping track of these little nuances may seem slight, but readers can spot them immediately. Historical readers are bears about inconsistencies.

Contractions

Modern speech requires brevity. We don't use the same patterns our great grandparents used. Contractions are a part of our speech today. Using haven't instead of have not, couldn't instead of could not, and weren't instead of were not is expected by the reader. Not using contractions makes characters sound stilted and unreal. The only exception to this is found in science fiction and historical genres. Even in narrative, using contractions helps maintain the pacing of the story. Be sure to shorten these words wherever possible in your novel.

Foreign Phrases

It's always tempting to use a few romantic French words or some robust Spanish phrases that will add flair and enhance a character's dialogue.

There's nothing wrong with doing this, provided that you keep it down to a minimum. An occasional German profanity is enough to make the reader understand that the character reverts to his native language when he gets upset. It works the same way in the middle of a great sex scene. Any strong emotion or simply a slang that the character picked up can be effective.

Avoid overdoing it, though. Too many foreign phrases will take your readers out of their story zone and send them scrambling for a dictionary—just like a movie with too many foreign words will have you shouting, "Subtitles!"

FACT

Science fiction novels have created a host of "foreign phrases" that allow the characters in the book to express themselves. Because they are frequently from other planets or times, their words may be gibberish but they are important to the story. Use them sparingly to create the alien feel you're trying to portray.

Dialogue Tags

Attributives, or dialogue tags, separate dialogue from narrative, indicating who said what and the action that takes place in the dialogue. Dialogue tags appear before, after, and between the words of dialogue.

Today's fiction tends to use few dialogue tags, relying on them only when they are absolutely necessary. Even then, they are frequently action tags, referring to the speakers' action rather than simply saying "he said" or "she said." Dialogue tags are particularly useful in conversations that involve more than two people.

Finding the right number of dialogue tags to use in your work must have a commonsense approach. If you use too many tags, you risk interrupting the story line; using too few makes it impossible for the reader to figure out who's talking. The only way to learn about using them is by trial and error. When you've written enough of them, you'll get the idea.

When to Use Them

The placement of dialogue tags complicates the matter even more. There are no rules except what sounds right. Finding a "natural" place for them requires reading the dialogue out loud and deciding for yourself.

For example, you could use a dialogue tag several different ways with the same piece of dialogue:

He said, "Everyone must leave. Go out the back door."
"Everyone must leave," he said. "Go out the back door."
"Everyone must leave. Go out the back door," he said.

The best way to judge this is by the text around it and listening to find the place where you pause to put the dialogue tag. You have to develop an "ear" for speech and its placement. Try to avoid too many of the same placements on a page of text. It's not essential to use other attributives than "said." Try not to get too colorful. And remember that the words you use must be able to describe speech. The following just won't work: "You are silly," *he laughed* (you can't "laugh" dialogue).

Action Tags

Action tags, for want of a better term, are attributives that describe action and help mark which character is speaking. These indicate the movements that characters make before, during, and after speech. They can help sustain the pace in a story by providing information that keeps the reader from having to slow down to decide who's speaking.

Like dialogue tags, their more sedentary counterparts, there are several different ways to use action tags. Using the sentence from the previous section, action attributives would change it this way:

He rushed into the room. "Everyone must leave. Go out the back door."
"Everyone must leave." He pointed toward the far end of the room. "Go out the back door."
"Everyone must leave. Go out the back door." He opened the door and ushered them out.

Remember that you don't need to add another attributive to this unless you change subjects or you're worried about the reader getting lost in a large paragraph. Like passive dialogue tags, action shows who's speaking.

When you must use passive dialogue tags, be careful not to get too creative. A good he said/she said will get you through most situations. You don't need to spend a lot of time with your thesaurus to research other ways to say it.

Dialogue can be used to create a feeling of movement in the story. If you find some spots in your book are not as lively or well paced as they could be, try adding some dialogue. It will move the story forward without bogging it down.

Be Aware of Bad Dialogue

Because dialogue is unique to each character and each story, it's difficult to say what's right and wrong. You'll have to use your own best judgment. If you read everything aloud, it should help you make your characters' speech realistic and right for them.

Characters in books have said some memorable things. Ask yourself if your characters have anything important to say. Do their words touch you? Do they make you laugh when they're supposed to? Do they make you cry at the right moment? Do they move the story forward and reveal things about your characters that are important to the reader?

Obviously, not every novel is going to change the world. Not every piece of dialogue will be picked up and mimicked by readers. Don't strive to reach those lofty goals. Let your dialogue tell your story with an honest and fresh approach. Then let history take care of the rest.

Avoid Clichés

Like bad stereotypical characters, some words and phrases keep coming back and have become stale from so much use. Someone should have put them out of their misery a long time ago. But they've become so familiar that many times writers don't realize what they're saying—or worse, what their characters are saying.

Avoid clichés like the following:

- "It was blacker than pitch outside."
- "The bar was hotter than an oven."
- "Her eyes were bluer than the sky."
- "When in Rome . . ."
- "When life gives you lemons . . ."
- "She was happy as a clam."

These are only a few of the many clichés that you don't want to use. It's best to avoid all clichés, especially in narrative. It may be argued that it is okay to use clichés in dialogue because people speak that way. Readers may understand clichés and relate to them. Writers frequently use them to express comedic characters in novels. But by avoiding clichés, your work will seem less tired and your dialogue will be more unique.

ALERT!

Be sure that your novel is a comfortable blend of dialogue and narrative. Too much narrative will leave your readers yawning but too much dialogue will leave them gasping for air. Keep an even balance between the two and make sure both enhance plot and character.

Too Much Dialect

In *The Elements of Style*, Strunk and White put it bluntly: "Do not attempt to use dialect unless you are a devoted student of the tongue you hope to reproduce." Dialect can be a useful trait to show the reader where your character is from. It can be quaint or romantic. It can tell the reader a great deal about the character without any narrative to describe him. Used cautiously and sparingly, it can enhance your novel.

But when it becomes overdone, dialect is tedious and boring. There's no reason to reiterate a character's dialect in every piece of dialogue. If the character is from the South, he doesn't need to end every *–ing* word by cutting off the *g*. If he does it a few times, the reader gets the picture.

The same thing can be said for using the Irish brogue. Once or twice is fine, even in historical novels. Continuing to use it every time the character speaks would be like repeating the character's description in each paragraph. It's unnecessary and can be distracting.

Dialect should be like sugar sprinkles on a doughnut. You don't have to cover the entire doughnut; a nice dusting does the trick.

Chapter 8

Choosing the Setting

If you think that when and where a story is set doesn't matter, think again. Whether the background is a creepy English moor or a distant desert planet, setting creates the picture you're trying to portray. If you don't believe it, take the same story about the desert planet and put it in the English countryside. How many things that you thought were basic to your plot and characters would have to change?

Time Period

Think of the setting for your novel like the resting place of a brilliant diamond. The diamond may be the most important part of the equation, but where it rests adds or subtracts from its overall effect. The diamond, in this case, is your brilliant combination of plot and character. It's a masterpiece of sparkling wit and intricate facets that will mesmerize readers. Now, will you put that diamond in a lovely antique setting, large and heavily carved? Or will your setting be something lightweight and comfortable, something more in keeping with modern times? Or will your diamond rest in a high-tech platinum setting, one that challenges the mind and questions the future?

Whatever your choice, remember that the setting is the showcase for your work. Give your story the perfect background and your characters will shine. Take the time to choose carefully. Every novel deserves the best!

ESSENTIAL

Use enough pertinent information about your setting to give the reader the feel of the place without making it too specific. When it comes to personal detail, less is better. You may even want to change some names so that they're close to the real thing without being exact.

Historical Setting

If you decide that your perfect setting is Italy in the 1400s, expect to do a lot of research. But don't let that put you off if this is the right place for your novel. Certainly, if your main character is an Italian priest who knows Christopher Columbus, Italy in the 1400s would have to serve as your setting.

Every place, every time period is different. Historical settings allow some things to happen that couldn't happen in present day. You can explore the world with Magellan or participate in the Civil War. The past creates the possibility of exciting events and people who could take part in your novel.

If you're a mystery writer, your sleuth doesn't need to find DNA to solve a crime. Like Cadfael in the Ellis Peters's series, he can use his sense of curiosity and knowledge about the world to solve crimes. The possibilities are as numerous as the days of our past.

Remember that your setting is important to your plot's believability. It may seem unlikely that many readers know much about fifteenth-century Italy and that getting the details right doesn't matter. But your lack of detail won't convince you or your reader and you'll lose the illusion that your story is "real."

Contemporary Settings

Maybe your sleuth is a monk like Cadfael but he lives in a modern-day monastery and uses a computer to solve crimes. Contemporary settings are a little easier to write. Still, you'll need to research places you've never been and certain aspects of the plot or character. You'd want to know about tools your characters might use (guns, computers, cars) or things they might do (skiing, being a stockbroker, skydiving). But there's a lot you already know about contemporary life. You know what clothes people wear and how they talk. You know what sports and other activities people have as hobbies.

Possibly the easiest of all locations is your own hometown. This includes your house, your basement, your front porch and other miscellaneous personal locations. You can use your neighbors or even the postman as templates to create your plot. There is nothing too mundane that it can't be made grotesque or ridiculous. Conversely, in mainstream fiction, there is nothing too mundane that can't be explored with a writer's eye for emotion and compelling personal detail. Even a visit to your doctor can yield material that you can be weave into your plot. From small towns to big cities, writers make use of what they know. It's the most common and time-tested means of creating your fiction.

Futuristic Settings

What do you see when you look into the future? More than 100 years ago, Jules Verne saw men in flying machines, living and traveling underwater, and walking on the moon. Was he a psychic? Or was he just an imaginative writer?

The future is wide open. Because no one really knows what's going to happen, your characters can go anywhere and do anything. They can live on an Earth that has become a barren wasteland. Or they can live on a distant planet that is a garden paradise free of hunger and disease. The choice is yours. As long as your characters are at home there, your futuristic setting can become as well known as the one in *Star Wars*.

The only limitations are the ones in your mind. As long as the idea works in your book, you're free to play with it. As you create the world of tomorrow, remember that writing about something in the future has to be as detailed as describing life today or 200 years ago.

QUESTION?

Where's the line between historical, contemporary, and futuristic fiction?
Most publishers consider anything before the 1900s as historical fiction and anything set after current times as futuristic fiction. Consult guidelines from individual publishers to be sure.

Geographic Location

Your characters' stomping grounds might be something as simple as living in a cardboard shack behind a convenience store. Your characters could live in a huge tree house on a deserted island, like the characters in *Swiss Family Robinson*. Your characters could be Nazi agents living in Poland during World War II. Whatever suits your plot and creates the perfect setting for the people in your novel to reach their goals is fair game.

Many times the locale for your story will come to you as part of the whole package. Your character emerges. You discover what the character wants and how he'll get it. The setting falls right into place because the only option for this character is to live in present-day Minnesota. All of that can happen on a good day.

On a bad day, the character you thought could only live in Minnesota suddenly takes a turn. He has to go to Russia to find his long-lost daughter. You don't know anything about Russia except what you hear on the news. Your locale shifts with your story and you find yourself doing research.

Be flexible. If your character needs to go to Russia, let him go. He can always come home again.

Exotic Locations

For some authors, the more exotic a locale, the better they seem to like it. Many of them have traveled to these places. For instance, James E. Michener's own travels were the inspiration for *South Pacific*. Author Rudyard Kipling went to India before writing *The Jungle Book*. Anna Leonowens wrote *The English Governess at the Siamese Court* about her time with the king of Siam.

There are many exotic locations to choose from and many different time periods to find them in. This includes science fiction and fantasy. Just as some science fiction takes place in present day on Earth, other novels depict lush, spectacular worlds that exist only in the minds of the authors.

Details are essential to writing about an exotic port of call. You want your readers to feel the heat of the jungle or the cold of the lifeless tundra. You have to know what animals exist there, if any. What does it smell like? What does the water taste like? Because many of your readers will never travel to these locations, you have to include everything to make them feel like they've been there.

Your Own Backyard

Writing teachers always advise their students to write about people and events that they know. That's part of the beauty about writing something ordinary that you've experienced. Let the others write about perfumed harems and gilded palaces. You're going to write about taking your kids to school and going shopping.

It's not as far-fetched as it sounds. Amy Tan's *The Joy Luck Club* doesn't take place in an extravagant setting. Its comfortable setting serves it well in its exploration of relationships between people. Judy Blume's novel of youthful discovery, *Are You There, God? It's Me, Margaret*, doesn't have an ostentatious background. But the strength and problems of this young girl living in New Jersey doesn't need an elaborate backdrop.

Many horror novels are set in the most ordinary of circumstances and places. The rationale behind this is using something everyday that suddenly becomes alien. Romances usually take place in a hometown setting because the only thing important is the developing relationship between the hero and heroine. You'll have to decide if your setting needs to be exotic to add to the plot or if your story can be told over a cup of tea in someone's sitting room.

ALERT!

Be aware of time zones when considering times in your writing. A good place to get this information is the World Clock, at ✑*www.timeanddate.com*. This site will tell you what time it is in Sydney when your character is in Moscow.

Sequencing

You're writing for people who live by the Atomic Clock. They wear watches on their wrists while their computers click off the minutes and the clock on the wall moves slowly forward. People are aware of what time it is, and they need to feel like they know what time it is in the scenes of your novel.

How do you achieve regulating time in your novel? One way is to make sure the movement in your book runs according to your reader's expectations. When morning follows night and lunch follows breakfast, you're assuring them that everything is right in the world.

Time of the Day

How do you decide what time it is? Do you look out of your office window and see the people flooding into the streets to know it's time to go home? Does the smell of cinnamon rolls waft up to you from the cafeteria bakery to let you know it's lunchtime?

There are plenty of creative ways to let your readers know what time it is without actually telling them. You don't have to force your character to glance at her watch every five minutes. It's not necessary to proclaim that it's evening like an old-time watchman in London. Give the reader hints about the time by what your characters and the people around them are doing.

Your characters wake up in the morning. They go to bed in the evening. They can watch a sunrise or sunset. They can eat lunch or dinner. Their children come home from school in the afternoon. All of these things show the passing of time. Dialogue never needs to discuss the current time unless your character is on a schedule or a bomb is going to blow up in three hours.

Day of the Week

Monday always follows Sunday. That goes for present-day and historical novels. It's fine to mention days of the week in the novel. It's not unusual to let a character say that it's Tuesday and the trash needs to go out. Or the narrative can tell a reader that it's Sunday and the character always sleeps late on Sunday.

Other ways of showing what day of the week it is could include having the character attend Shabbat services at the synagogue, which implies Saturday. If a character ends the workweek, you know it is probably Friday.

Time of the Year

Seasons are different for everyone around the world. When it's spring in the United States, it's autumn in Australia. One group of people is planting while another group is harvesting. Besides the obvious spring buds and golden leaves of fall, writers need to keep in mind what time of year their book takes place.

ESSENTIAL

Remember that there are certain limitations on time, particularly associated with seasons and locations. If your character is going to be in New York during the winter, he won't be wearing shorts and a tank top unless he just moved down from the Yukon. But even that could be explained in the text.

It makes a fuller, richer background for the reader to feel the cold of December in Maine or the hot sun during the summer on the coast of France. People's activities change according to the season. They dress and eat differently. Letting your reader experience these changes, even if your book only takes place during one season, sets the mood and makes the action more realistic.

Seasons don't have to be observed by remarks from characters. No one has to open their front door and declare, "It's winter!" Subtle reminders keep the reader in the season. Maybe the heroine has to put on a coat and gloves to go out for a walk. Maybe she has to have a raincoat. Or her air conditioner or furnace could be broken, creating an uncomfortable problem. Holidays can also tell the reader what season is taking place.

Details That Evoke the Setting

There's more to setting than simply time and place. What are those details that add dimension to the setting of a story? The five senses are powerful ways to describe settings. What does the beach smell like? What does sand feel like between your toes? What do the waves hitting the beach sound like? All of these things represent the psychology of setting. They are the nonspecific points of recognition that contribute to the reality of your locale.

Another small but important detail that can be used to evoke the setting is food. What people eat varies from place to place, so a character's favorite food can help define a character and setting.

When you think of home, what comes to mind? The easy chair in front of the television? The worn spot on the carpet where the dog lies? The comfort of your bed after a hard day? Close your eyes and envision the small details that make your house special to you. So many things create a home.

It takes just as many details to create homes for your characters. If you want your readers to really know a place in your book, you have to include the little details that make it come alive in their minds.

Customs and Traditions

The special things that people do every day make up the customs of a place. In your home, it may be customary that you always eat dinner on Sunday afternoon with your whole family. That creates a piece of the tapestry that surrounds your life. Customs can be the small aspects that are part of your daily life. Particular customs might be used in your book to create conflict. They are pieces of the setting for your character to explore. He may not like the customs he finds, and he may even try to change them.

The customs may also be related to celebrating holidays and special events. These can be famous like the Mardi Gras in New Orleans or less famous like a Founder's Day Festival in a small town. Different places celebrate holidays like Christmas and Chinese New Year in various ways. Each of these contributes to the flavor and flair of your setting. They bring the reader closer to understanding the character through understanding the place he's from or his reactions to the place he finds himself.

Latest Fashions

The clothing your characters wear can also be part of the setting. Basically, descriptions of clothing aren't a part of most plots. There can be exceptions to this idea, but mostly, clothing is part of the backdrop of your story.

What your character wears can help describe where they are and what they do. For instance, if it's summer and your character is at the beach, she's probably wearing a bathing suit. If it's winter and she's hiking in the mountains, she's probably wearing a snowsuit and boots. It's not so much that clothes are essential to the story as that they contribute to the description of your character and setting.

The exceptions to the importance of clothes in your novel could be if it takes place in the garment district of New York. Or if part of the plot is that your heroine is left naked in the woods. In circumstances like these, the description of clothing becomes essential to the plot. You'll have to decide the difference for your book when you start writing. But even if your novel doesn't take place on the fashion runways of Paris, telling your readers what your characters are wearing is another piece of the images you want to create in their minds.

Would hairstyles be considered as part of the setting?
Unless the hairstyle is important to the plot, you could consider hairstyles to be part of the time and place of the setting. It adds an interesting touch when you know even small details.

Creating the Backdrop

A setting is your novel's backdrop, and you create it much as you would weave a tapestry—by weaving together all kinds of details that all fit into place to create a larger picture. You know where you want your story to take place. You know where that place is located. You know what time of the day, week, and year it starts. Each is a part of the various colors of thread that will come together to draw your reader into the story.

You'll want to be sure that your characters and plot create a warm glow within the other colored threads. The picture that emerges as you put everything together will be what your readers see when they look at your book. Can you see the complete image? Do all of the threads blend together? This is a good time to question how the character, dialogue, and setting mesh. If one seems out of place, now's the time to change it. It's easier to change something before you start writing. There will be plenty of things that you don't see beforehand to change later.

There isn't always a way to know if everything is going to work together. Until you begin writing your manuscript, there's always the chance that what you've already put together isn't going to be what you want. But the more time you spend thinking about the pieces and trying to put them together before you start, the better your chances that they will be exactly what you want.

Do Your Research

Many writers hate this word. They don't want to think about what they're writing; they just want to write it. The best advice on this: Don't write anything that requires research. If you stay exclusively in your field of knowledge, you don't have to look up anything. The same goes for worlds you create. That information is stored in your own mind.

But if you want to write about a gunslinger in the Wild West, prepare to research. Even if you only watch old Westerns to learn about that period, you have to know what you're talking about.

Going There

If you want to write about Cairo, there's nothing like going there. You can taste the food, visit the pyramids, and feel the sand. You'll get first-hand knowledge of the people and how they live. You can drink coffee and talk about politics. If you're writing a historical novel, you can visit the museums and the actual locations where the events took place.

Writers dream of going to their favorite places on Earth to write a book. Whether it's a beach on Maui or a castle in Scotland, writers are sponges taking in information that is stored to be written later. Visiting the places in your book can add realism and detail that might otherwise escape your awareness. By all means, if you can visit the setting of your book, whether it is around the block or around the world, do it.

Virtual Travel

When the Internet became readily available to writers, they gained an important resource in research. We can now contact people around the world with just a few clicks of a mouse. We can visit museums and see virtual exhibits, view photographs of places from around the world, and even look at live cameras. In short, writers never had it so good or so easy.

For far less than a trip to London, anyone with a computer and access to the World Wide Web can enter the Tower of London Web site and review its grim history. It may not be as romantic or exciting as getting on a plane and going there, but for many writers, it's as close as they can get to the real thing.

FACT

You don't have to own a computer to use one for research. Most libraries in the United States have computers for their patrons to use, free of charge. They can also be found in some malls and coffee shops. Take advantage of the opportunity to try the Internet before you invest in your own computer.

Read Other Books

Many generations of writers have used books for research. It's not surprising since books are writers' familiars. Libraries have been their friends because they could use the books without paying for them. Many money-strapped, would-be writers are on a first-name basis with their local librarians. They haunt the musty rows of older tomes looking for information about past civilizations.

Travel books that describe contemporary places around the world are a favorite. Writers can get the flavor of a locale without leaving home or knowing how to use the Internet. For some novels, intimate detail isn't necessary and travel guides can give a writer all the research she needs.

Travel Groups

If you can't go to China and you're challenged by the Internet, and dry accounts in books aren't giving you what you need, consult your local paper or phonebook for travel groups. These are individuals or groups of people who have recently visited China, or whatever locale you are researching. They take lots of pictures, then come back and share their experiences with others. Usually, they do this for free or a group sponsors them. Either way, you can learn all about the details of the area and even ask questions.

Chapter 9

The Building Blocks of the Plot

"Plots come a dime a dozen," according to author Joan Aiken. They're found within the mind, within the late-night news, and at your grandmother's feet. They're simple. They're easy. But if you don't have one or the one you have doesn't work, they can make you miserable. Hobbling a great character with an inadequate plot is like giving a superhero the superhuman gift of opening canned goods. It might work but who would want to read it?

Who: The Characters

Plot is primarily built around characters. Think about how the characters and plot move together and enrich each other. It's not enough that you have the greatest character since Moses. The plot needs to back him up and make him stronger. In turn, the characters make the plot believable.

Sometimes plot is generated by the characters' needs. If your story involves a powerful Southern matriarch, it would be difficult to place her in the middle of a European yacht race. If you see her as dominating her family's lives to the point that they are willing to murder her by pushing her down an old well, your characters have dictated your plot line. This act of murder would either be covered up in some way or create a rift that destroys the family. Or it might even set off an angst-ridden dark comedy.

> **ESSENTIAL**
>
> As you plot your book, you must consider every character. Their movements, what they do or don't do, their thoughts and fantasies are important to creating your world.

Primary Characters

It's the job of the primary characters to focus the reader's attention where it needs to be and to move the plot forward. To do this, the primary characters must help enhance every aspect of the plot.

In a romance, what happens between the hero and heroine is the plot. What they do together, how they meet, and how they finally end up as a couple constructs the novel. In many mysteries, it's difficult to tell if the primary character is the sharp police captain looking for the killer, or the killer himself with his psychopathic tendencies. The bad guys fascinate readers. The bad guys move the plot forward. A weak detective can almost be tolerated if the bad guy is fascinating enough.

Secondary Characters

Many writers neglect their secondary characters, like that zany sidekick or the morose aunt. But minor characters can be used to enhance your plot. They can say and do things that your primary characters may not be able to say or do. They can ask questions and find answers, like the well-meaning neighbors who manage to help a couple solve their romantic difficulties. They can keep your plot on track and help bring together your primary characters and plot shifts.

In many novels, the side character is essential. Mystery seems to benefit most from characters that understand and help the reader relate to the main character. But it's not unusual in horror or dark fantasy to find side characters that help alleviate some of the tension. Mainstream fiction novels sometimes find that their side characters are not only essential to the plot but also stay with the reader. In *Gone with the Wind*, the secondary characters Ashley and Melanie almost eclipse the main characters, Scarlet and Rhett. They certainly drive the plot and the primary characters forward.

ALERT!

Be careful to keep your secondary characters from stealing the show. The main plot should belong to the primary characters. Sometimes secondary characters can be so much fun to write that you can lose track of where they belong.

What: The Action

What's going on? What's happening? Both of these questions could be the beginning of your plot and your novel. What happens when the Texas Ranger faces down the man who killed his brother? What happens when a woman on vacation in Greece meets a sweet-talking con man?

"What" is the catalyst for many writers' thought processes. While you may not know yet exactly where your novel is going, you can begin to understand the vehicle that will get you there.

The question of what happens has ignited writers' imaginations forever. People are consumed by reading newspaper accounts of murder trials to learn the details. Everyone slows down to view an accident on the highway. We have Internet access and cable television, satellite uplinks and minute-by-minute descriptions of events from wars to royal marriages. They all have the same thing in common: our need to know what happened.

Plot Is Based on Action

Everyone says that action speaks louder than words. As a writer, words are all you have to work with. You have to create action with your words. Action can be exotic, like catching snakes in India or climbing Mount Everest. But mostly action is everyday things that we do to survive. It's the simple things that are wonderful and terrible. You don't have to look any further than your own experiences to create action in your novel. Here are a few examples:

- A bicycle ride in the country
- A car breaking down along the side of the road
- A honeymoon to Hawaii
- Getting in the shower
- Going for a jog
- Going to work

All of these basic actions have been used to jump-start plots in novels. They can be used as the catalyst for evil, love, or redemption. They are the most basic of plot devices stretched or agitated by an author's imagination.

Framework of the Story

Just as a house is built by first creating a frame of wood, metal, and concrete, a fiction novel must begin with a strong frame as well. If characters are the base or the floor of a structure, plots are the walls. It supports the roof (the setting) and creates space for what happens inside (dialogue).

As with any house, you want to make it as strong as you can so that storms (editors) and general wear and tear (reviewers) don't pull it down to the ground. Writers do that by asking questions that yield answers that shore up the structure of their manuscript. What happened may start the story but thousands of other questions must follow.

Don't be afraid to question your plot. If the answers aren't available, look for them. If you don't understand what happens you can't expect your readers to understand either.

Where: The Setting

Does your setting establish your plot? Or does your plot create your setting? The answers to these questions will be different for each writer. Of course, your location is important and must encourage your characters and plot. But your setting can be a plot in itself.

In the case of many sci-fi, fantasy, and men's adventure novels, the setting is essential. The mountain that the character must climb becomes the adversary. Its avalanches and freezing temperatures drive the story. In this instance, if there is no mountain, there is no plot. This makes your setting of primary importance. You need to understand it and express it just as you would any primary character or plot device.

The fantasy novel you're writing doesn't take place in real time or even the real world. But where would your characters be without this place that you've created? Whether the novel takes place in the past or the future, the plot must ring true for readers. They will believe what you believe. If you believe that a place with wizards and magical creatures exists, your words will carry your plot.

FACT

Works of fantasy don't have to be set in fantasy worlds. A fantasy novel can take place in the mind of the main character. This occurs in *The Secret Life of Walter Mitty* by author James Thurber.

Because of the nature of fantasy realms, they must work closely with the plot. Your hero is bound by the rules of your universe. Even character must have guidelines. Just like in real-life plots that are driven by setting, fantasy plots are frequently intertwined with their location. If your realm is in the clouds, your question of what happens begins with the people who populate this lofty domain.

When: The Time Frame

The time frame of your novel defines a great deal of your plot. Is it set in the past? Is it set in the future? Does the entire novel take place in twenty-four hours? Is the scope of the novel several generations?

These are all questions that the writer must answer before he or she begins to write. Some answers will require a lot of research. If you write futuristic fiction, the answers to these questions will come from your own imagination. In the case of a thriller mystery, lack of time to diffuse the bomb and save the world becomes the issue. But no matter what the answer, time is important to what happens in the framework of your plot.

Time Sequence

All the events in your life follow a certain order. You get up at 6:00 A.M., get on the train by 7:30, arrive late for work at 9:15, and take an early lunch at 11:30. Your boss hassles you at 1:15. You close the biggest deal of your career at 2:45. You call your wife at 4:00 to let her know that the boss is taking you out for cocktails to celebrate at 5:30 so you won't be home until 8:00. You go to bed at 10:30 and the day is over.

Life unfolds in a series of events that follow the natural order. Tuesday always follows Monday. Fall always follows summer. Some laws are immutable (except if you change the laws of the universe in fantasy, sci-fi, etc.).

Keeping track of time within a novel can be done in many ways. It can be as simple as glancing at a watch or more complex, like knowing what time the sun is going to set. Be creative. Don't limit your character to mundane ways of knowing the time.

In the Present

It's easy to write about current events. If it's important for your plot to know who the president of France is, all you have to do is pick up a newspaper or look on the Internet. Maybe that's why so many books are written with contemporary settings. It makes it easier for the author and the reader to relate to the plot.

Your plot still requires that you be accurate as far as important information is concerned. A car trip between New York and Chicago can't be accomplished in two hours no matter how fast a man drives (again, alternate universes excluded). There are only twenty-four hours in a day and seven days in a week.

Historical Novels

Some writers love research. They love to sit in libraries or museums and soak up the atmosphere of 1800s England or ancient Rome. So, they build their plots in historic settings around the world. Unless you're a history major, this means a lot more work in writing your novel.

Accuracy in detail is just as important if your book is set during the Spanish Inquisition as during a congressional hearing today. You have to know how long it takes a carriage to travel ten miles or how long it takes mules to pull a barge through the Great Lakes. Time restrictions change according to the age you're writing even though basic time remains the same. Queen Elizabeth I had the same twenty-four hours a day that you have.

FACT

A good place to start looking up historical information on almost any subject is the World Wide Web Virtual Library, at *http://vlib.org*. Their history section will lead you to other places for more complete information.

Why: Motivations and Explanations

Why? Inventors and philosophers have asked this question for generations. Their questions have ranged from the practical to the metaphysical. Why do people get married and have children? Why are some years abundant with rain and others are dry? Why does the Earth continue to rotate around the sun?

You don't have to be a philosopher to ask the big questions. As the creator of the world that becomes your novel, it's important to probe for answers. Just because you think of a basic plot doesn't mean that you understand all the underlying aspects that you'll be working on in the next 50,000 words. Asking yourself why something happens can be the beginning of understanding why something happens in your novel. It doesn't matter if it's murder or a trip to the moon; many discoveries begin by asking why.

Coming Back to Motivation

Why did your neighbor paint his house pink in the first place? There are no other pink houses in your neighborhood. He's a quiet, shy little man who never goes out of his way to make trouble. Yet, here's his house, bright pink in a sea of white and gray. What motivated him to take that action?

You may never understand your neighbor, though you might be guessing that his action is a cry for attention. But asking why begins the process of looking for motivation. We are all motivated to action by something. For some people, the edge between action and thought is very thin. The least thing can set them off. Others have to be prodded, even pushed into action.

What motivates your plot? Is there a volcano erupting that causes an ordinary man to take action? Is there a final straw that comes from a demanding husband that causes a frustrated wife to kill him? Finding the motivation behind the action in your plot will help you stay on track and understand your characters.

Asking What If

If you're a murder mystery writer, you might be asking yourself a question right now. What if your next-door neighbor mysteriously painted his house pink overnight to hide the ghastly bloodstain in the back? What if his demanding wife finally pushed him to the edge and he killed her?

Alternately, if you write science fiction, you might be asking what if your neighbor painted his house in what looks like pink paint. But it's really an alien phosphorescent that will signal a transport to pick him up.

Still, if you're a mainstream fiction writer, you might ask what if painting this house pink is a call for attention. What if this quiet, shy man just wants to be noticed by his uncaring, insensitive neighbors?

You can see how different questions from different points of view can achieve different answers. Certainly, these answers would create totally different plots. Why your plot flows in any direction can be a direct result of asking "what if."

ALERT!

It's important to ask the questions that move your plot. But don't get so caught up in the questions that you spend all of your time on them. They are only the preliminary to writing your book.

How: Putting It All Together

Another piece of the puzzle falls into place when you begin to wonder *how* things are done. Have you ever stopped to consider how cheese is made? Or how a plane flies? Or how DNA samples are gathered?

Many writers are walking encyclopedias of useless tidbits of information—until that moment when they finally put pen to paper (or fingers to keyboard). That's when all of that knowledge about widgets and physics finally gets used. Knowing a little bit about many different subjects is a good thing in this case.

How does your plot begin? How do your characters react within the plot structure? How do the loose ends tie up? How do you get from point A to point B? Plotting requires depth and understanding of many different facets of human nature and wondering how things happen in life. Before you begin to create anything, you have to ask how you'll create it.

How Is It Done?

If you're writing a murder mystery, you're going to ask how the murder is committed. What is the sequence of events leading up to the murder? How did the killer get into the locked room and lock it from the inside after committing the crime?

Science fiction writers ask how their characters got to Planet X or the Fourth Dimension. They need to know how their futuristic gizmos work and how their characters battle the bad guys. How does a Star Trooper keep his indestructible uniform clean during a long battle? Mainstream writers want to know how their characters interrelate. They want to know how Aunt Sally got to be so disagreeable.

There is no end to the "how" of writing a novel. How will the book end? How will you ever get the hero and heroine back together again after they break up? Sometimes pondering how things work can take some effort. You might find that you have to step back from the plot to get an objective thought.

How Characters and Plot Relate

In the Destroyer series (men's adventure), Remo Williams makes blowing up the bad guys looks simple. The plot moves quickly but it doesn't move without Remo. He manages to save the world in each exploit as well as getting the girl.

In Barbara Hambly's *A Free Man of Color*, Benjamin January plays piano and solves a murder in the midst of 1833 Mardi Gras. His story is one of a black man who has lived in Europe as a free man. He returns to his home in New Orleans and finds himself in a world he doesn't recognize. The plot's movement is dependent on his surroundings and the time period.

In the books readers remember and read again, characters and plot mesh so well that you can't imagine one without the other. These novels don't limp from chapter to chapter. The characters bring the plot to life and the plot sustains and showcases the characters.

Secondary Plots

In most modern books, subplots are as easy to find as brown leaves in November. Very few novels contain only one main plot. Secondary plots strengthen and add to the main plot that threads through the book. This can be a dilemma or character that adds tension, comedy, or complications to the life of the main characters. It can be used as a red herring to draw readers' eyes away from what's really going on. It can be a device that takes the main plot where it needs to go.

It's not unusual for a novel to contain many different subplots. As long as all the loose ends are tied up by the end of the book, these plots are a welcome addition. As you add additional plots, consider how they relate to the main plot and how they advance the story line. You don't want to use a side plot that doesn't have anything to do with telling the story.

QUESTION?

Can there be too much plot?
It's always possible to have too much of a good thing. The plot should never overpower the characters. They should always create their world together.

How to Find Secondary Plots

In a romance, a subplot could be a budding relationship between two side characters. The relationship complicates the main romance between your primary hero and heroine because these people are their parents.

A secondary plot for a fantasy could be a wizard who is battling evil and finds himself being followed by a fairy that wants to help but can't control her power. This leads to complications that the wizard doesn't need and adds humor to what is otherwise a dark book.

Many thriller/slasher mysteries use a humorous side character that gets himself and the hero into difficulties. But because he gets them locked in a basement, it helps the hero solve the crime.

Finding secondary plots that work within the framework of your main plot can add whatever you need to make your novel a more enjoyable read. Use them to add conflict, solve puzzles, or as ways to show more detail about your hero or heroine.

Where to Put Them

In Ann Maxwell's *A Dead God Dancing*, the primary plot is about a special rescue team that is trying to save a dying planet. In this book, secondary plots evolve around each member of the team. All the characters have their own background and their own private reason for being on the planet. Some of these reasons jeopardize the main objective and cause conflict. Some are as simple as a love affair between two of the members that could end in tragedy.

Deciding where to put your secondary plots can be as easy as understanding the goals of your main plot. Even a simple romance can have complications. These complications and how the hero/heroine handles them become your subplots.

Plot Progression

Even when you have all of your plot information together, writing it as a whole may not be as simple as it sounds. Sometimes even if you've asked all of the questions and have all of the answers, everything won't fit together.

If you put together puzzles, you understand. Some pieces look exactly like the right fit. Yet, when you try them in the slot, they just don't go there. Other pieces don't look right but they fit anyway.

You can only do so much planning. Ultimately the true test is writing the book. The plot may seem fine in your head. You can see everything coming together. You can even write it down and it looks fine. Yet, when everything reacts together, the plot falls apart.

When this happens to you, don't be afraid to let go of whatever doesn't work. It may be something large like how the murder is committed or how your adventure hero gets amnesia. It may be something small like a side plot that was supposed to add humor but falls flat. Whatever it is, it can be rewritten, reworked, or revised.

ALERT!

Even though you may be very excited about your plot, don't begin to write it until you have a full understanding of your characters as well. Character and plot must always work together. Trying to write one without the other will only end in painful revisions.

How It Begins

It can't be stressed too often that how your plot and your novel begin is important. Like all good beginnings, it should start full of hope and promise—or beyond the depths of what one man can endure. Whatever the beginning, it should be strong and believable.

Even though it is the beginning, your plot should begin in the middle. This may seem like a contrary idea. But you're trying to place your reader in the thick of things. You don't want to start out with long explanations that take them into the plot. You want them to feel the icy finger of death on their necks in the first paragraph. You want them to be standing at the edge of the volcano with your hero just before he slaloms down the lava flow.

Don't give them a safe place to be. If your book starts out at high tea in England at the turn of the century, spill the tea, or show the characters gossiping maliciously. Engage the reader in your plot from the get-go.

The Buildup

Even though it's essential to grab your reader in the beginning, what you have to say next is just as important. You've connected with your readers; now bring them into the story more deeply. Follow the plot points you established in your outline or summary. Don't be afraid to add on anything that seems important. Let the tension build as you add blocks to the story's foundation. Carefully take your readers from place to place. Don't leave them stranded or let them fall behind.

The progression of your plot should follow a logical, understandable line that your readers can easily follow. Don't leave essential information out, thinking that they will "get it." Sometimes they will, but sometimes they won't. There's nothing more frustrating than reading a book and suddenly feeling that you don't know what happened.

Make sure the actions your characters takes helps add to the feeling of movement in the plot. Sometimes a character might want to just sit down and take a rest. But the plot must continue to build, drawing the reader closer as the story races like a runaway freight train toward its inevitable conclusion.

How It Ends

Author Sidney Sheldon says that no author should ever know how the book is going to end. Some writers work that way. They allow the plot to meander like a river until they feel it has reached its goal. They believe that knowing too much information can ruin the author's creativity and make the book flat.

You can't argue with Mr. Sheldon's success, but not all authors feel this way. Many authors have a clear picture of their book's plot from beginning to end. Sometimes a character or secondary plot may not react in exactly the way they expected. But overall, they know where they're going and how they want to get there.

QUESTION?

Do most writers know how their book will end?
It seems that about half the writers do and half don't. Some have the entire plot outlined and figured out. Others are waiting for the characters to take them where they need to go. It doesn't matter which path you choose, as long as it works for you.

Beginning writers have a hard enough time staying focused on their work. Sometimes having a plan, knowing the goal, is the only way to finish the project. If you decide to plan your ending, remember that you can always change it. If you decide not to plan your ending, you can always revise it if you don't like it.

But remember that your plot ending must live up to the promise of the book. Your readers have trusted you to provide them with a satisfying conclusion. Ⓔ

Chapter 10

Making Up Your Mind

Your preparation for writing a novel is as important as actually writing it. True, if you don't sit down and write your ideas out, they'll never make it into a novel. But how you prepare can mean the difference between frustration and creativity. Very few writers simply sit down and start typing. The thought you give to your characters and plot will shine through in your finished product. If you don't take the time to prepare, that will be clear too.

Identify Your Genre

By now, you've done your research and you know what type of book you're writing. If you don't, you must be writing a mainstream fiction novel or you are just willing to live dangerously. In this case, living dangerously means plenty of rewrites after you finish your book. Do yourself a favor. Don't start writing until you know what you're writing. It can be confusing to be able to tell the difference between a cozy mystery and a thriller, but you have to take the time now or take it after you've finished and made mistakes.

QUESTION?

Where does the term *wing it* come from?
It comes from the theater, where actors gave impromptu performances in response to prompts from other actors in the wings. The phrase has gone on to be applied to anyone else who does something without a script.

Genre Novels

Are you planning to write a genre novel? Is it a fast-paced mystery? Is it a sweet romance? Is it a combination of romance and mystery and possibly has science fiction overtones? By this time, you should know the difference. If you want to write a novel, you should understand the terminology. Think of it as the difference between knowing if your car needs an oil change or a tune-up. One is very different from the other. You'd feel like an idiot if you went into a car care facility and asked for one when you meant the other. Understanding the differences between the various types of genres is no different. You're a writer who hopes to be a published author. Learn everything you can about it.

Mainstream Novels

If you aren't writing a genre book, you're writing mainstream fiction. You aren't bound by all those rules and regulations that hamper genre writers from giving full rein to their imaginations. The sky's the limit. You can write about anything you want in any style you want.

True? Yes and no. Yes, you don't have to worry about choosing between a sexy romance and a more prudish one, where the hero and heroine barely kiss. But you'll probably write some part of a genre into your novel. Not all mainstream writers do this. You might be one of that rare breed. But just in case, review the rules about genre before you start to write. Don't get so carried away with your belief that you can do whatever you want that your work becomes unmarketable because no one understands it.

Formulate Your Idea

By now, you've sifted through all of the ideas that have been floating around in your head. You've settled on one particular idea for a novel that's exciting to you. You believe you can write it. You've done the appropriate research to feel confident in your writing. You've scheduled your commitment to writing by finding time to sit down and do it.

Can you see it clearly? Your idea should be as clear in your mind as your name. Now's the time to find out how strong your idea is and how much you understand it.

Having the big idea is one thing. Writing it down is another. If you find yourself sitting at the computer or with your pen poised over paper and nothing coming out, try it in smaller gulps. Try it one paragraph or page at a time until it begins to flow.

One Sentence

The following exercise will show you how clearly you understand the idea for your novel—or that you don't understand it at all. It's very simple. Condense the entire story line down to one sentence.

Right now, you're probably gasping for air. How can you possibly condense an idea that's big enough to write a 100,000-word novel into one sentence? Can that be a paragraph-long sentence?

No, it can't be a paragraph long. And yes, it's not only possible, but imperative as well. If you truly understand the ideas that move your story, you can do it. Here's how it can be done:

- A young boy discovers that he's a wizard and has adventures at a school for magic.
- A Roman soldier turned monk solves the mystery of dead woman found in a frozen river.
- An obsessed sea captain hunts for a white whale and loses his life trying to kill it.
- A Southern woman finds her way of life changed forever by the Civil War.
- A regency gentleman makes a wage that he can win the heart of a spinster.

The novels broken down into one sentence are: *Harry Potter and the Chamber of Secrets* by J. K. Rowling; *The Virgin in the Ice* by Ellis Peters; *Moby Dick* by Herman Melville; *Gone with the Wind* by Margaret Mitchell; and *Knave's Wager* by Loretta Chase.

Blurb—125 Words

Next, try writing a paragraph or blurb that describes your novel. It's good practice in case you get published and your editor asks you to do it. It can also be something you can use to attract an editor to your book if you go to a conference.

If you can't reduce your novel idea down to a basic form like the ones listed here, you need to do more work. Take the time to figure out exactly what your book is about. Start by understanding your characters, knowing what they need to do and where they need to go in the story.

A blurb is nothing more than the highlights of your novel. It's the back or inside flap on a published book that's supposed to excite readers into buying it. In most cases, publishers pay editors to create this part of the book. But pretend that you're creating a blurb for your book yourself. Think about the following questions. What stands out? What makes your book worth reading? Without telling all the details, why would anyone want to read your book?

Review Your Characters

Now's the time to make corrections and changes to your characters. If you have any doubts about anything, make the change now. As difficult as it may be, it will be a lot harder later when the story is already written.

Make sure you know everything necessary about your characters to make them seem real. Even something as small as your hero's hair color can be important. Consider how it changes someone when they go from being a brunette to a blond. The plot rests on the shoulders of your characters. It revolves around them. Make sure they're strong enough to handle it.

The Protagonist

Your hero is foiling a plot to take over the world. He's brave. He's ruggedly handsome. Women love him. Men fear or respect him. But what is his weakness? What tiny seed of imperfect humanity was planted in him? That's what your readers are looking for. That's what makes him like everyone else.

Your heroine is beautiful. She's fearless in her pursuit of justice. She champions the rights of the underdog and stands up to the wrong in the world. But does she have a hobby? Is she a tough cop who likes to read romances? Does she have a problem with spiders? These smaller aspects define her as well and help readers relate to her even if she does super-human things.

Before your fingers strike the first keys, know your characters inside and out. Everything else will be easier if you aren't fighting with the people you create. Once you've done this, let the story find other things about them that you didn't know existed. Let yourself be surprised by where they'll take you. Give your hero/heroine a compass and a map and let him or her lead the way.

Secondary Characters

Your hero has a zany sidekick. Or his partner in crime is serious and always worried. Or maybe your heroine/sleuth has a meddling aunt who moves in with her and finds clues that the heroine misses. What does that secondary character do to enhance the story?

Don't let these characters merely take up space in the story. They have important functions that make the book better. They should never take over the plot, but they have an active role in the novel. They can move the story along and help the reader see the main characters in a different light.

Before you start writing, have an idea of where the secondary characters come into the story and how large a part they play in it. Decide beforehand if they will have point of view or if we only see them through the eyes of the main characters.

Visualize Your Setting

Why do you think Margaret Mitchell chose Georgia as the setting for *Gone with the Wind*? Chances are, she chose that setting because she knew it so well. Familiarity is an amazing tool. The book might have been the same if she'd written it in Virginia. She could've used the burning of Richmond in place of the burning of Atlanta. There were plenty of plantations in Virginia as well. But she wouldn't have been as comfortable or possibly as knowledgeable with that setting.

Setting does matter. If you've chosen your setting and you're happy with it, integrate it completely into your novel. Help your readers feel as comfortable there as they do in their own home. Let them see what you see and experience everything you've imagined.

Specific Places

Where does your novel take place? Maybe you've decided to put it in your hometown or you've researched an exotic island in the South Pacific that you visited last year. Or maybe it takes place on a world that's only visible in your own mind.

Will you use landmarks in your novel? Your heroine fights a villain at the top of the Eiffel Tower. The bomb your hero is looking for is hidden in the eye of the sphinx. Specific place information can give your reader a sense of being there. Everyone has an image already in mind when they read about specific, well-known places.

Remember that the five senses are an important part of showing readers what you want them to know about your setting. Know what kind of food your shepherd in Spain is eating for lunch when Great Aunt Matilda visits him. Decide what kind of clothing your alien species wear.

Don't Be Afraid of Adding Details

Pretend you're a real estate salesperson. If you've ever done business with someone trying to sell you a house, this should be easy. Real estate people are memorable. If you haven't had this experience, pick up a real estate magazine. Read through the elaborate descriptions of what the kitchen counters are made of and when the new floors were put down. The house comes with draperies or blinds. The unfinished portion of the attic is wired and plumbed for an additional room.

Every real estate agent knows his houses. He can tell you when they were built and how many people have lived there. He can wax poetic about the oak trees in the yard and the sod that was recently put down.

You need to be that person when you begin to write your novel. Help your readers envision your setting with carefully chosen words. Tell them where the sun comes into the house in the morning. Don't let them forget about the enchanting fountain in the backyard. Sell them what you want them to experience in your world. Make them want to move in.

Establish Your Time Frame

You've made your decision about when your story takes place. In some cases, there's no decision to make. If you're writing a book about intrigue in Napoleon's court, it can only take place in one time.

If you're convinced that your family saga has to take place in the 1950s but you can't imagine writing it without the family having a computer and cable television, it's time to rethink your story. The time period you use as your setting has to fit the story because the two need to work together.

If you're writing in an alternate reality, you have your character's sense of time to guide you. If you're writing in a historical framework, you've done your research and you know the difference between family life in the 1860s and 1960s. If you're writing in a contemporary setting, you've observed life around you to add realism and spice to your novel.

When Does It Happen

You're ready to begin your book if you know when your story happens. If you're unsure, that will show up in your text. If you're writing a time travel novel, you'll have to decide if it will encompass more than one period of history as well as contemporary lifestyles. Just let the reader know when the changes take place and let your imagination do the rest. Pay attention to the clues you present to your readers—overexplaining is too distracting, but leaving the readers completely lost won't work either. Invoke your time frame with details like the clothes, food, hairstyles, and technology.

ESSENTIAL

If you're interested in playing with time and space, you might want to join the Society for Creative Anachronism (✍ www.sca.org). They're a group of like-minded thinkers who'll help you make sense of time and show you unique ways to play with it.

The Time Span

Also consider the time frame of your novel—the time period that it will cover. Some novels, like *One Day in the Life of Ivan Denisovich* by Alexander Solzhenitsyn, cover just one day. On the other extreme, family sagas like *The Thorn Birds* by Colleen McCullough span many generations. The time frame that governs the lives and minds of your characters will affect your reader's perception of the book.

For example, when you're writing a romance, deciding how long it's going to take for your hero and heroine to fall in love is an important part of your plotting. It can be a matter of moments, weeks, or months. It can be a difficult courtship that spans a lifetime. How long they are together before they tie the knot is another important decision.

Making these decisions will help you avoid problems as you begin writing. You won't have your heroine talking about something that happened yesterday in the beginning of the book, then tell the reader in Chapter 10 that it happened last year. It will mean fewer revisions for you and less confusion for your readers.

Finalize Your Plot

If you understand your plot at this point, you're ahead of the game. It's not always necessary to know exactly what goes where so long as all of it fits in together. Give your characters some leeway with what you expect them to do and how you expect them to do it. Remember that your plot doesn't need to be complicated. The story should be simple and elegant. Even detailed stories can be told in a simple way.

What Happens

Even if you opt not to write it down, you should have a timeline for your novel. That way you know approximately what happens and when it happens.

Most mysteries follow similar lines. The sleuth finds the first body. The sleuth finds the first clue. The sleuth finds carefully placed red herrings that throw off the reader. The sleuth solves the mystery and takes out the bad guy in a believable manner.

If you're writing a romance, you'll need to show how the hero and heroine meet for the first time. They share their first kiss. They have their dark moment when they break up. They get back together and plan for their future.

If you're writing a science fiction or fantasy, you'll need a catalyst or threat that begins your story: A world on the verge of collapse or some new technology is threatening the existence of a group of people. Your hero or heroine becomes involved in finding the answer to the problem. After overcoming difficulties, he or she solves the problem.

FACT

The great debate in romance rages on. When should the hero meet the heroine? A good guide is that series romances like Harlequin expect the lovers to meet on the first page. The longer standalone books can manage to make the introduction a bit later. Figure out which kind of romance you plan to write, then check with a potential publisher for details. Read plenty of romances that seem like yours to give you a basic understanding of the genre.

How It Happens

To get an idea of how the events of your novel will play out, you have to understand what your characters will contribute to the plot. If your heroine is going to solve a murder, how is she going to do it? She'll probably talk to the friends and neighbors of the dead person. She might find clues by sorting through the dead man's garbage. She might be friends with the dead man's wife. How does she put all of the information together and come up with her conclusion?

The Earth's orbit has suddenly changed in your novel and your hero creates a machine to pull the Earth back into it. How does he do it? He has basic skills that make him believable as a character who can accomplish this task. You explain to the readers your vision of how he creates the machine and how it works. Then you show them the consequences of using it.

If a family suddenly discovers that the matriarch they all know and love is responsible for the death of her husband, how do they handle it? They may cover it up to protect her, even if they're secretly appalled. But there are terrible repercussions that stem from their deceit. Your story emerges from showing the reader how the family stays together and survives this terrible secret.

Consider Back Story

What is back story? Some might say it's the boring part you have to wade through to get to the good stuff. For readers, it's the part that they hope will be brief. For writers, it can be the kiss of death. Basically, back story is what happened *before* the story begins, the background information readers need to know in order to be able to follow the plot.

How much back story is too much, how much isn't enough, and where you put it are always topics of interest for writers. Years ago, authors used a lot of back story to take the reader through the terrible events that shaped their characters. Today's authors don't have that luxury. In the words of Chris Tucker's unforgettable character DJ Ruby Rhod in *The Fifth Element*, "It must pop, pop, pop!"

But the problem still remains. Too much back story and your reader falls asleep. Too little and he has no idea why anything has happened.

Telling the Back Story

Because the back story establishes facts about your characters, plot, and setting, it's essential to your novel. How will anyone understand your heroine's reluctance to get involved with a gorgeous, sexy, wealthy man unless they know that she lived with an abusive gorgeous, sexy, wealthy man? That's back story. Unless your hero has amnesia, he has to have a back story.

The back story also affects the setting. Your tiny town in the Ozarks isn't as mysterious without the reader knowing that people have randomly disappeared from there every year for the past twenty-five years. Suddenly those little white houses take on a sinister bend. The reader shivers just thinking about it.

Distributing the Back Story

Creating a spine-tingling back story that won't put the reader to sleep isn't always easy, but there are ways to give your readers the information they need to grasp the complexities of your plot without shoving it down their throats. First of all, consider using dialogue. Your characters can tell readers about past events. For example, a local woman can impart the knowledge about the town in the Ozarks to your heroine. In turn, that information motivates her to investigate the disappearance of her aunt. Maybe it wasn't just something that happened randomly, the sheriff suggests.

You can use narrative, when you have to, if your heroine suddenly finds herself alone out in the woods—when there are no other characters that can help her out. There is information that the reader has to have to understand how and why things are happening. Just be sure to break up this vital information. Your heroine and your reader can only take in so much at one time.

ALERT!

Putting too much back story at the beginning of the book can cause your readers to lose interest. Give readers a chance to get to know your character before enveloping them in back story.

Choose the Point of View

There are plenty of books and workshops on what point of view is and how it can be used to your advantage. Basically, point of view (POV) refers to who is telling the story—whether it's a first-person (I) account or a story with an outside narrator who describes all the characters in third person (he, she, it, they). Some novels have more than one point of view, which may alternate from chapter to chapter. If you don't decide how point of view will work in your novel before you begin writing, you should expect to make major revisions.

First Person

Are you going to have one character tell the story from her point of view? If you go this route, every bit of information has to be filtered through this character. For instance:

I knew what Jean was talking about. I hated for her to go but she never listens to me. I said, "Jean, don't go there. You'll only get in trouble." But would she listen to me? Probably not.

Remember that the first-person narrator cannot know everything. Everything that this narrator recounts must have happened already. Because this places limitations on the narrator, first-person point of view is not used as frequently as third-person.

Third Person

This point of view allows the author and the reader to explore all the characters in the novel. You don't have to limit yourself to what one character is thinking and feeling. If you take the previous bit of story and change it to third person, it would look like this:

Betty knew what Jean was talking about. She hated for her to go but Jean never listened to her. "Jean, don't go there. You'll only get in trouble." Jean wasn't listening. She wanted to go and nothing Betty said was going to stop her.

FACT

A good book that can help you further explore and understand point of view is *Mastering Point of View* by Sherri Szeman. This book can aid you in escaping writer's confusion about fiction, but you'll have to keep it straight after you start writing!

The Omniscient Narrator (Second Person)

Third-person point of view gives the readers direct information about more than one character, but second-person point of view goes beyond that and introduces another character—the omniscient narrator. This is an almost godlike figure that knows what's going to happen in the story and may speak to the readers directly (in second person).

Most books written today don't include narrative that speaks directly to the reader. Books written in this manner include some fairy tales and classics like *The Hobbit*. Here's how our example would look in second person:

You can see what Betty was talking about. She hated for Jean to go but her friend never listened to her. Would she listen this time? Probably not. Jean was stubborn. Not unlike people you might know.

Head Hopping

Switching points of view is known as head hopping. Modern novels are frequently written from more than one character's point of view, rather than the viewpoint of a single person. This can get tricky for the writer who doesn't want to lose his reader in the flurry of multiple POVs.

QUESTION?

How much is too much POV change in dialogue?
The only way to gauge whether or not there are too many voices is to carefully read through each page of your manuscript. Don't change POV unless it is important to the story.

Dialogue can help keep up with transition points between characters. By using a combination of dialogue and narrative to anchor the reader's focus, it's possible to successfully change points of view without confusion.

Don't be afraid to use dialogue tags in this instance. It's more important not to have the reader asking "huh?" than it is to keep your attributives down to a minimum. Use them wisely. Don't let them take over your story but allow them to guide your reader.

Whose Story Is It?

How do you decide which point of view to use in your novel? Take the cue from your story. Who is it in your story that should be the one to tell it? Should there be an obvious storyteller (omniscient narrator), or should the action be presented seamlessly (third-person narrative)? It's often the case that the main character's experiences are the pivotal part of the book. Their thoughts and emotions are what the reader is bonding with. What is the best way of presenting them?

In some novels, the author chooses a secondary character to tell the story. In the Sherlock Holmes series, the narrator is his sidekick, Dr. Watson. But in most cases, your steely-eyed police detective who's solving a string of gangland murders is going to speak for himself. The reader experiences what he experiences. The reader learns information from other characters through dialogue.

ALERT!

If you decide to use multiple points of view, be careful to identify who's thinking and speaking. Too many pronouns can leave the reader wondering who he or she is. Using a proper name too often can give that repetitive feeling to the text. Use the narrative and dialogue to identify changing points of view.

Chapter 11
Outlining Methods

Writers all disagree on whether or not novels should be outlined. The ones in the "no outline" camp feel that it would stifle their creativity. The ones who outline religiously feel that it's an important part of their process. Even the writers who agree with the importance of creating an outline disagree on what kind of outline is necessary. Whether or not you decide that outlining is a good approach for you, it's good to have a basic idea of how outlining is done. Many publishers request an outline as a part of a manuscript submission.

Formal Outlines

This type of outline is the kind that makes many writers cringe. It's the kind you did in school. It follows certain rules and guidelines. Nonfiction writers do them all the time to sell books. Fiction writers are more hesitant. How can an outline, especially a formal outline, possibly reflect the flexibility necessary to create a novel? Once you write an outline, how can you change it?

FACT

Since many publishers expect outlines from writers, learning to outline in some form can be useful as a skill. Creating an outline shouldn't keep you from being a creative writer any more than taking a photograph of a tree would stop you from painting it.

The answers to these questions are simple. The outline may be formal but it reflects what you want to write. You're writing the outline just like you're writing the novel. It can be as flexible as you want it to be. If you want it to be exactly what you plan to write, you can follow it letter by letter from beginning to end. If you want it to be a guideline of where you want to go, it can be that too.

Many fiction writers are scared by the formality of a regulation outline. They're afraid they will be overshadowed by it, stifled by its very existence. But an outline is as flexible as the writer who wrote it. Don't be intimidated by anything except your own limitations.

Basic Structure

The structure of a formal outline hasn't changed for at least fifty years. Its regulation and order can bring cohesion to your ideas. It can take characters, plot, and setting and put them together in a way that's easy to see. Take a look at the basic structure and don't let it scare you. You can use the formal outline to break down your idea into characters, plot, setting, and so on. Here's what the first section of your outline might look like:

The Title of Your Book Here
- I. Characters
  - a. Main Characters
    - 1. Hero
    - 2. Bad Guy
  - b. Secondary Characters

This is one way you could use a formal outline to work with your novel. Another way would be chapter by chapter. Either way accomplishes the same goal, which is to organize your thoughts and have a game plan to get your novel from the beginning to the end. (If your publisher requests a formal outline, be sure to ask for guidelines.)

While this gives you a very basic idea of a way to use an outline, most outlines for novels would be much larger. They need to be as detailed as your thought processes regarding the work.

Check a publisher's guidelines to see if they require an outline of your work. If they do want to see an outline, ask what form they prefer. Different publishers like to see different types and lengths. The only way to know is to ask.

Putting It Together

Once you've established your basic outline, where do you go from there? How can your outline contain all of the information for your story?

If you decide to use the outline with characters, you could simply name each character in the novel and write a short description of them. Include who they are in the story, what they look like, something about their goals and motivations. Create something you can glance at as you're writing to keep track of the characters. Then move on to plot. List the major events in the story and write a short paragraph about each event. Under the major events, include the smaller events that are related to them. Then move on to setting and do the same thing.

If you decide to use a chapter-by-chapter outline (the kind most publishers ask to see), you would start with chapter one as your first Roman numeral. Write a paragraph or two about the chapter. Include the characters and major events that take place. The letters and numbers under them will include side characters and approximate places they're introduced. Subplots can be charted this way as well.

ALERT!

Don't get so caught up in the outlining procedure that you become afraid to deviate from it. Writing requires creative changes at times that can't be foreseen when you make the outline. Consider it part of the process, not the whole thing.

An Informal Approach

Most writers prefer to use a less frightening way of outlining. This could be called informal outlining. It's not something you could send to a publisher but it's something that you can use to guide your writing. Individual writers seem to have their own style of informal outlining. Ask a roomful of writers how they outline their ideas and you'll get a roomful of different responses.

The best way to find what works for you is to try different methods. Whatever is easiest and expresses what you want to say is what's best. Nothing else matters.

Basic Structure

One option for putting together an informal outline is using a bulleted list. Basically, this follows the same kind of structure that you'd use in a formal outline, but you use bullets instead of Roman numerals, letters, and numbers. For example:

- Your Title Here
- Characters
- Plot

- Setting
- Subplots
- Secondary Characters

Inside the bullets, after the headers, would be information about characters, plot, setting, and so on. How much detail you choose to use is up to you. Usually a paragraph or two is enough.

A bulleted list outline could also be made of the chapters. In that case, each bullet would contain information about what happened in that chapter. This could be as much or as little description as you need.

Putting It Together

Suppose you were using this method to outline a murder mystery. You've decided to go chapter by chapter. Here's an idea of what something like that would look like:

- Title: She Murdered Her Husband
- Chapter 1: A man is found dead after not showing up for work. The members of his carpool find him in his garage, face down in a pool of oil.
  → Red herring—he never worked on his car.
- Chapter 2: The members of the carpool (these are the sleuths) are suspicious of their friend's wife after they hear her lie to the police.
- Chapter 3: The sleuths decide to investigate the wife's alibi.
  → Note—she catches them following her and tells them to leave her alone.
- Chapter 4: The sleuths tell the police about their suspicions but the police have already arrested a man they think is responsible.

The information here probably isn't enough to write a murder mystery novel, but it should give you a good sense of how to go about it. If this were a real outline, you'd include more information about the sleuths, the wife, and the crime.

Another way of creating an informal look at your story is through a timeline. To create one, start with the first event that begins your story and move forward. This can be a graph that is an actual line where you insert events or it can be just a listing of events. Characters and setting can be added where appropriate.

Freeform Outlining

The art world has used the term *freeform* for years. It denotes a lack of structure in artwork. That basically means that anything goes. Think Picasso!

Freeform outlining is based on the same idea. You can choose any form or lack of form to convey your thoughts. There's no limit to how you do it. Remember that this is an exercise in thought, for you and no one else. Whatever comes to mind is possible.

The key to freeform outlining is organization. As long as you understand how the process will help you organize your ideas, it should do the trick. There are no specifics on how to create your individual style in this form. You'll have to fly by the seat of your pants to reach your destination.

If you simply can't stand anything that resembles an outline, freeform outlining is better than nothing to organize your ideas. Be aware that this type of outlining can lead to greater amounts of revision for the beginning writer.

Listing Your Ideas

One thing that most writers don't lack is ideas. Normally, they're overflowing with them. If this applies to you too, your freeform method of outlining might include simply writing all of those ideas down. That way you can look at all of them as you write.

Since even freeform needs some structure, you could consider writing the words "main character" on the top of the page. The rest of it could be whatever your ideas are about your main character. You could write "handsome" or "swarthy" or "rich" or "beach bum"—anything that comes to mind about that character. Think of it as a kind of word association about each character, place, and plot point in your book.

Writing Out Summaries

Many writers are able to keep track of their ideas by simply writing a paragraph about each thing. For instance, you would write down a list of your characters, then write a paragraph about each one. The same thing applies to plot points and setting.

There doesn't have to be any particular form or way of doing this. You can begin with the setting, if you like, then continue on to character or whatever comes to you. You can go on this way and expand the paragraphs for as long as you like. You can always add to them or take something out of them at your discretion. No Roman numerals or numbers or even bullets are necessary.

The only thing you'll want to do is give yourself enough room between paragraphs to make corrections. You can do this on the computer or a legal pad. The hardest thing is keeping track of what you've written so that it makes sense to you. You can put the character's names, dates, places, or plot points in bold to separate them. Or you can use colored markers. Whatever works for you.

Puzzle It Out

This is an elaborate and creative way of outlining your novel that isn't always difficult to keep track of. To create a puzzle outline, you'll need a large space (a tabletop will work well) where you can lay out the puzzle when you want to use it. When you don't need it anymore, it can be put away in a box or folder.

Why go through all the work of creating a puzzle to keep track of your ideas? Because some writers are more visual or prefer a hands-on approach. They need a way to coordinate their work that is stimulating and keeps them interested. The puzzle method is a creative way of stretching your imagination to work with your manuscript.

Fitting the Pieces Together

In his book *A Whack on the Side of the Head,* author Roger von Oech details a way for everyone to be more creative by using puzzles. Though von Oech's book's title might seem unorthodox, sometimes it's exactly what every writer needs. Puzzling can help with this dilemma by giving your brain another way to expound on the information you've fed it for your novel. It may feel like a waste of time. But anything that helps your brain to make sense of writing a 100,000-word manuscript is always a good thing.

ESSENTIAL

Roger von Oech has also created the Creative Whack Pack, a deck of cards that provides creative-thinking strategies. Think of them like puzzling; they give your brain a chance to step out of its usual thought habits.

Puzzling can be done with words or pictures—whatever works best for you. The most important thing is to relax. Let yourself play with the words or images. This is not a life or death exercise. Its sole task is to help you think more creatively about what you're writing.

Whether you decide to use words or pictures, the important thing is to keep them straight in your mind. For instance, you have various paragraphs that represent your characters, plot, and setting. You fit these together by putting your main character first then adding pieces of the plot. Maybe the paragraph about the original setting would fit here. Progress as you would with any other puzzle by adding and subtracting pieces as you tell yourself the story.

Some writers use both pictures and words to create the images in their minds. You can use different colors of paper or ink to represent the characters, and so on. Using colors and pictures appeals to another portion of your brain that will help add texture and new thought to your creative process.

Keeping It Straight

Don't worry about taking your puzzle apart each time you finish using it. That's part of the appeal of puzzling. The pieces that work together will find their way back together again. The pieces that don't work will find new partners. Remember that this is more a creative exercise than a strict outline of your story.

Taking Notes

Notes can serve as the writer's best friend. If you decide to travel to Spain to experience firsthand the life of a Basque sheep farmer, be sure that you take some serious notes and lots of photographs. You can't just rely on your memory to record all the little details. Keep copies of your notes for reference and to prove that you were working in Spain and not just eating olives and lying out in the sun.

FACT

A good book that explains how the brain learns to work more creatively is *Writing the Natural Way* by Gabriele Lusser Rico, Ph.D. If you don't understand it on the first time through, try again later. It's a fascinating subject, and understanding it can help you be a more creative writer.

Good notes can be used as an outline for your manuscript. By placing them in the correct order, you can see where your first ideas came from and where you thought they were going. Some writers even scan their notes into their computer so they can write directly from them. This way your prose is as fresh as when you first got those ideas.

Good Note Taking

Good notes contain as much or as little material as it takes for you to understand what you were looking for with a particular experience. For instance, if you went to a Laundromat to experience the situation, what would your notes look like? They might include descriptions of the machines, what the building looked like. You might write notes about some of the people who were there, how they dressed, what they did while they were waiting for their clothes to be washed and dried. You might take note of how much the machines cost and if a customer could bring in a pet with them. Some Laundromats are also bowling alleys or arcades. If you wanted to connect something to the Laundromat in your book, you could get ideas from your notes for this purpose. Include in your notes the smells and sounds, the heat from the dryers and you'll have the experience of a Laundromat in your notes. When you go back to your notes a month or a year later, they will re-create that experience fresh for your mind.

FACT

For those of you who are looking for more structure for your note taking, you can check out the Cornell Note Taking System. Developed forty years ago by Walter Pauk, this system is designed for students in college but can be used by anyone who wants to be more organized with their notes.

Organizing Your Notes

Your book is about a Spanish sheep farmer who comes to America and goes to the Laundromat to wash his clothes (among other things). Your notes are extensive about both sheep farming and the Laundromat experience. How can you keep track of them in an orderly way so that you can look at them while you're writing?

Organizing your notes is important if they are going to be any help to you. You can't write the whole first part of your book about your sheep farmer's life and then realize that you forgot four of five important incidents because your notes for those occurrences were in with your notes about the Laundromat.

One good way to keep up with the notes is to organize them into separate files. The sheep farmer files would be separate from the Laundromat files. You could look at them while you're writing, then put them back into your files. Another way would be to write or type them all together, then keep the individual notes in a file. You wouldn't access the individual notes creatively, only if you needed them to validate your work.

Remember that your notes are only for you. They don't have to be complete sentences that are punctuated and spell-checked. It's more important that they convey the feelings or sense of the people, places, or events that you want to remember. Good note taking and organization can take you back to Spain or to the Laundromat at any given moment.

Writing a Rough Draft

One other way you can choose to outline—and the most involved—is actually writing down your story as a rough draft. This draft may look nothing like the final version, but just knowing that what you're writing down is more like an outline than the final text makes it easier for writers to just start writing. And the resulting draft becomes the master plan for their novel. If you can get down the basic idea and aren't put off by a lengthy rewrite process, this approach may work for you.

Take a look at this list of authors who readily confess to using an outline: Sue Grafton, Connie Shelton, and Barbara Taylor Bradford. Authors who don't outline: Jane Fletcher Geniesse, Sidney Sheldon, and Erica Silverman.

Writing It from Beginning to End

You have a story to tell. It involves magic, murder, romance, and betrayal. It has a large cast of characters. Its setting is in another world totally different from present-day Earth. The plot keeps you up at night just thinking about it. You know it's a winner.

Even if you are the type of writer who requires perfection with every word, you can still use a quick, rough draft method to get your ideas down. The reason for doing this is just to see the whole thing from beginning to end. It doesn't have to be perfect. You can even write it with pen and paper.

All you have to do is take the thread of your story and start writing. Don't worry about punctuation, spelling, grammar, or paragraphs. Just run through until you've told the whole story from beginning to end. No one is ever going to see this except you. Don't worry about mistakes, because they don't matter here.

Whether you do this on paper or the computer, leave room for ideas that come up after you finish this draft. Doing this gives you an opportunity to find weak spots and loopholes in your characters and plot before you begin to write the manuscript. If you're one of those writers who must create the perfect draft the first time out, repress your urge for perfection. Think of this as an exercise in simply writing what's on your mind. Use it to free your imagination from the constant nagging of your novel that wants to be written. And maybe you'll find the imperfections in your ideas before they become major flaws.

Writing When You Get into Trouble

Oh no! Your plot has unraveled. Your main characters have flaws that can't be mended. Your setting isn't right. Your dialogue isn't good. There are too many mistakes. Maybe the best thing to do is start over. There's probably no point in rewriting this book. You might as well start from scratch.

There should be a word for this event. Every writer goes through it at some point. Beginning writers usually have more difficulty getting past a crisis of this nature because they have no confidence in their work. It's dropping the ball. Trading in the car rather than getting a tune-up. Looking for a new job because you think your boss doesn't like you.

QUESTION?

What flaws should I look for in the outline version of my story?
Plot points that look weak, characters who can't engage the reader, and dialogue and setting that don't put you in the proper mood to continue reading are all flaws you should look for.

There are times when you do have to give up. There are times when you have to shelve a manuscript. But not at this stage. This is still fine-tuning. No matter how many errors you find or how many holes are in your plot, it's probably not hopeless. Even worse, this hopping from manuscript to manuscript without ever finishing one to the stage where you can send it out into the world won't make you a better writer. The only way to become a better writer is to stick with what you have and fix what's wrong with it.

Your characters are weak? Go through and find out what makes them weak. Look through your notes about them. What can you change to make them stronger and more vibrant?

Your plot has bad spots? Where are they? What makes them weak? Why doesn't it work? Take each plot point and follow it through. You should be able to see where your brilliant ideas got muddied in the writing.

Your setting is wrong? Change it to one that works for the characters and plot. And next time, be sure to take extra time before you decide on the setting.

Your dialogue sounds like a B movie? Carefully read each piece aloud. What's wrong with what's being said? Correct it by making it sound more natural and right for each character.

If you have to give up, only do it after you've reworked the manuscript. Give it, and yourself, a chance to be brilliant.

Chapter 12

E Writing the Rough Draft

The first run-through of your novel is sometimes called the discovery draft. Think of it as a dress rehearsal for the finished product. Most writers create some form of rough draft for their books. Then, authors revise and refine that less-than-perfect text until it says exactly what they want it to say, the way they want to say it. You can choose to skip this step, and write each paragraph as if it were your final draft, but many authors feel that this is too much pressure and prefer to put the entire story down on paper and then go back to make it perfect.

The Best Part of Writing

Many writers consider the storytelling to be the best part of writing a novel; they see revisions and editing as necessary evils and don't enjoy those parts of the process. Writing the rough draft is their chance to tell their story from start to finish without interruptions. They don't worry about the details of grammar and spelling because they know they'll fix everything later.

You can choose not to write the entire story and then revise. But you have a better chance of finishing a novel if you get the whole thing down first, then worry about making it perfect. Too many first-time writers are so concerned about their initial work, crafting each sentence and phrase, that they end up unable to complete their story.

QUESTION?

Do I have to create a rough draft of my manuscript?
It would make a better book, but it isn't technically necessary. No editor is going to ask if you wrote a rough draft first.

What's a Rough Draft?

The rough draft of your manuscript should be exactly what it sounds like—rough. No smooth edges or rounded corners. It might bulge out in some places or sag in others. Maybe that's why some writers prefer to call it the discovery draft. It sounds so much neater.

Whatever you choose to call it, sit down and write all of your heaped-up ideas, the pictures in your mind, as short scenes—whether or not they come in order. Play with words like a child plays on the playground. Let all of the research you've done come together. It doesn't have to be coherent. Shift it around like a puzzle until you know exactly how everything goes.

This is where you have the chance for your writing to really be creative. Throw wild colors at your canvas. Don't be shy. Let it all come out and worry about it later. No one else has to see this version of your story.

FACT

Writers talk about "writer's trance," moments when the story seems to take over and the text begins to flow without the writer thinking about it. For most, this is the best writing they will ever do, and it usually occurs during the rough draft process.

In a Trance

The first draft of your manuscript frees your mind from the world you inhabit at this moment. It allows you to inhabit the world you're creating. This is absolutely necessary if you hope to describe it for your readers. If you don't believe that, try describing people and places you've never experienced. Try it using 100,000 words. If you've never been to India or done serious research on that country, you'll find that words fail you after the first few hundred.

This place and these people that you're excavating from your soul are real to you. The challenge is to make them real for the person reading your book. You can know all the pretty words and all the right ways to express them, but if you aren't writing like you're really there, the reader won't be there either.

Choose Your Approach

There are many approaches to writing a rough draft, and you'll have to figure out which works best for you by trial and error. There is no right or wrong way to do this. There are no editors here, no reviewers—just you and the story that keeps you up at night. The important thing is that you sit down and tell the story from beginning to end.

Freeform

This is probably the simplest way to accomplish your goal. Take your outline, or whatever you've chosen to keep track of your ideas, and start writing. There doesn't have to be correct spelling or punctuation. You don't need margins, chapter breaks, or even paragraphs. Start at the beginning and write until the whole novel has spilled out of you.

If you can get past the fact that you have to sit at the computer, you'll save yourself a lot of extra work that isn't creative. Ignore or turn off spelling and grammar checkers. Unplug the phone. Lock the door. Tell the story. It's the only way you'll ever get those images out of your mind.

A good book to look through for ideas on the creative process is *Telling Stories: An Anthology for Writers,* edited by Joyce Carol Oates. With witty words of personal wisdom on the creation process shared by well-known authors, this book will help you realize that you aren't struggling alone.

Chapter by Chapter

If you can handle a little more structure, you can write your rough draft chapter by chapter. You have your outline, so you know approximately what you expect to happen in each chapter. You don't have to limit each chapter to what your original thoughts were in the outline. It just gives you an idea of where to go.

Doing the rough draft this way can help organize your thoughts more clearly. It enhances your perception that you are writing a book. For some people, that makes all the difference. They can deal with not checking the spelling of each word as long as there is some structure. They can't abide the unregulated, freeform style of thoughts flowing without any vessel to contain them.

It doesn't make you neurotic or obsessive to create your rough draft in chapters. In fact, it will be easier to revise and edit this way.

Character Sketches

Another way of creating a rough draft of your manuscript is to sketch your characters. Many writers feel that their books are character driven. Because of this, they can relate better to lengthy studies of the important characters in their novel. They actually tell the story from start to finish through their characters.

You can do this too by choosing your cast of characters, then telling something about who they are and what they contribute to the plot. Start with the most important characters, then progress to the ones who have only bit parts. By the time you finish, you should have a discovery draft of your story. It will have to be pieced together, but that's what revisions are for.

What is character-driven fiction?
The term *character-driven* is used to describe books in which the plot revolves around the characters, rather than the characters following the plot. Most of today's fiction is considered to be character driven.

Main Characters

The primary players should have the strongest voices. You should understand the workings of their minds like you do your own. By now, you should be able to see them clearly. All you have to do is take the snapshot from your mind and put it on paper.

As you write character sketches, be sure you know the answers to these questions:

- What do they look like?
- What is the face they show the world?
- Who are they in private?
- What are their personality traits?
- What are their strengths and weaknesses?
- What are their goals and what motivates them?

If you know the answers to these questions, you're ready to write a character sketch for each of your main characters. If you can't answer them, you aren't quite ready. You can't use your characters to understand your plot if you don't understand your characters.

Secondary Characters

Don't underestimate the power of your secondary characters. They may be bit players, but they can steal the show from your hero or heroine. Understanding who they are and how they think is important even if you don't convey these details to the reader.

Sketches for these supporting actors may not be as long or as detailed as they are for the main characters. But don't neglect them if you want to tell the whole story. These people add charm, wit, and information to your book. They make the main characters look good or bad. The story may not revolve around them but they make it more interesting. The same rules that apply to the main characters also apply to the secondary characters. You should ask yourself the same questions and know the answers.

ALERT!

Your story's villain should get some special attention, particularly if you're writing a mystery or if your novel incorporates some mystery in it, because villains often drive the plot in this genre.

Let the Writing Begin

You already have all your ideas in one place, and you might even have a detailed outline to get you started. But you can't start actually telling your story until you begin writing your rough draft.

The rough draft should take all your ideas and turn it into a manuscript with a distinct beginning, middle, and end. It may not be perfect but it should give you a rough idea of what the finished product will look like. By doing this, you work out the "bugs" in the story that the outline doesn't catch. Maybe the hero isn't all he could be. Maybe he doesn't relate well to the heroine. This is your opportunity to resolve those issues.

Use the rough draft to see if the road map (outline) works. Don't be afraid to make corrections in your travel plans. There may be obstructions and you may have to alter course, but you can still get where you're going. Consider the obstacles minor detours that will strengthen your novel and give your characters a better way of getting from point A to point B.

Let Yourself Go

Because there are no rules for this part of your work, relax. Have some fun. Don't be worried about making mistakes. That's what rough draft writing is all about. Explore the possibilities.

Maybe you thought your heroine was a natural blond. She turns out to be a redhead. Maybe she isn't a stereotypical redhead. She's calm and rational to the point of being cold. Maybe you thought the hero related to her because she was the product of a broken family, just like him. But in the discovery draft, you realize that it would be better for their relationship if she had a wonderful, big family. These are things you can't see until you start writing. Characters don't relate to each other in an outline. They don't interact until you have them face to face in a situation.

FACT

Sometimes, the dreaded writer's block is unavoidable. Your mind refuses to move another character even a step forward. When this happens, most writers find it helpful to get away from their work and focus on something else. After a while, interest and enthusiasm usually return. Another option is to stop writing and move on to the next chapter.

Turn Off Your Inner Editor

Many writers seem to be natural editors. All of their lives, they've annoyed their families by correcting their spelling errors. They notice if there is a question mark where there isn't a question. They don't mind pointing out mistakes they see on signs and billboards or in the newspaper.

All of that makes writers their own toughest critics. They may not be able to see holes in their plots or character flaws because they're too intimate with them. But the bloopers in spelling, grammar, and punctuation they see in their work haunt them like an irritating jingle.

It's difficult, but you'll have to let those things go. Don't let your inner editor keep you from telling the story by making you worry too much about mistakes that you can handle in later revisions. It will distract you from telling the story. Learn to ignore these minor problems. Resist the urge to correct everything you see.

Leave It Out

Sometimes what you leave out can be as important as what you put in. This is definitely the case when you're writing a rough draft. What should you leave out? Anything that doesn't directly pertain to telling the story. Focus on the story and nothing else. That's the best rule of thumb in this case.

If you allow yourself to get caught up in a lot of useful information that has little or nothing to do with the core of your story, you're defeating the purpose of writing the rough draft. Try to remember that revisions and editing will come later. Anything that doesn't look right can be corrected. If you don't know something, it might be better to leave a blank space and go on. You can always find the answers to fill in later.

Before you begin writing, plan that you'll have some places to fill in when you do revisions. Keep track of those spots in a notebook or in a computer file while you're working to make it easier to do corrections and revisions later.

Research Information

You've thoroughly researched the setting for your book. The story takes place on a charming island in the South Pacific. You know everything about this place from what the cabana boys wear to the type of soap they use in the hotel. You begin writing your rough draft with confidence. But halfway through, you realize that you missed a few details that would make it difficult for you to describe a certain scene. You could decide to stop writing and look it up, but that means the end of writing for the day.

Instead of ruining your creative moment, leave some room for the research you'll do later. Unless the details are at the core of your plot, that information can wait. You can always look it up later.

Minor Problems

Don't let minor problems distract you from your goal. If you just can't find the perfect word to describe the color of a flower, leave yourself a note and move on. Or skip the flower altogether. While you shouldn't ignore major problems, peripheral difficulties must be overlooked.

If you have to change the fact that your murder victim died going over a cliff in his car, that's a major change that could continue to affect the plot. Changing what kind of car he's driving when he goes over the cliff isn't a major plot point. It can wait until you do revisions.

Deciding on whether something you've written is a problem can be a matter of distance. Your emotional connection to the story can make some aspects seem wrong, even though they fit the plot and characters. Set it aside and come back to it later. You may see that what you did was exactly right for the story. If not, you can revise.

When You Finish

Finishing the rough draft is a huge accomplishment. What you should do next is simple: sit back and relax. Sure, you still have a lot of work ahead of you—it's possible you'll need to make major revisions, do more research, and then revise again. But for now, consider what you've accomplished. You've told your story from beginning to end. All of the problems have been solved. True love has conquered all. Your sleuth has found the killer. The world has been saved.

The best thing you can do now is take a break. Refocus your eyes. Try to let it go. You've done your best for now.

Leave It Alone for a Few Days

As hard as this advice may be, it's a good idea to get away from your work for at least a few days. It's not always possible, especially on a tight deadline. But when you can, leave the manuscript alone for a while. This will give you a fresh perspective when you come back to do revisions. It doesn't mean you can't think about what you've written. It just means ignoring the impulse to edit.

This is a great time to reward yourself for a job well done. Take yourself out for dinner and a movie. Open a bottle of champagne. Take the time to pat yourself on the back.

Every writer wants to correct those glaring errors as soon as possible. Some writers have terrible dreams at night about too many adverbs chasing them. If you can't sleep, then you have no choice. But your ability to see errors will increase after a few days without the story going around and around in your head waiting to be written. Your emotional ties will change as well. Like letting your baby go off to school for the first time, letting go of your story will make you more objective.

It's Time for More Research

Now's the time to look up the information you were missing. Doing this first can help you ignore the impulse to start editing. If you're busy doing more research, you don't have time to ruminate over the finer points of your story that may be out of place.

Take the time to reread all your reference materials. It may be the last effort you put into research for this book. Do a good job. Don't be satisfied with half answers because you're in such a hurry to get back to your manuscript. If you need to go to the library, go. The work will still be there when you get back.

Problems to Look For

You took a few days to finish your research. You put your manuscript into a drawer where you couldn't see it for a while. You developed an objectivity to allow yourself to look for errors beyond whether or not something is spelled right. You targeted a long weekend where you'd have plenty of free time to carefully examine the manuscript.

Now nothing seems right. The plot isn't what you thought it would be. The characters don't interact, or react with the force of a sledgehammer.

You didn't realize there could be so much dialogue in a book. You're considering throwing the whole thing away and starting over.

Hold on. There are cures for almost anything that ails a rough draft. Remember, this was never meant to be the finished piece. You were supposed to make mistakes. Now, it's time to correct them.

Weak Characters

You thought your character was like Superman. Instead, he's more like Bizzarro. He stumbles when he should be walking confidently. He mumbles when he should be taking charge.

Even when you mean to write great characters, they can be less than great in the rough draft. Your hero isn't a man of steel? Why not? Figure out what the problem is and correct it. He's still your character. You have the final say on everything he does. If he stumbles, help him up. If he mumbles, change his dialogue. Consider how you saw him the first time in your head. Reshape him to fit that image.

Bad Dialogue

It's always easy to know what you mean to say. It's not as easy to say it. Your characters' dialogue can be the same way. If you don't like what your heroine says or how she says it, decide why. Is she too mild-mannered when she was supposed to be outspoken? Is she too abrasive when she was supposed to be sweet? Go through her dialogue and decide what you don't like about it. Change her words to suit what you first envisioned and what the plot needs. Make sure that the rest of her character changes with her.

Not Enough Plot

Your novel is supposed to be 100,000 words. Your rough draft is a mere 50,000. And even with half the amount of words that you need, the plot runs out before the end. Go back and find the place where your plot started winding down. What can you do to bring it back to life? Maybe you need a larger subplot. Either possibility exists and could help you understand and revise your work.

Deciding how much plot belongs in your book can be difficult. But if you take the time before you start to think through your plots and subplots, problems in either direction can be resolved.

Too Much Plot

The only thing worse than not enough plot can be too much plot. Half-solved theories, partially developed characters, and story lines that go nowhere are the hallmarks of this problem. You want to keep your readers engaged. You want to give them plenty of action and excitement. But too much excitement that doesn't fit in or causes the book to be too "busy" isn't good either. It leaves readers feeling like they've been run over by a car at an intersection. They wonder what happened and how they missed it. Correcting this mistake can be as easy as removing an extra, unnecessary subplot. Focus on what's important to the story. Make that exciting and you won't need anything else.

E Chapter 13
Basic Structure

A haiku is a Japanese poem that has seventeen syllables arranged in three lines. A sonnet has a fourteen-line frame, and each line contains five feet. Poets who write in either of these mediums know exactly what type of structure their writing will have. Novels aren't structured as rigidly. There is a basic, accepted framework and structure for novels, but they aren't as specific. This chapter reviews the basic structural requirements of the novel.

Chapter Breakdown

Most novels are broken down into chapters. A chapter may be as long or as short as necessary. Some writers prefer to keep all their chapters at about the same length, like 5,000 words. Other writers vary chapter size: One chapter may have 1,200 words while another may have 6,000 words. Most publishers don't seem to care about the size of the chapters, so long as there are enough words in the book.

How much should happen in a chapter? That's up to you too. Sometimes lots of events will happen in a single chapter. The hero will meet the heroine, fall in love, and break up. But sometimes, only one earth-shattering event will take place in a single chapter. You'll have to decide what's best for your story and the reader.

FACT

If you're interested in checking out a good book on the structure of creating fiction, *Scene and Structure* by Jack Bickham can help you. It's loaded with lots of creative ideas for building your book from the ground up.

How many chapters are in a book? That's up to you. Some writers prefer to have many short chapters. Other writers break up the number of words and set them in chapters accordingly. For instance, a 100,000-word book at 5,000 words per chapter would mean twenty chapters. Publishers rarely have rules that govern the number of chapters in a book. They leave that up to the author, who makes that decision based on where and when the story needs breaks.

How to Begin

The first line in every chapter should be a sentence that draws the reader into the story. Even if the beginning hook in your story is powerful and persuasive, the reader needs to be reminded. Starting with dialogue or a strong piece of action can convince the reader not to go to bed. They want to keep reading to find out what happens next.

Back story is never a good way to begin a chapter. Even though you've thoroughly introduced your plot and characters, beginning anything with back story is always a mistake. Save it for a time when the reader isn't as likely to put the book down.

Don't end something that you're carrying over from a previous chapter at the very beginning of the new chapter. Add to it in the first few sentences. If it's thrilling, make it more thrilling. If it's emotional, make it more emotional. Get the reader hooked into the chapter before you end the scene and begin another one.

How to End

Except for the end of the book, where you have to tie up all the loose ends, never end a chapter by solving anything. If your hero is having a problem catching the bad guy, don't let him catch him on the last page unless the bad guy turns around with a gun in his hand. Chapter endings should be dynamic and energetic. They should be the heroine leaning against a wall and feeling it slide open behind her. They should take the reader's breath away and force them to continue reading.

QUESTION?

What is the average number of chapters in a novel?
It's difficult to say because it varies so greatly. Most books between 60,000 and 75,000 words have about ten to fifteen chapters.

Never let your heroine or hero go to sleep at the end of a chapter. This may be a signal for your reader to yawn, put the book down, and go to sleep as well. It doesn't mean that your hero can't ever go to sleep. It just means he can't go to sleep at the end of the chapter.

The end of the chapter should automatically cause the reader to flip the page and start the next chapter. There shouldn't be a question of whether or not to read on. The remarkable discovery the hero just made should be too exciting to let go of the story so easily.

Paragraphs of Text

Each chapter is further broken down into paragraphs. Paragraphs are versatile and flexible; they may be a page long, or just a few sentences. Use paragraph breaks to tell the readers that you are switching points of view or moving on to your next thing.

Usually, you begin a paragraph with a sentence that leads the reader into more of the text. This sentence can be transitional, helping the reader make a change between paragraphs that are about different topics.

Breaking your manuscript into paragraphs should be done with a keen eye for readability. Huge blocks of text can be mind boggling for a reader. Many of them will give up before wading through that much information. You may be reluctant to break up a single thread of thought that runs through a page-long paragraph. But it's for the good of your story that you offer it to your readers in a way that they can understand it. That's what paragraphs are all about.

Dialogue Format

Each line of dialogue constitutes its own paragraph. For instance:

She walked into the house and closed the door.
Her mother looked up. "Back already?"
"Yes."

Dialogue is usually set off with paragraph breaks because it's so easy for a reader to get lost when more than one character is speaking. Even with punctuation, it can still be difficult. Always keep in mind that you want to make it as easy for the reader as possible. She may be reading in a roomful of crying toddlers or on the bus as she goes to work. A fascinating story will keep the reader's attention. But a well-ordered page makes it simpler for readers to forget that they're reading and lose themselves in the book.

Don't worry that there are too many empty places, or white space, in a page of dialogue. Readers are familiar with that. It would be far worse to have dialogue jumbled together without paragraphing. The dialogue paragraph makes it instantly recognizable when a different character is speaking, even without dialogue tags.

> *White space* is the term editors use to refer to areas of a book that contain no text or graphics. Researchers claim that this makes a page easier to read. This is part of what makes dialogue valuable.

Narrative Paragraphs

Narrative paragraphs may not be as exciting as dialogue paragraphs, but they're just as important. They keep the tone and pace of the book so that the reader isn't bored until they get to the next exciting event. They create mood and movement when there's no one for the heroine to talk to. They express emotion, opposition, and awareness. It would be difficult to constantly refer to setting with dialogue. Narrative has to support your character's thoughts and words.

It's important to use paragraph breaks correctly with narrative text. Because there are no quotation marks to break up the text, readers rely on the writer to create breathing places for them. Think of that as you tackle breaking up your story. Look for paragraphs that are too long or convey too much information. Don't be afraid to break these up into smaller groups. Shorter paragraphs convey more movement. Excitement and agitation can be expressed with choppy, short paragraphs.

Use paragraph breaks every time you change the mood or place. Give your reader plenty of room to take in all of your words.

Sentence Structure

Each paragraph is made up of sentences. Nothing to it, right? Well, there are plenty of books written about sentence structure. Each sentence should make sense and get to the point. You only have so much space. Be concise and don't ramble. Let your sentences show as much about you as an author as they say about your characters.

How do you write good sentences? Use strong verbs and interesting nouns. Be sure that you have something to say. Create your sentences with your reader in mind. Do what feels natural. Watch out for awkward ways of saying something. Human beings are very young when they begin creating sentences in speech. Polish that skill and your text sentences will be interesting and easy to understand.

FACT

Dialogue paragraphs may certainly be a sentence long, but narrative paragraphs need to be longer. As a rule, a single sentence cannot stand as a separate paragraph of narrative text.

Sentence Length

What is the best length for a sentence? The answer depends on the writer and what he's writing. Nonfiction writers who write books as well as newspaper articles are encouraged to use shorter sentences to get their point across. The reading public has a short attention span and would like you to get to the point. Fiction writers aren't as strongly encouraged to use shorter sentences, yet editors are always looking for better ways to make text more readable. Genre writers tend to lean toward shorter sentences. Mainstream writers tend to use the classics as guidelines. Some of the older novels had sentences that went on for days.

Which is right? There really is no right or wrong. Some novels work better with longer sentences. Some are better with shorter sentences. Overall, the market tends to favor writers who write shorter sentences. This work is viewed as being more exciting and energetic. However, if you feel you just can't write the story without using longer sentences, go for it. Just stay away from sentences that become chapters.

Grammatical Structure

A good sentence should have a subject and a verb. For instance: "The cat saw the dog." The subject here is *cat*. The verb is *saw*. The object of the cat's action is the *dog*. Pretty simple, right?

It would be, if you only wrote books for small children. But novel writers use sentences that are much more complex. Take a look at the following paragraph:

He'd always been afraid of elevators. As a small child, he avoided them. But as an adult, they became a necessary evil. Now he faced the ultimate challenge. His new job required him to ride an elevator that went up ninety-nine floors.

These aren't bad sentences but they could be made better:

He faced his new enemy. An elevator that went up ninety-nine floors. Yes, he was afraid of elevators. He managed to avoid them as a child. But now he had no choice. He had to ride the elevator or not go to work.

The second paragraph is more active, more to the point. Don't be afraid of using sentence fragments if it enhances your text. Keep your sentence form as simple as possible. Even great things can be said in short, straightforward ways.

Clauses and Phrases

A sentence may contain clauses or phrases:

- A clause is a group of words that contains a subject and a predicate.
- A phrase is a group of words that doesn't contain a subject and a predicate.

Using phrases and clauses is part of speaking—you probably use them a hundred times a day. When you're talking, you don't think about it. Neither does anyone else. For the most part, you won't think about it when you're writing either. But understanding these two parts of a sentence and how to use them can make it easier for you to write good sentences.

Dissecting a language is never easy. Think about it like high school biology. You have to take things apart sometimes in order to know how they work when you put them back together.

Using Clauses

Clauses are divided into two groups: Independent and dependent. Independent clauses are parts of sentences that can stand on their own. Many times, they make up sentence fragments that a fiction writer will use to create tension or movement in his or her story. For instance: "How many times he walked down that street."

It can become part of a larger sentence if it's connected to other clauses or phrases by a semicolon or coordinating conjunction: "How many times he walked down that street and she met him there." Or: "How many times he walked down that street; she was always there."

Dependent clauses are like your kid brother. He looks like you but he can't pay his rent by himself. A dependent clause relies on another part of the sentence to make it complete. For instance: "How many times he walked down that street before he met her." The word *before*, in this case, creates the bridge that helps the dependent clause, "he met her," stand by itself.

If you combine more than one independent clause into one sentence, remember to use correct punctuation: Independent clauses are always separated by a semicolon or a conjunction, never by a comma.

Using Phrases

Phrases can be considered as a group of words spoken in one breath. It can be something catchy or repetitive. When you're writing, be careful not to use the same phrase too many times—they can be addictive. Common phrases include:

- *After midnight:* After midnight, she left the ball.
- *In a flash:* In a flash, she realized she'd lost her slipper.
- *Faster than a speeding bullet:* She ran home faster than a speeding bullet.
- *Less than perfect:* His response to her flight was less than perfect.
- *By the way:* By the way, he was a prince.
- *Out of season:* It looked like royal weddings were out of season.

Phrases can be used in a sentence as a noun, verb, adjective, or adverb. A phrase that is necessary to the meaning of a sentence is called a restrictive phrase. For instance: "The computer in my office is invaluable to me." The phrase here is "in my office."

A phrase that is actually a comment about the sentence is called a nonrestrictive phrase. For instance: "The computer, which isn't mine yet, is in my office." The phrase here is "which isn't mine yet."

Great Beginnings

There's nothing like scrunching down in your favorite chair with a cup of coffee to read a book by one of your favorite authors. Or maybe your favorite place to read is at the poolside with the sun beating down on you.

Whatever your ideal reading spot, it should be exciting to begin a good book. It has promise and possibilities that you hope will be fulfilled in the hours and days that follow. If you're a reader, there's nothing else like it.

Then suddenly, the unthinkable happens: Your favorite author forgot how important the beginning of the book is to you. Instead of hot passion, dead bodies, or an immediate emotional moment, the author drags you through a quagmire of back story. You tap your fingers on the side of your chair and read on, hoping it will get better. If you're lucky, it will. If not, you're going to be a little more cautious when you pick up another book by your now second favorite author.

Are there certain types of books that use prologues and epilogues more than others?

Mysteries and books with historical settings tend to use prologues more than others. This helps the author set up what's to come for the reader. Romances and science fiction tend to favor epilogues.

One way to start is with a prologue, or introduction. Although some editors are wary of prologues and have been known to reject a manuscript for including one, others consider prologues to be an integral part of the novel. If you think that you need a small section to set the tone of your novel, introduce information about the characters that the characters themselves can't know, or address the readers and welcome them into your world, then a prologue may be a good idea for you.

Ending with an Epilogue

The epilogue finishes a book. It can take readers outside the main lines of the story to tell them what happened after the conclusion of the book. Maybe the hero and heroine that ended up together at the end of the novel will go on to have a child. If you're careful, you can use your epilogue as a plot device to introduce a sequel. The child to be born to the hero and heroine might grow up to be the main character of your next novel.

Like the prologue, the epilogue can give readers information beyond the knowledge of the main character. This can be useful if the novel is written in first person, or from the point of view of only a few characters.

Should you use an epilogue for your book? Only if it seems right for your story. Not every book needs this extra touch. But it's nice to know it's there if you need it.

Chapter 14
Reviewing Grammar

You didn't worry about grammar usage as you were writing your rough draft, but now it's time to make revisions and fix all those grammar mistakes. But are you comfortable with grammar, or are you totally lost? Many writers seem to have an almost innate sense of what to say and how to say it. If you're one of those writers, this chapter will help you brush up on your basic knowledge. But if you aren't so blessed, pay attention. This may be a good time to begin taking a look at your language and how you use it.

The Importance of Good Grammar

Overall, your book should adhere to the established rules of grammar, unless you're trying to make a specific point by changing them. True, you might veer off the path in your dialogue if you feel that your character speaks in a different way and you want to be able to express that. But remember this: When a reader picks up your book, you don't want your story to be hampered by unacceptable grammar. Learn the rules so you can apply them as you write, then do careful revision to catch what you missed. If you're not sure about something, look it up.

FACT

Daily Grammar, at ✑ *www.dailygrammar.com,* is an easy way to get a handle on using and recognizing good grammar. You can sign up to receive short grammar lessons five days a week. You can even take a quiz about what you've learned on the sixth day.

Learning the Rules

Even though everyone learns the rules of good writing in school, most people don't remember them by the time they graduate. They take for granted that what they say and write is correct. But like anything else you learned in school, unless you use it professionally, you've probably lost most of it.

You don't have to go back to school to learn to use grammar correctly and effectively as a writer. A short refresher course will be enough to do a good job, and then you can look up the answers to any questions you might come across as you edit your work for grammar mistakes. There are plenty of books and online resources that can help you do both.

Bending the Rules

Everyone has heard the phrase, "Rules were made to be broken." Writers don't break the rules of grammar; they bend them. Writing fiction is different than writing a school essay or a report for work. A fiction writer has more room to modify his or her grammar to fit with the story. Many fiction writers seem to create their own brand of grammar that suits their needs. Once you learn the rules and know what's right, don't be afraid to bend them a little if that will help you achieve a certain effect.

Examples of bending the rules of grammar can be found in almost every contemporary fiction novel. Authors like Mickey Spillane, Nora Roberts, and Piers Anthony play with grammar usage. Hard-boiled detective novels and science fiction are famous for it. They don't so much reinvent grammar usage as enliven it.

Know Your Nouns

If you've ever listened to School House Rock, you know that a noun is a person, place, or thing. That sounds pretty simple—everything you see, everything you touch is a noun. Most words are nouns. Rock. Tree. Dog. Car. Elephant. Their usage depends on the sentence you put them in:

- The rock fell on the tree.
- The dog chased the car.
- The elephant sat on the dog or the car.
- Elephants can sit wherever they want.

It gets more complicated from here. But this is where you start.

Using Nouns

Nouns are everywhere because they name everything. They can be simple or complex. They are one of the first things to change in a language. Dancehall became ballroom, ballroom became nightclub, and nightclub became disco.

You can't write a sentence without using nouns. Every sentence has to have a noun as its subject. These words express so much of what writers have to say that they keep up with the times better than most people. Strong, descriptive nouns that accurately portray what needs to be said are the backbone of the writer's vocabulary.

Proper Nouns

The names of certain people, places, and things are called proper nouns. These include names of people: Janice, Mike, Bill. Also names of places: Paris, Washington, New Orleans. Even some specific things like the Eiffel Tower, the Empire State Building, Buckingham Palace.

Proper nouns always refer to something in particular. They are always written with a capital letter. Whole phrases can be included under this umbrella. This can apply to book titles and specific groups such as the United Steelworkers Union.

Watch out for nouns that may seem like they should be proper nouns. A good example of this is using words like mother and father. These words aren't capitalized, unless they're taking the place of a name.

Pronouns

A word used to substitute for a noun is a pronoun. Most common pronouns (subject pronouns) are *I, you, he, she, it, we,* and *they.* These pronouns help you refer to people without repeating their names. Instead of using your heroine's name, you can switch to *she*: "Sally went to the zoo." "She went to the zoo."

There are other pronouns as well. Pronouns like *my* and *his* are possessive pronouns, because they show possession. Instead of saying "Sally's visit to the zoo," you can say "Her visit to the zoo."

ALERT!

Using and understanding pronouns is especially useful when you have long proper nouns. This means that the United Steelworkers Union may simply be referred to as *it.* By correctly placing pronouns, you can keep your readers in the loop without getting them lost in all those repetitions.

Verbs: Words of Action

Whether you choose to write mystery or romance or any other kind of fiction, you'll have to use verbs. Whether your main character puts on his socks, goes dancing, or murders his wife, you'll express everything he does with verbs. The verbs you use say something about you as a writer. They should be crisp and clear. They should tell readers exactly what they need to know. They convey the imagery from your words to your reader's imagination.

A Basic Definition

Verbs express existence, action, or occurrence. Basically, that means that verbs move your characters around in your story. "Sally walked to the mailbox." In this case, the verb *walked* moved Sally from wherever she was to the mailbox.

Subject and verb must always agree. Compare the following sentences:

- Lucy has a great idea.
- Lucy and Bill have a great idea.

The verb *to have* must change in order to agree with the subject "Lucy" and "Lucy and Bill."

Using Verbs Wisely

A writer should always be aware of his or her verbs. Using the right ones in the right way can make the difference between passionate prose and plain prose. Compare the following:

- She was scared.
- Terror filled her heart.

The second sentence paints a clearer picture with the verb *filled*.

Be creative. There are plenty of verbs out there waiting to be used. Your heroine doesn't just walk away after her fight with the hero. She flounces. The villain in your mystery novel doesn't just kill people. He maims and tortures them. He plays with them. Let your imagination find elegant, wonderful ways to express your characters' movements.

Describe It with an Adjective

Writers eat adjectives for breakfast, lunch, and supper every day. This may be because writers know that adjectives are a powerful part of writing. You can use adjectives to create a mood or help the reader understand something more about your characters. But be careful: If you begin to overuse your adjectives, you'll end up muddying your text and lose the clarity you were trying so hard to create.

Adjectives are words that modify, limit, identify, or describe nouns (people, places, or things). In the phrase "blue car," blue is the adjective that describes the car. There are also degrees of describing nouns, such as "the bluer car." Just as there are proper nouns, there are proper adjectives too: American cars, British oil, or Hungarian goulash.

Using adjectives is simple, but using them effectively isn't always so easy. How do you know when a detail you add with an adjective is helpful or distracting? Details don't have to be dramatic but they have to explain whole worlds of emotion, wonder, and discovery. It's all in the adjectives and how you use them. Use the right one, and you get exactly the reaction you were hoping for. Overdo it and your story descends into mediocrity. Writers tend to get carried away with wanting their readers to experience everything that's in their imaginations, so they overemphasize. The elephants weren't just big and gray. They were enormous, gargantuan, bigger than life. The food wasn't just delicious, it was spicy, hot, four alarm, sinus clearing. By this time, your reader is saying, "Enough already!"

Finding the right adjectives is usually part of the revision process. It can change a day into a sunny day. It can make a tall, brown-haired woman into a leggy brunette. And it can change those elephants to gray and enormous.

What Adverbs Are For

Writers are constantly nagged by editors to live without the lowly adverb. But what would life be like without them? For one thing, the first sentence of this section would have to be revisited. The words *constantly* and *lowly* would have to be replaced.

What is it about adverbs that editors dislike so much? Apparently, they feel that verbs don't need adverbs. If a verb is strong enough on its own, it won't need anything except a strong noun. This may be true. But most writers continue to use adverbs when they write. They probably always will.

It's true that some writers do use adverbs unnecessarily. Take a look at the following sentence: "They returned back to the house." Anything wrong here? The adverb *back* is completely unnecessary, because the verb *to return* means "to come back." Dropping unnecessary adverbs will help you avoid redundancy.

What Is an Adverb?

An adverb is like an adjective, except instead of modifying or describing a noun, the adverb modifies or describes a verb (or, less often, an adjective or another adverb). These words specify when a verb happens, where it happens, how much it happens, and in what manner it happens. For instance: "The dog barked loudly." Another form of adverb would be: "The man remained quiet."

Many but not all adverbs end in *ly*. These simply seem to be the greatest offenders of all the adverbs. You can write without them, most of the time. But, sometimes, a good adverb is necessary.

Using Adverbs Wisely

To make your adverbs more effective, consider their placement in the sentence. For instance, look at the usage of the adverbs *only* and *almost* in the following sentences:

- The man made only one mistake.
- The man only made one mistake.

- It almost seems impossible to go to the moon.
- It seems almost impossible to go to the moon.

The meaning changes slightly according to where *only* and *almost* appear in the sentence.

Judicious use of adverbs is necessary to good writing. You'll use adverbs and adjectives in your writing all the time. The best you can do is to try not to use them in every sentence. Dialogue requires more adverb usage than narrative. Basically, this is because people speak with plenty of adverbs. Dialogue would sound stilted without them. Again, use them carefully and they won't come back to haunt you.

FACT

Using adverbs that end with *ly* in dialogue tags is one of the most abused ways that writers lean on adverbs. "He said sheepishly," "they agreed blindly," and "she screamed madly" are all examples of this problem. Don't use adverbs as a crutch for better dialogue.

Plurals and Possessives

Many people have trouble keeping straight the rules for spelling plurals and possessives. Like the multiplication tables you learned as a child, the best thing to do is learn these rules by heart. You might still have some trouble remembering them from time to time, but you can correct those issues.

Plural Nouns

Most nouns have a singular and a plural form. Most commonly, the plural form is created by adding *s* as an ending:

- horse—horses
- dog—dogs
- door—doors

Some nouns that end in *f* and *fe* change these letters to *v* and add *es*:

- thief—thieves
- wife—wives

Nouns ending in *s, sh, ch, x,* and *z* take on *es* as a plural ending. For instance:

- annex—annexes
- witness—witnesses
- beach—beaches

Nouns ending in *y* preceded by a consonant change *y* to *i* and add *es*; nouns ending in *y* preceded by a vowel simply gain an *s* ending:

- army—armies
- city—cities
- key—keys

Rules for nouns ending in *o* differ. Some form their plural by adding *s,* while others add *es.* For instance:

- hero—heroes
- radio—radios

A few nouns are the same in plural form, such as deer and sheep. Some nouns are always plural, such as acoustics and athletics. Phrases like brother-in-law are made plural by changing the first word: *brothers-in-law.*

Possessives

Noun possessives are much easier to figure out. All nouns show possession by either adding *'s* or *s'.* If the noun is singular, *'s* is used; if the noun is plural, use *s'.* For example:

- brother's wife (one brother)
- brothers' homes (more than one brother)

Additional confusion arises if the noun in the possessive form ends with *s.* For example, which is correct?

- Ross's book
- Ross' book

This depends. Some grammar manuals prefer the former and others the latter. Pick one and stick to it; if you're writing for a specific publisher, you can check with them to see which they prefer.

QUESTION?

What is the book most writers and editors use as a guide to editing grammar and style?
The Chicago Manual of Style is the most commonly accepted guideline by publishers and writers. It was originally published in 1906 and has been updated every few years since.

Active and Passive Voice

All writers have to worry about how their writing impacts their readers. Whether you're writing an insurance statement, a business proposal, or a novel, you have to write with your intended audience in mind. By thinking about your reader and how you want him to react to your work, you create more effective text.

Understanding the concepts behind active and passive voice will help you become a more effective writer. While this is good practice for all writers, it's crucial for fiction writers. You have to create reality with your words. Your characters, plot, and setting are counting on you to be able to describe them in a forceful, active manner. While using the best voice is important in dialogue, even narrative descriptions can be enhanced by the right language.

Active Voice

In active voice, the verb shows the action of the subject:

- He ate his supper.
- She walked to the store.
- They drove the car off the cliff.

In these examples, the readers can easily figure out who it was that ate, walked, and drove. Active voice makes the action more direct and immediate. It can help you take your characters from place to place without slowing down the pace.

Passive Voice

There are some cases where you have to use passive voice. Usually writers do this with a form of *to be*:

- She was attacked.
- It is taken care of.
- It will be done.

Sometimes you want to avoid stating who it was that performed the action of the verb. In the first example, maybe you don't want the readers to know who it was that attacked her. But more often then not, withholding this information is not intentional. In this case, see if you can revise the passive voice sentence by figuring out what the subject is: "The killer attacked her in the dark."

Read carefully through your work when you revise. There are many ways to change passive voice to active voice. Don't forget to look for these opportunities. You don't want your readers to feel disassociated from the story.

Common Usage Problems

There are some grammar problems that continue to plague writers. They can be as small as individual words or as large as not understanding what verbs to use. All of them make a writer's job more difficult.

Most of what a writer does is a learned experience. While it's true that there has to be that fire to tell a story burning in a writer's soul, all the rest is expressing it. Talent will take a person to great heights. But even the most talented writer has to know how to say what she wants to say. The more she writes, the better she gets because her experience in language and storytelling grows. No one remembers all the rules all of the time. Learn as many as you can and work on the rest as you edit. Don't be afraid to ask questions. It's one of the best ways to learn.

Its and It's

These two little words seem to be the most difficult to understand and use correctly. There is really a very simple explanation that can take you through your text without ever confusing them.

Its is the possessive form of the word it:

- The dog's bowl—Its bowl
- The organization's personnel—Its personnel

That's not to be confused with *it's,* a contracted form of *it is.* For example:

- It is sunny—It's sunny

There and Their

Similarly, people sometimes have trouble figuring out when to use *their* and *there. There* is used to show location or presence:

- She's over there.
- There are no more chips.

Their is a possessive form of *they*:

- Kenny and Joanne's home—Their home
- The students' homework—Their homework

Subjects of Confusion

Some words are easily confused with others. Here's a quick rundown of the usual suspects:

- **Affect/effect:** To *affect* something is to influence it. *Effect* is a noun that refers to the outcome of being affected.
- **Leave/let:** Don't use *leave* when what you mean is *let*. "Leave go of that girl" is incorrect usage.
- **Irregardless:** Although this word is beginning to make its way into English dictionaries, it really should be *regardless*.
- **Nauseous/nauseated:** Use *nauseous* as a synonym for "sickening" and *nauseated* as "sickened."
- **Or/nor:** Many people overuse *nor* when *or* should be used instead. "He can't run nor jump" is incorrect. Use nor only in combination with *neither*: "He's neither tall nor short."
- **Regretful/regrettable:** *Regretful* is used to describe a person who is full of regret. *Regrettable* is an action or circumstance that shouldn't have happened.

There are other words that can be difficult to use; you should carefully analyze them before using them in your text. Check your dictionary if you aren't sure.

Overused Phrases

There are some phrases that have been overused to the point of being comical. While some letter writers may constantly use the same phrases, fiction writers need to be aware of redundancies. Most of these phrases are too stiff and formal to use in modern fiction. Here are a few examples:

- **Due to:** "He was due to leave on the next plane." Use "had to" instead.
- **Different from/than:** "He was different from other people." Use "unlike" instead. Don't ever use "different than."
- **As to whether:** "He couldn't tell as to whether or not she loved him." Use "whether or not" instead.
- **Each and every one:** "Each and every one of them had ice cream." Just use "all" instead.
- **He is a man who:** "He is a man who is very angry." Simply use "he" instead.

• **In terms of:** "He wasn't her type in terms of looks." Just drop the phrase altogether.

There are many other phrases that you should avoid, including your own favorites that you'll find repeated too many times in your text. Keep a sharp eye out for them to keep your story crisp and vibrant.

If you find some of these phrases in your work, look for ways to work around them with fresh text. There's always more than one way to say something. Try to make your way exciting and interesting rather than dull and repetitive.

Chapter 15

E Rules of Punctuation

The glue that holds a manuscript, or any other form of writing, together is called punctuation. Without it, these sentences would be difficult to read. You wouldn't know where you were supposed to stop or the difference between statements and questions. Needless to say, correct punctuation is very important. When you were writing your rough draft, the punctuation probably fell by the wayside. Now, as you're revising, it's time to place those commas and periods where they belong.

Common Comma Problems

For one reason or another, the comma is one of the trickiest punctuation marks. There are many rules that govern their usage and placement. Punctuation specialists (English teachers) can go on for hours about the do's and don'ts of using commas.

Proper placement of commas is an art and a science. Because there are specific rules for where and when to use a comma, it's a science. But because comma usage may be subjective, it's also an art. Every novel writer knows that their writing has certain rhythms. Commas, as well as other punctuation, are an integral aspect of this rhythm. How you punctuate your writing makes the book easier or harder to read.

A good place to go online for punctuation answers is Punctuation Made Simple, at ✍ *www.stpt.usf.edu/pms,* put together by Gary Olson. This site gives you the rundown on major forms of punctuation and how to use them.

Correct Usage

Because there are so many rules to using commas, and this book can only provide a quick overview, the rules will be broken down to their simplest form:

- If you use a series of three or more items with a single conjunction, use a comma after each item. For instance: green, red, and blue. (Be aware, however, that in some style guides, you'll be advised to drop the final comma: green, red and blue.)
- Enclose expressions that interrupt the flow of the sentence with commas: Going to the store, unless you have a car, can be a long journey.
- Writing out the month, day, and year will require a comma: January 5, 1968.
- A comma should go before a conjunction that introduces an independent clause: The trip was bad, but the food was great.

- In dialogue, a comma separates the spoken words from the modifiers: "Mary went to school," she said. She said, "Mary went to school."
- Use a comma to add phrases to the front or back of your sentence: Surely, she'd listen to reason. She believes in Santa Claus, obviously.

ALERT!

While using a conjunction with a comma to separate independent clauses is correct, most writers avoid doing this by creating two separate sentences, or fragments. While grammarians frown on the use of fragments in writing, they can successfully be employed in novel writing.

Don't Overdo It

Commas are great, but if you use too many, your readers will get thoroughly confused. A good rule of thumb is to avoid using more than three commas in a sentence. If you feel the need to do so, your sentence is too long. It would be better to rethink and revise. Remember that you're trying to create a feeling of movement. When you're writing an action scene where your hero and villain are fighting, the sentences should be even shorter, with very few commas. Here are a few examples of comma overuse:

- The swollen river, fed by streams from the mountains, fraught with ice, was dangerous, if not impossible, to pass.
- Tomorrow's stock market, reaching new highs, falling to new depths, rushing toward disaster, is nothing if not, we predict, overzealous.

One way to adjust these comma-heavy sentences would be to create more than one sentence:

- The swollen river was fed by streams from the mountains. Fraught with ice, it was dangerous and difficult to pass.

The meaning remains the same but there aren't so many commas and the reading is more casual.

Editors look for excessive comma usage as a way to tell how experienced you are as a writer. The more experienced the writer, the fewer the commas. Don't let them catch you on this. Even if you don't have tons of experience, your manuscript can read as though you do.

Quotation Marks

The most important application of quotation marks in fiction is to signal dialogue. For writers, it's not enough to hope readers realize where the dialogue is. They have to be shown. You can imagine the problems that would come up if quotation marks were gone:

- Mary said, I'm going to the house. This bucket is breaking my back. She went back to the house.

Who knows what Mary said, and what she did. Sure, if you reread the section three times, you'll figure out that Mary said, "I'm going to the house. This bucket is breaking my back." And then she goes to the house. But if you had to read an entire novel like this, how far would you progress? It would have to be pretty interesting for the readers to continue struggling through it.

Double Quotation Marks

Double quotation marks are used for direct quotation. In fiction, this is likely a direct line of dialogue:

- "I'm going home," she said.
- She looked confused. "What about it?"

These marks are also used with the titles of short stories, magazine articles, and songs:

- Have you ever read "Indian Camp" by Ernest Hemingway?
- Is "Never Again" the name of that song?

Finally, you can sometimes use double quotation marks to denote irony, in a sense that something is "so-called."

FACT

Modern writers tend to use italics to set off words or phrases that used to be set in quotation marks. For instance: She was really "messy." She was really *messy*. It makes it easier for the reader to tell when someone is speaking. Writers also use italics to denote thought.

Single Quotation Marks

Double quotation marks are used to enclose a direct quotation. But what if there are is a quotation within a quotation? In this case, single quotation marks have to be used: "He read the book and said, 'That was great,' and so I gave it to him." This is the only way that single quotation marks are used in American English. On their own, the right-hand quotation mark is known as an apostrophe, and it is used in possessive forms (Mike's, students') and contractions (they're, I've).

Correct Placement

Here are basic rules for using quotation marks with other punctuation:

- Quotation marks always go outside of the comma or period: "It's time." "It's time," she said.
- With a semicolon or colon, quotation marks come first: Read the short story "Days of Our Lives"; discuss. Take a look at "The Hour": Isn't it a beautiful story?
- For question and exclamation marks, it depends whether the mark belongs to the section inside the quotation marks: "What did she want to know?" Have you read "The Hour"?

Punctuating Clauses

Keeping sentences from running on together can be complicated. Some people feel that it's just a matter of style. They consider their short, choppy sentences or long, epic-poem sentences to be a matter of personal choice.

To a certain extent, that's true. Every novel should have a combination of short and long sentences. The short, choppy kind is good for action. The long, epic-poem kind is good for emotional difficulties. Like dialogue and narrative, these two techniques should enhance each other. No one wants to read too much of either of them.

If you're thinking of writing like the classics, forget it. Most people wouldn't be able to get a classic novel past one of today's editors. Sentences were longer fifty years ago. So was length of narrative versus dialogue. These books, though highly prized for their literary merit, aren't good examples of how a contemporary novelist should write.

But how do you decide whether a sentence is too long or too short? How do you know if it needs breaking up of if it's best to join it with another sentence? Don't worry so much about using complete sentences. Sentence fragments can work very nicely. The most important thing is that they make sense. As far as being too long, if you read the sentence out loud and you have to pause for breath, it's too long.

Colons and Semicolons

The colon may be used to introduce a list or a long formal quotation. You can also use it after a formal salutation in a letter. Numbers used to indicate hours, minutes, and seconds—12:30:10—also use colons.

The semicolon has almost been replaced by the comma in contemporary writing, but there are some circumstances when only a semicolon will do. One of them can be between clauses in a compound sentence:

• I found the evidence; you can't look the other way.

The semicolon can also be used to replace the serial comma if one or more of the terms in the series include other punctuation:

• She bought plump, fragrant oranges; juicy, succulent nectarines; and ruddy apples.

Punctuation for Pause

Creating a pause in writing is more like drawing a breath than a complete stop. It's where the hero takes time to think over the problem. It's the unspoken moment that follows a first kiss. Without this quiet space, you'd have too much going on in moments when life would at least seem to slow down.

It's not something you'll want to use in every sentence. Too many pauses would take away the effect and make the reader feel disengaged from the story. But the right number will bring a tear or a sigh. It's the response you're looking for as you present your reader with an emotional moment.

If you think back on your life, you'll see how these poignant pauses come around. Sometimes, it can happen as you're thinking, or as you're speaking. It can happen for your characters that way too. Even the most despicable villain can take a moment to realize the completion of his terrible plan.

When a Dash Would Be Appropriate

Dashes (—) are often used in fiction to create the effect of an abrupt stop, when you need the reader to realize that something important has happened. Maybe the hero just realized that he is in love with the heroine. Maybe a conversation has ended suddenly, leaving a feeling of ill omen behind. Here's an example:

He saw her walking toward him. She looked better than he remembered. He searched for somewhere to put the mop he was holding. What an awful time for her to—
"Hi, Max. Nice mop."

When a dash is used to indicate a break, no period is needed.

FACT

Have you been wondering how to type the long dash? Try typing two or three hyphens together, and see if they are auto-corrected into the long dash. Otherwise, you can do this manually. On a PC, use the keys Ctrl + Alt + hyphen. On a Mac, try Apple (command) key + Alt + the number pad hyphen.

Ellipses

Another option for making a pause is to use ellipses (. . .). You may use this punctuation mark to indicate a thoughtful pause or a lingering part of speech. It's not the abrupt cutoff caused by the dash. It's something that the person has chosen not to say. Perhaps because the person he's speaking to would already know it. Perhaps because the speaker has lost his nerve.

If the ellipsis is used in the middle of a sentence, there is a space left before each dot and after the line of dots. There is also a space between each dot. Space, dot, space, dot, space, dot, space. It would look like this; "You left me . . . what should I have done?"

When the ellipsis is used at the end of a sentence, it finishes the sentence with no other punctuation needed. For instance: "I looked for you . . ."

Question and Exclamation Marks

A question mark (?) is placed at the end of a phrase to indicate that it's a question. Easy enough, right? There's not much to learn about question marks, other than the fact that novelists tend to overuse them. Try not to use an abundance of question marks. Obviously, if your characters ask questions, go ahead and type in the question mark in the dialogue. But don't go overboard with question marks in the narrative.

Exclamation marks are equally overused. Many times, even though a character is very excited, a period is just as appropriate. An entire conversation filled with exclamation points will tell an editor that you haven't been writing very long.

On the other hand, if you save your exclamations for important occasions, they can really help you make your point. An exclamation point can express irony, surprise, and dissatisfaction. "Imagine how stark that would be!" It can also be used after a command. "Go and get it!"

Brackets and Parentheses

Other than the physical use of brackets to hold up bookshelves, most fiction writers don't use brackets very much. But their traditional use is to enclose words and phrases that are independent of a sentence. This can include explanatory notes, omissions, and comments. For instance:

• The following day [Monday] was good for her.

Note that no punctuation is needed with brackets, unless they contain an entire sentence.

For "aside" comments and other phrases that don't belong in the sentence itself, it's best to use parentheses:

• She asked him for help (or so he thought).
• The house payment was past due (along with everything else) but the bank wouldn't work with them.

Don't use a comma, semicolon, or colon in front of the opening parenthesis (the singular form of the upright punctuation). You can use a comma, semicolon, colon, or period after the last parenthesis.

By including subject matter in this way, the author calls attention to what is inside the parentheses. Of course, commas or long dashes may also be used to set off parenthetical text.

One very funny Web site you can visit when you just need to laugh at punctuation is the Parenthesis Conspiracy (✍ *http://patrick.wattle.id.au/cameron/brackets*).

Showing Emphasis

There are different ways to emphasize words in your text. But before you think about how to do it, consider when to do it. Most fiction writers use emphasis in dialogue. It portrays the way something is said as well as exactly what is said. Sometimes, you'll want to use emphasis in your character's thoughts. You'll rarely use it in narrative.

Before the advent of word processing, putting emphasis in text was much different than it is today. Writers today have various options.

Capital Letters

Some writers still use capital letters to emphasize text. Most editors don't really like this. There are some cases where capital letters are used in text (besides proper nouns or the beginning of sentences). These aren't so much for emphasis as distinction: Doctorial degrees (M.D.; Ph.D.; M.A.); initials that take the place of a proper noun (J. P. Magnus); states or countries referred to by initial (NC or USA).

Showing emphasis this way was popular when people used typewriters. But today, we have so much more.

Italics

Basically, italics is a style of type. Its *slanting letters* create emphasis by appearing different from the text around it. Most word processors do this fairly easily. Just look for the big *I* in your toolbar.

The beauty of italics is very simple. It appears to show the tone of speech, then disappears. Readers have come to know what this means. If it's in dialogue, it shows readers where to emphasize the word in their own mind. It's also come to represent thoughts shared with the reader directly from the point of view of the character. In science fiction or paranormal fiction, italics are frequently used to create the impression of telepathy (mental communication).

Bold Type and Underlining

Another type of emphasis is using **bold type** and <u>underlining</u>. Fiction writers rarely use these in text, and underlining is particularly discouraged. If you want to be sure, check the submission guidelines of the publishers you're planning to submit your work to.

Expressing Numbers

All novelists use numbers at one time or another. You have the street address where the murder took place, the amount of money stolen from the bank. Even in mainstream fiction, you could have to talk about age or how many slices of pizza your character ate. While numbers will never be as important to writers as words, it's important that they're expressed in clear ways that everyone understands.

Numbers Within a Sentence

Always spell out numbers from one through ninety-nine. Use figures to express definite amounts as well as numbers over ninety-nine:

- Eighty years
- 7,000 members
- 3.25 feet

Spell out ordinal numbers (numbers that refer to order, like first, second, third, and so on). Also note that all numbers in dialogue must be spelled out.

Time of Day and Date

When writing down the exact time, use numerals and the letters a.m., p.m. or A.M., P.M. (to create small caps, go to Format, Font and check the box next to small caps). For instance: 1:30 a.m; 6:30 P.M. When you spell out the time, however, abbreviations should be dropped: "She left the station at one-thirty in the afternoon."

Sums of Money

Everybody likes to think about large sums of money. When writing a large sum in your text, anything over a million is spelled out. For instance: He won 12 million dollars. (Or: He won $12 million.) Don't use the dollar sign if you write out the word "dollars."

Don't use figures and words for sums of money. If you aren't sure your reader will understand what you're saying, you can use parenthesis. For instance: I have forty (40) dollars.

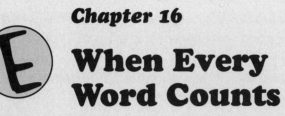

Chapter 16

When Every Word Counts

Deciding what to put in and what to leave out is a hard job for every writer. Writers tend to fall in love with their words and ideas. How do you decide which child stays and which child gets deleted, never to be seen again? A writer needs to be objective. No matter how much you like the idea of your heroine finding her true love in Manhattan, if she's from Boise and the crux of the story takes place in Yellowstone National Park, the city life just doesn't seem to fit in.

Clarity: Saying What You Mean

A writer should be willing to sacrifice anything in the name of clarity. If the reader has no idea what you're talking about, the greatest story ever told has no meaning. Telling your tale clearly and brilliantly should be the goal of every writer.

But sometimes what you mean to write, and what you end up writing in the heat of a frenzied writing trance, are two different things. Even an outline won't save you from this experience. The characters go one way and the plot goes another. What started out as a simple story becomes a monster of epic proportions.

How do you tame the beast? Don't give up on the story unless it's so far gone that you can't recognize it at all from where you started. If you've used the wrong words, find the right ones. Clean up muddied sentences where the meaning is obscured by words that refuse to come to the point. Don't worry about showing off your extensive vocabulary. Worry more about being understood.

Experts claim that people read for pleasure at about a fourth- or fifth-grade level. That means that writers have to relate to them on that level. You have to say what you mean to say. Say it clearly and carefully. It only takes three words to say "I love you." Yet some writers feel compelled to use something much more complex to say the same thing.

Orthodox Spelling

Despite Mark Twain's observation that there is always more than one way to spell a word, for the sake of clarity, use the accepted spelling. If you don't know what the accepted spelling is, look it up. There are many resources available. Don't let anything get in your way. Editors are looking for interesting material, not material that they have to try to figure out.

Robert Fulton, Jr.'s *"But . . . You Know What I Mean" An Editor's Point of View* is a good book that will tell you how editors look at work. Written by writers and editors, it begins to explain why editors reject and why they select certain work.

Avoiding Large Words

Stay away from million-dollar words. These are words that the average person doesn't know and doesn't want to know. In particular, these are words that should be replaced with simpler words. There's no reason to extend your vocabulary in your novel. Everyone knows you're a writer. You don't have to prove it by showing off your extensive knowledge of the language.

Take a look at this horrendous sentence:

• There were odiferous emanations coming from his masticating orifice.

How many people will know that all the writer really means is "He had bad breath." Here's another example:

• He afforded approach by grasping the protuberance in his hand.

In other words: "He opened the door." Keep your words simple, short, and to the point. Remember that you're writing for a pleasure-seeking audience. They don't want to run for their dictionaries every five minutes while they read your book.

Check out the bestselling authors. Their words aren't there to impress anyone. Your book should be the same way. Don't let your story and your characters get lost in a maze of words that fascinated you while you were writing.

FACT

Your dictionary and thesaurus are both wonderful tools for converting large words into small words. But this process shouldn't take place until you reach the stage where you're ready to revise. Before that time, it will only take you away from the story.

Be Specific

Mean what you say, say what you mean. That is, when you have something to say, go ahead and say it. Even if you're purposely trying to be obscure, at least give your readers the impression that you're telling them what's important. That way, they can be surprised when you need them to be surprised.

If you aren't sure what words you need to use, get a thesaurus. They're available in print, in your word-processing software, and online. Don't use a word unless you know what it means. If a word means something close to what you're trying to say but not exactly, find the word that means specifically what you want to say. And this doesn't just apply to particular terms or knowledge. You should know the words of your trade, whether it's romance or mystery. But you should also know the difference between common words like window blind and window shade.

Brevity Is a Writer's Virtue

Being succinct is an art. Telling a story in a few words is a talent. Even though a book has 100,000 words, brevity is all about keeping the story fresh and vital. Say what needs to be said in each scene or piece of dialogue, then move on. Don't belabor the point. Give yourself plenty to say.

If you feel the story is dragged out for too long, so will the reader. The story should hold the reader's interest from beginning to end. There should be enough interesting material without repetition. You should not dwell on one scene or theme too much.

Some authors feel it's their responsibility to educate the reader. They can feel this way about anything from spirituality to world events. They have to drive home their point over and over again in a way that would make a children's book on manners or good behavior look interesting.

There's no reason to be preachy while you write. People are reading fiction to be entertained. If you are lucky enough to get some small point that you believe in across to them, good for you. But be entertaining first. Tell your story clearly and concisely. Let readers get what they can out of it.

Overwriting Descriptions

Beware of being too Victorian in your work. The Victorians had a great love of layers. Lace doilies over velvet cushions. Throw rugs over carpet. Plenty of bric-a-brac, pictures, and anything that could take up space. They didn't believe in meaningful pauses or leaving room to breathe. The result was nice and comfy most of the time. But sometimes it got to be too much. Everybody needs a little blank space.

When you layer your work with too many metaphors and clichés, the effect is similar to a Victorian living room. Flowery phrases shouldn't be used to explain simple things, or your text becomes too heavy, too full. There isn't any room for the important elements of your book.

Watch out for page-long descriptions of the room your heroine finds herself in. Stay away from telling the reader about the world your hero discovers in long sentences that become long pages. Description is fine in small doses. Find ways to interject it into conversation. If it has to be in narrative, make it brief. Remember that you have an entire book to fill. You can add descriptions and explanations all the way through it. Alien flowers that smell like chocolate will smell just as sweet on page 239 as on page 2.

ALERT!

If you decide that you need to use profanity in your work, check with the publisher, then go out and read what the market can bear. Too much of anything can be bad. If you use profanity, you don't have to use every swear word ever written.

Overstating Your Point

Finding something you want to write about can be difficult. Maybe that's why some writers feel compelled to direct every word in their book back to this one thing. Like Ahab, they want to drive the point home with their obsession.

Readers don't care about obsessions unless they have something to do with the story. You can try to make your readers feel guilty about not eating meat or supporting terrorism within the framework of your story if you like. But don't expect them to like having your lecturing shoved down their throats.

If you have something to say, find a way to do it without sounding like you're championing a cause. Even if the point is as simple as how beautiful or sexy your heroine is. Readers can only stand to be told something like that so many times. Then they begin to develop an antipathy for your character. Instead of empathizing with them, the reader wishes they'd just go away. Not the kind of thing a writer likes to hear.

Overexplaining the Story

Mystery novels aren't the only place where you can explain too much. Any book that tells too much about the plot, the characters, or the setting can be just as bad. In a mystery, you'll give away secrets you wanted to keep. In a romance, you might explain more about the heroine's past than the reader ever wanted to know. You might be entranced and fascinated by what kind of food the Greeks ate during the Trojan War. But unless your book is about that subject, don't go into it at length.

You're only trying to give the reader a feel for the place, the time, or the people. But you have to do that in less than twenty-five pages of text.

Your readers want you to get to the point. Maybe not to the end of the book, but certainly to the meaning behind what you're telling them. If there's no purpose in the reader understanding what kind of thread was used in a Roman toga, you've explained too much.

QUESTION?

How can you know if you've explained too much?
Look for repetition. That is the hallmark of overexplanation. Put the text away for a few days and look at it again. If you don't understand it, neither will anyone else.

When describing settings or other side issues (like the exact shade of brown of your heroine's hair), think about *CNN Headline News*. They don't describe every detail of everything that happened today. Instead, they tell you what you need to know. You can keep up with conversation around the water cooler at work. Unless the facts pertain to or move the plot forward, less is better.

Show, Don't Tell

One of the biggest differences between fiction and nonfiction is the principle of showing instead of telling. Compare a documentary about Africa to Isak Dinesen's *Out of Africa.* In a documentary, many of the facts can be presented by simply telling the viewers. Sure, it's also important to include images of what it is you're talking about, but showing in a documentary is secondary to telling.

In a novel, showing must come in first place. Rather than telling the readers what happens to the characters, the novelist must show the scenes as they are happening. Only occasionally will the reader accept text that simply tells what has occurred without describing it.

There are probably passages in your rough draft where you simply said what happened, or what the characters did, or how they felt, without really showing it to the readers. Now is the time to go back and rewrite. But before you do that, let's look at how both telling and showing can be used to your advantage in your novel.

Show It

Showing readers what's happening and what they need to know about characters, plot, and setting isn't hard. Just remember not to talk about them so much. There are ways to do this that will keep the reader engaged in the story.

Use dialogue. Don't tell the reader what a mountain looks like. This way doesn't show your readers anything. It tells them what you want them to see. It's passive and doesn't draw the reader into the story. Instead, use your characters to describe what the reader needs to see:

> "Are you sure it's safe to climb today?" She looked up at the mountain that seemed to touch the sky. "Those snow packs look pretty heavy. It wouldn't take much to bring them down."

Both ways accomplish the same thing. The reader knows the mountain is tall and covered with snow. But the second way doesn't act like a travelogue. It engages the reader, helping them to see through the character's eyes.

Tell It

Novelists are always cautioned to show, not tell, but there are times when you have to tell the reader what's happening or how it's happening. At these points, you'll have to tell them what's going on.

One of these times is during tense or active scenes. For instance:

They struggled for the gun. Max kicked it across the room. But Sam shoved him against the door and pulled out a knife.

Scenes of this nature don't have time to be pleasant or descriptive. And it's important that they aren't. In this case, you have to worry more about breaking the tension or mood. Terse, almost staccato words describe these best. When you're writing this kind of scene, stick to the bare minimum and tell your readers what's happening. You can think of it as a play-by-play account—sort of like an announcer at a baseball game. You're excited or scared and your characters are too.

ALERT!

Like hammers and saws are the tools of the carpenter's trade, words are the writer's tools. Be sure you know your tools. If you write mystery, you should know the keywords that professional mystery writers use. For instance: Do you know what GSR is? It's gun shot residue. There are other words and phrases like this for every genre.

Room to Cut

In real life, there is a surfeit of words. People don't consider that what they're saying might be repetitive or unimportant. No one worries about making every word count. They don't have to think about how everything they say and do fits together to produce a single effect.

Writing isn't like real life. Writers observe real life to know more about people and situations. They mimic real life, but a novel is too small to really encompass even a single day in the real world. Think about how many things you and the people around you talk about in a day. How many situations are you involved in or do you see happening? Even 100,000 words doesn't cover it.

That's why writers have to choose their words carefully. They have a limited amount of space to tell their story. Like a painter whose canvas is only so big, the writer has to learn how much of real life can fit between the covers of his or her book.

Condensing Narrative

Because you're on a limited budget, you need to consider how much narrative you're going to need to explain any given scene. The chances are that you'll write the scene, then go back and cut it down. Not every scene will have action or tension that propels it forward. But every scene needs to know why it's in the book and what its function is for the story line.

QUESTION?

What should I do if I'm too short on word count but need to trim back my writing?
Look for places in the text that you can shore up. Even as you cut away the deadwood, there should be some new seeds you can plant.

How do you cut back those pretty words it took you hours to think of? How do you maintain the integrity of your story without sounding like you're rambling? Know your story. Don't stray too far from its heart. Don't use six words when one word will do. Look for spots where you added text because you found a hole in your plot and you were trying to plug it up. Don't use narrative to describe what dialogue can show. Don't overexplain, overdescribe, or exaggerate. Leave something to the actions of your characters and the imaginations of your readers.

Shortening Dialogue

"Mary, where are those fuzzy red slippers that you gave me last year for Christmas when I was sick with the flu and my aunt was visiting from

Scotland?" That sentence is enough to make a normal person experience information overload. No matter what you mean to say, saying it in this manner will never work. It's not impossible—though unlikely—that someone could talk this way in real life. But you can't write dialogue this way. If you come across dialogue that rambles on like this, get out your scissors and prepare to cut.

How could you use this dialogue differently? First of all, decide if it's important to the plot to have this information. Do your readers need to know about the red slippers being a gift? Do they need to know they were a Christmas present? Do they need to know that this character had the flu last year at Christmas? Do they need to know that this character's aunt was visiting from Scotland?

Even if all of this is essential information, it could be said in a better way: "Mary, have you seen my fuzzy red slippers? I was just thinking about Christmas last year when you gave them to me. Do you remember? My aunt was visiting and I had the flu. What a time!"

Developing Your Personal Style

Many people who've been fortunate enough to get published will tell you that it was their "style" that got them where they are today. But what exactly is style? Many writers define style as a personal voice that makes their writing distinctive from the writing of others.

FACT

Style is often blamed for deviations from grammatical norms. Do you have a paragraph that's three pages long? That must be your style. Do you insist on dropping dialogue tags? That's style again.

Style can make your writing original and distinguish you from the pack, but it can also hurt your writing. Writers who become stubborn about their style and refuse to modify their writing to make it more "mainstream" are vulnerable to rejection. If no one understands your style, you have two options: Give up hope of publication, or change your style.

Listening to Your Inner Voice

There are tons of books and Web sites that tell people that they have an inner voice. The inner voice is supposed to speak to everyone. Rather like the Porky Pig cartoons, where he has an angel on one shoulder and a devil on the other.

Artists and writers listen to their inner voices. These voices are what encourage you to continue even though you just got another rejection. They whisper brilliant things to you when your brain is numb at three in the morning and you should be asleep. They cause that tiny moment of "Aha!" that happens when a character reveals himself. You couldn't be a writer without them.

It stands to reason that your individual style comes from these voices. They tell you what to write and how to write it. They help you decide who the bad guy really is in your story. They show you how to get your hero and heroine back together after a devastating fight.

Listen to them with an open mind. Learn to trust them. Feed them enough information and give them time to work out the unsolvable problems in your story. They won't let you down.

What Comes Naturally

The word *natural* has been bandied around a lot in the last few years. There are natural clothes, natural foods, and natural environments. People are chastised for living unnaturally and for not seeking their natural abilities.

But what comes naturally for a writer? Some may say writing and, to a certain extent, that's true. Although, not many writers realize the amount of time they will have to do "what's natural" for them to get through the whole process of writing a book. Sometimes, that effort may seem very unnatural.

Your style should be a natural extension of who you are. That's why people write differently. It's how you see the world around you and how you express that vision back to others. Writers can change their styles. It doesn't mean that any way you choose to write is unnatural. The words that come to you and the characters you create are a part of you.

But don't use this realization as a crutch. You can always improve your style and what comes naturally to you. There is always something new to learn.

Finding Your Voice: How to Put Personality in Your Writing by Les Edgerton is a good book to look up when you begin to worry about what your voice is saying. It will help you without giving you a crutch to lean on.

Putting Life in Your Words

"It's alive! It's alive!" Victor Frankenstein shouted to his assistant. It would be nice if everyone could say that about every book they read.

Sometimes you come across a book with a great cover. You pick it up and you read the blurb on the back. It sounds like a great story. You've never heard of the author before, so you can't compare this book to another one you were liked. You open it up and read the first few sentences, maybe even a paragraph. Then you politely put it back on the shelf. You sigh as you walk away. Too bad the great idea and fantastic cover didn't go with the dead words on the inside.

Every reader is different. What you like and what your friend likes can be worlds apart. You may think a bestselling author who's written many books doesn't have enough talent to write herself out of a paper bag, and you're entitled to your opinion. It means you don't have to buy any of her books. No matter how good a writer you are or how hard you work to make your book vibrant and alive, there will always be people who don't like it. That being said, what can you do to make your words electrify your readers?

Making Language Vibrant

Have you ever considered the word *stodgy*? It actually sounds a little like what it means. A stodgy person is a dull, stupid, or commonplace one.

The one thing you don't want your words to be is stodgy. Yet many writers allow that to happen by choosing less than brilliant—or even half-dead—words to represent their work. They spend days, even years, coming up with wonderful characters and intelligent plots. Then they forget that they have to write them in an intelligent and wonderful way.

It's easy in the revision process to replace less than vibrant words with words that will resonate in your reader's brain long after he or she has put the book down:

Stodgy	Vibrant
He was thirsty.	His throat was parched.
The house fell in on her.	The walls caved in on her.
Her face got smaller as she got older.	Her face withered with advancing age.
He sailed with the wind in his face.	He sailed into the teeth of the wind.
She was standing in the cold rain.	She stood in the icy grip of the freezing rain.
Her hair was blond.	She was a burnished blond.

Flowery phrases, phrases that should only be in real-world conversation and not in a book, can be as bad as stodgy words. For instance: He gave in to his passion; He kissed his darling's rosy cheek; She swooned with ecstasy. That should be enough for you to get the idea.

Keeping the Story Alive

It would be nice if just by making your words vibrant and alive, your story would follow suit. Unfortunately, that's not the case. You may have all the wonderful words and they may be sharp enough to cut diamonds, but if you've lost the feel for your story, they won't help you.

Keeping your story alive is difficult at the best of times. An idea has to work through 100,000 words, the flu you had last month, your son's soccer practices, and your own fear that your work is a waste of time. That's a lot to ask from any plot and characters.

For some writers, the answer is to review their work from the previous session before beginning a new scene or chapter. If you can do this and resist the temptation to continue whittling away at the old material, the idea can work. If you get too caught up with what you've already written to write anything new, writing a single book could take a lifetime.

Another way is to constantly refer back to your original idea. What motivated you to write this book? What was it that you loved about your heroine? What scared you in the middle of the night and made you want to write horror? Look at your notes and images, if you have them. If you feel the story slipping away from you, remind yourself why it's important for you to write anything.

Try to work consecutively. Even if various scenes from different parts of the book come to you, write them down as notes and forget them until you get to those parts. It's hard enough to keep up with where you are in a story when your time to work on it is limited. Trying to write scenes from all over the plot could end with you being completely confused and your story losing its life.

Chapter 17
The Final Edit

Editing your work is a serious job. Some writers really enjoy this part of the process. Other writers don't even want to try. They hire an editor to look at their work before they submit it. If you want to edit, you'll have to learn the rules and how to be objective about spotting them. Editing your own work means you have to be willing to look for flaws. If you refuse to accept the possibility that your manuscript has any mistakes in it, it's best to save up your pennies and hire someone who can set you straight.

Choose Your Approach

There are several ways to get a good edit on your book. The first decision you need to make is whether or not you want to take your manuscript to a professional. This approach has some advantages as well as disadvantages.

The biggest drawback to editing your work yourself is not knowing if you've done a good job. Only experience and a willingness to do your best can give you confidence. Like any other job, you're bound to feel insecure at first. Read reference books and learn by doing. It may not be perfect (it never is), but you'll end up with a good manuscript.

The biggest drawback to professional editing is the cost. It can be fairly expensive. You might have more confidence in the end result but it might cost you your next vacation.

QUESTION?

How much does a professional editor charge?
Anywhere between $3 and $10 for each page of text. Sometimes, you can find an editor with a flat fee for the whole book.

Reading Aloud

If you choose to edit yourself, one approach is to read your manuscript aloud. Learning to read your words out loud may sound deceptively simple. It isn't. It takes stamina and focus to read through a 100,000-word book like a children's story. You have to stay alert, looking for errors as you go. It can take a while to get through the text—it may take you a week or longer, depending on how much time you have and how strong your vocal cords are.

Basically, the technique consists of starting on page one and reading every word out loud. Words that don't sound right in the text will show up quickly. Bad dialogue will become easy to spot. Too much narrative will put you to sleep as surely as any other reader.

You can correct mistakes as you go. Doing the corrections immediately keeps them fresh in your mind. Or you can make notations on a separate piece of paper to change later when you've finished reading. The advantage to waiting is finding errors that compound on each other. If you try to correct them as you go, you'll end up coming back again as new errors are spotted.

FACT

Writers seem to have trouble reading from the computer screen. Even though they earn their living using their word processor, most writers print out a copy of their work to use when they're editing. They say they can spot errors more efficiently on paper than on the computer.

Critique Groups

Groups of two or more people looking at your manuscript for errors may sound daunting. Nevertheless, a critique group can be a lifesaver for a writer. The people in your group can help you look for mistakes, question your choices in plot and characters, and cheer you on if you get rejected.

But before you rush off to meet with your group, consider this. If you don't feel positive about the quality of your work, a critique group may undermine your confidence. And if you do take the critique group approach, be sure you select your critique partners carefully. Know who they are. Make sure you respect their judgment and you feel comfortable letting them read your story. If there are any petty jealousies or problems with the group, look for another one. No one needs that kind of input.

Never have your rough draft critiqued. It's okay to discuss ideas or scenes with the others, but wait until you've had a chance to come up with a finished product before you share it with the group.

QUESTION?

How do I find a critique group?
The best way is through a writing group like the Mystery Writers of America. Many local and online writing groups offer critique help as well. Find a group of like-minded writers whose advice you value.

Professional Editing

There are two types of editors out there: editors at publishing houses and freelance editors who edit manuscripts for a fee. Editors at publishing houses can review your submitted manuscript and give you a few pointers on how to make your work marketable to the public. Don't expect an editor at a major house to walk you through all the mistakes you've made and tell you what you need to do to get published. It won't happen.

For detailed help with editing, look for freelancers—they can be found on the Internet and at writing conferences. Before you pay someone to edit your book, you should check the editor's credentials. A freelance editor should have a solid background with a publisher or be able to supply you with names of clients they've worked with. Talk to the editor's clients. See if the editor did a good job for them. Then look at their work. Does it seem to mesh with yours?

Working with a good editor can be a rewarding experience. Paying someone hundreds of dollars who doesn't do anything to help you can leave a sour taste in your mouth.

Before accepting a professional editor's help with your manuscript, check them out. Preditors and Editors (✍ *www.anotherealm.com/prededitors*) is a good online resource for keeping tabs on scams and dishonest editors and agents.

Looking for Flaws

If you do decide to edit your manuscript yourself, you need to train yourself to become a hunter of flaws. You need to be able to spot problems and then find solutions. This isn't always a painless process for a beginner, but the more practice you get, the easier it will be. You can train yourself to do a good job editing your work just like you learned to keep a checkbook or cook dinner. Most people don't go to school to learn these basic skills. They learn them through practice and persistence.

If you're serious about being a professional writer, you have to think of it as part of the job. You've created these characters and set up their story. Now it's time to evaluate the results. There are plenty of books and courses at a local community college, adult education center, or online that can help you. Even if you decide to use a critique group or a professional editor, you should read as much as you can about the process. If you don't, you won't know if the editor knows what she's talking about.

The Glaring Mistakes

The first thing you should do is to look for obvious flaws. These are things that just don't look right. Like walking into your house and finding that a single piece of furniture has been rearranged while you were gone. There are certain things that are noticeable even if they're subtle:

- Too many characters are introduced too quickly in the first few pages of your book.
- You are telling your reader what's going to happen before it happens.
- Back story is introduced too early, before the readers are drawn into the story.
- Your character's name is mentioned more than once or twice on the first page.
- There is immediate confusion as to whose voice is telling the story.
- The plot unravels too quickly.

These are very basic things, but they'll give you a place to start. Your list of flaws should be much longer, or you're not doing a good job.

Check out *Line by Line: How to Edit Your Own Writing* by Claire Kehrwald Cook. It's a good book, if you can find it. It has lots of practical advice on the subject.

Training Your Eye

Teaching yourself to see errors is something that comes naturally to many writers. It can be more difficult with your own work because you don't want to see errors, you don't want to change anything, and you'd like to finish the book. All three of these excuses are powerful motivators not to look for mistakes.

But if you push yourself past the obvious problems, you can train your eye to catch them all. The process will be faster as you go along and learn more about editing. Learn right away to have some confidence in your judgment. This isn't brain surgery. The worst that can happen is that you'll send off your manuscript and it will be rejected. By the time you look at it again, you should know more than you do right now. You can always make changes and submit again.

Read books about editing. Pick up plenty of fiction in your field and critique it. What's right about the book? What's wrong with it? Go to lectures given by writers and editors. They can help you hone ways to see errors in your work.

Looking for your personal demons in your text can be a strange experience. How many times did you use the word *finally* in your text? Some writers use the search mode on their computer to help pinpoint their overuse of specific words.

Edit Spelling

Maybe you were the class spelling bee champion for ten years in a row. Maybe you regularly contribute to the *Oxford Dictionary*. Maybe every word you write is always perfectly spelled. If so, you can skip this part.

If you're like so many other mortal humans and spelling isn't exactly a challenge for you but after thirteen chapters you become a little hazy, you're going to need help. Fortunately, you are in good company. Many writers can't spell. Just because you can tell a good story doesn't mean you can spell every word without looking it up.

Spelling correctly is an important first impression for editors. It means you took the time to make sure everything is in good shape. It shows that you care about the quality of your work. Remember, you can't afford to be arrogant about your manuscript. You've spent quality time creating this work. Don't make the mistake of letting it go out the door without being the best it can be.

Spell Checker

Computers come with a plethora of great tools that writers can use to make their work better. Sometimes, the tools can even make your work easier. One of these tools is called spell checker. It's located somewhere in your toolbar. Different programs will have it in different places. If you can't find it on yours, consult your help guide.

Spell checker is nifty because it can look through a manuscript for misspelled words in a fraction of the time that it will take your eyes. It doesn't get tired. Its eyes don't get blurry. It hunts out offenders and shows you where they are and gives you ideas on how to change them. Pretty cool.

The only thing it can't do is understand intent. It looks for potential mistakes, so just because a word is marked as wrong, it's not necessarily wrong in the way you use it.

Right Spelling—Wrong Word

Unfortunately, this is one part of spelling that the spell checker can't save you from. It can't tell the difference between to, *too,* and *two.* Other problem word groups include: there, their, and they're; our and hour; your and you're. You have to be able to read the text around these words to know which one is correct. As long as those words are spelled correctly, the spell checker will whiz by them.

ESSENTIAL

Ultralingua.net (✍ *www.ultralingua.net)* is a great online research tool for writers. You can look up words for their correct spelling and meaning in several major languages, including English. It's a good tool to have open when spell checker fails you. The site is updated regularly.

That means the grunt work is up to you. You'll have to go through each page of text and look for spelling errors. Paying attention to these details will make your presentation better. It's tedious work checking every word but it's part of your job as a writer.

Edit Grammar

Basic grammar is covered in Chapter 14, but if you need more help, find a good book or online tutorial to help you get comfortable with it. Fixing your grammar can mean the difference between a rejection letter and an accepted manuscript. If you get your manuscript back with the note "Check your grammar" on the margins, you'll wish you had taken the time to do this.

Your computer can run a grammar check for you. Sometimes, it checks grammar at the same time that it checks spelling. This is another handy feature, but don't expect it to catch everything that could be wrong in your manuscript. It can be cryptic. It sometimes will advise you to change text that is right.

The problem seems to be that it gets confused. While some of what it says is valid, you'll have to wade through all of it to decide what to change. It's a good place to start, but not the end of the road.

Keep It Simple

One thing spell checker or grammar checker can't tell you is whether or not you're using the right words to make your point. You'll have to ferret them out the old-fashioned way: You'll have to read the text.

FACT

If you're writing science fiction or fantasy, expect your spell checker and grammar checker to give out even more quickly than for a mystery, mainstream, or romance text. The use of extraordinary words completely throws off the computer. The chances are, halfway through the text, the system will tell you that it can't take it anymore.

It's hard to know which words are too big or too difficult to understand for your readers. You don't want to assume that the average reader is stupid. People who read tend to have above-average IQs. But that doesn't mean that a professor or lawyer wants to read difficult words for pleasure. Pick up a Robert Heinlein science fiction novel or a John Grisham mystery novel. If they don't use words like the ones you want to use, you're thinking like an intellectual.

Remember: Keep it simple. You don't have to talk down to your readers. You're just trying to give them a good read without straining their brains to understand what you're saying. If you want to write textbooks, you're in the wrong field.

Keep Your Tenses Straight

A common problem in beginner fiction writing is the confusion of tenses. Check to see if the scenes in your novel are presented properly, and that the verbs don't switch tenses back and forth.

Inconsistencies

Every book has a few inconsistencies. Every reader knows that. It's not that you expect them, but you've learned to live with them. No matter how many editors look at a book, some things just aren't caught. Some of the more famous novels even have groups of people looking for inconsistencies to post on the Internet. That's a challenge most writers could do without.

ESSENTIAL

If you find an inconsistency like your heroine having blond hair in the beginning of the book and red hair later, you can use the search function of your computer to find these problems quickly and correct them.

It's the big, glaring inconsistencies that can sink your boat. These can keep you from ever getting a serious read from an editor. How to avoid this problem? Keep your notes handy as you edit. If you have any questions about the details, stop editing and look up the answers. You don't want mistakes to go past the rough draft stage.

Time Shifting

Awareness of time is important to your novel. Check important times and dates to give your reader a sense of validity. For instance:

- When does your hero meet your heroine? What time of the day is it? On which day, week, month, and year does this meeting take place?
- Know if this day is an important one in your heroine's life. It could be the day she celebrates her divorce from her cheating spouse or her birthday.
- Show movement of time in your story. If the book opens on a Saturday when the sheriff finds a dead body, decide how long it will take to find the killer.
- Use information in your story that relates to time. If you're writing mystery, know how long it takes to process DNA. If the sheriff needs DNA evidence to solve the case, understand how that affects your timeline.

Keeping Your Setting Straight

How does your setting impact your story? If your story starts out on a 1,500-foot mountain, you have to make sure it hasn't grown to 15,000 feet by the end of the book. If oleanders are growing there at the beginning of the book, you have to make sure your reader understands that they grow there yearlong or that it's summer.

Remember to check mileage between places your character travels. A trip that may look like it takes an hour on a map may only take fifteen minutes in real life. Everything works together. An inconsistency in one part of your novel can lead to a problem in another part.

You should know where your story happens. How well do you know the place? Describe what it looks like in the summer. Know what kinds of plants grow there. Tell the reader what the air smells like. Make them feel that it's a place that they will either want to go or want to stay away from.

Character Details

Give your characters plenty of detail. Know the color of your hero's eyes and hair. Then be sure it's the same every time you mention it in the story. Decide what kind of clothes he likes to wear. Does he like to dress in sneakers and jeans at the beginning of the book? If so, be sure your reader understands why he likes to wear tuxedoes by the end.

Think about character traits. Is your hero sneaky but lovable? That combination is what helps him catch the villain. Tell the reader why he's looking forward to opening his own pizza shop at the beginning of the book but does an abrupt reversal twelve chapters later. Be sure you lay the groundwork so that your readers understand why he now wants to be a fireman.

Like a puzzle, every piece of your manuscript has to be cut to fit together. When you first start writing, all of the pieces are spread out on the table. By this time, you should have gathered almost all of them together. You should know where they go and how they affect the story.

QUESTION?

What is a line editor and what do they do?
The line editor (also called a copyeditor) looks over the text line-by-line for errors. Usually, these are errors in grammar, punctuation, and spelling rather than plot or characters.

Sentence Structure

Sentence structure is one of the things you should train your eye to see as you look through your manuscript. How does your sentence structure look? Is it sloppy or neat? Can you tell the difference between times of great excitement and times when things are going smoothly? Does your sentence structure reflect your story? Have you checked out your clauses and phrases? Are they punctuated right? Are they set up in the best way for readers to get the idea you want them to have? This may seem like nothing in comparison to solving the murder case or finding a new life form, but your readers will appreciate both story lines better if they can read your sentences.

Everything your characters do rests on the backs of these individual pieces of expression. As their creator, you have to make sure they're as strong as they can be. Each sentence adds to or subtracts from the whole.

Lengthy Sentences

You've seen examples of sentences that were too long. Do any of your sentences look like that? Have you trimmed them down and given the reader room to breathe? Have you considered the impact that will have on your reader?

Reading your work out loud should give you a better understanding of sentences and paragraphs that are too long. If you have to catch your breath when you've finished reading one sentence, you know it's too long. If you feel like you have to speak faster to get through the sentence, it's too long.

How do you trim a sentence that's too long? Usually, the best way is to break it up into smaller sentences. You don't have to lose the idea or the train of thought. Just make it more accessible to the reader.

Bad Wording

Rambling sentences aren't any fun. If you have to go back and reread a sentence because you don't understand it the first time, your readers will have to do the same—and they'll get distracted from the story. Some sentences are just badly worded. The solution is revision. Just moving a few words from the end to the beginning can make a difference.

When you're trying to get an idea down, you might ignore the best way to say something. There's nothing wrong with that. But catching the less-than-perfect sentence and correcting it is your saving grace. It may not always be easy. You might have to rewrite an entire paragraph to accommodate the changes in your sentence. But nobody said being a writer is easy. It's all about commitment to your work.

Chapter 18

E Rewrites and Revisions

Sometimes a publisher will reject your submission but will include advice for revision. Even though there's no guarantee following through on these revisions will get your manuscript accepted, it's probably worth the effort. True, all the extra time spent might not get you that book deal. However, even if the publisher doesn't accept your revised manuscript, it'll still be an improved version, and you might have better luck with it elsewhere.

In the Beginning

What makes a good beginning, and how do you know whether yours fits the bill? It's hard to tell if a reader is going to be enthralled enough to read the rest of your book. You need sincere objectivity or feedback.

If you decide to get feedback, you'll have to choose someone who can be objective. Most people think their spouse or another family member can give them a good critique. But most of the time, a spouse or family member doesn't want to hurt your feelings. They will say whatever they have to say to see you smile.

The Bulwer-Lytton Fiction Contest is looking for people who write terrible beginnings. Check it out on the Internet at ☞ *www.bulwer-lytton.com.* You might get a good laugh— and some ideas on the kinds of beginnings you should avoid.

You can choose a friend or fellow writer, but is her critique valid? Has she been too harsh or tried to spare your feelings? The only way to know this is by experience and developing an instinct for people who can actually help you. Since you have to become sincerely objective to do this, you might as well learn to trust your judgment on the novel.

The Hook

What is it in your beginning that's going to "hook" or draw the reader into the story? Because the reader isn't involved at all when he or she picks up your book to purchase it, the opening lines have to be special. Chapter openers need their own, though less dramatic, hooks that tease and torment your readers. They don't want to know what terrible thing is going to happen next, but they have to keep reading.

If you're having a hard time with the hooks in your book, pick up a novel by one of your favorite authors. Take a piece of paper and use it to track all the places that you can feel yourself being sucked into the story. This can give you an idea of where to put your hooks and what they should be.

Hooks are usually emotional in nature. Fear, anger, passion, and hate are the best hooks. Your heroine is angry after she and the hero have a fight. She's certain they'll never get back together again. Your reader sighs and turns the page. That's really all you have to understand about using hooks. If you can't find places like this in each of your chapters, it's time to revise.

FACT

If you're looking for a good book totally dedicated to revision, *Revising Fiction* by David Madden could be for you. This book will help you through a difficult process that requires stamina and forethought. Consider reading it twice before making any decisions about your work.

Back Story

If you submit your work to an editor or a critique partner and he or she tells you that you have too much back story at the beginning of your book, what are you going to do?

This is a common problem for writers. There are probably more rewrites done to correct back story issues than any other. Writers want the reader to understand what motivates their characters. They want the reader to experience the torment that made a character evil or good. Unfortunately, just telling the reader all of that information in the first ten pages of your manuscript won't work.

When you start rewriting to take out back story, think sneaky. Think subtle. How can you tell readers about your character's background without them realizing that you're telling it? Consider advertising. How do ads entice you to buy the products they are selling? Experts say that it is in everything from the mother's face as she hands her son a bowl of oatmeal to the flowers on the table and the dog on the floor. The ad says: "Here's a happy family and a mother who cares. Don't you want to be that way? If you give your child oatmeal, maybe your life will be this way too."

ALERT!

A rule of thumb in fiction is not to go more than three pages without dialogue. Some authors violate this rule on a regular basis. Consider carefully the needs of your characters and plot. But also keep in mind that you want to entertain your reader.

The Sagging Middle

How do you set about changing a middle that has no muscle to a hard six-pack that anyone would be proud to show off? Not just exercise, but the right kind of exercise. If your novel seems a little weak halfway through, you may have to work it. It may not be the most glamorous part of the book, but it has a major responsibility. It has to take your readers from your exciting beginning to your fantastic ending. Why would you want anything less than extraordinary to connect them?

How does the sagging middle happen? You're a determined, hard-working writer who plotted carefully and wrote the best story you could. But you probably focused so much on a sharp beginning and a satisfying conclusion that the middle was forgotten. But like a bridge, the middle is at least as important as the two ends.

Diagnose the Problems

There can be many problems associated with a weak middle. Do any of the following sound likely?

Lack of Emotion

You sound like you ran out of steam. The hot love scenes in the beginning peter out or the emotional turmoil that engaged the reader reached a conclusion too soon. What's the best solution?

Emotion is what drives your characters. It can't disappear in the middle and wait like an abandoned lover at a train station. Keep a steady diet of emotional moments flowing between your characters.

Lack of Action

You managed to keep up a good pace through the first part of the book. Now suddenly, there is this calm pond effect. No waves. Not even a tiny ripple. It may be the calm before the storm at the end of the book, but your reader doesn't know that.

If the beginning of your book is loaded with action, make sure it extends to the middle. If you have to, move up a few of your action scenes to the middle to keep the movement going.

Lack of Important Events

You were so busy putting enough excitement in the first part of the book that you suddenly ran out of events. The reader finds himself in a dead zone. Nothing important happens again until the end of the book.

Go back to your chapter-by-chapter summary. Was there something you forgot to add to your book? If you didn't plan for enough important events, come up with something new or move one of your events to shore up the middle.

FACT

Why not surprise your readers by writing a middle so strong that the end and the beginning pale in comparison? That would amaze most readers since they've come to accept that the majority of books will slow down in the middle.

Lack of Interaction

You created in-your-face interplay between the characters—but then you reached the middle and there's no more communication. The reader finds himself in a place where all of the major characters have gone to their corners. They're waiting for the next round, but will the reader be there?

The middle of your story is no time to send your hero to Iceland and your heroine to Australia. Alternately, if your villain has been torturing your hero, the middle isn't the place for him to go on vacation. Character interaction is what drives your story. Don't leave your readers stranded in the middle while your characters go off to collect their thoughts.

Too Much Back Story or Filler

You suddenly realized that your characters have run out of things to say to each other before the end of the book and the big reconciliation scene. Or the hero has been shot and has to have time to recover before he tackles his greatest enemy. The middle becomes the time that the hero reminisces about his childhood in Uruguay.

Because you understand back story, you wouldn't use it to kill time, would you? If that's exactly what happened in your rough draft, remember that the slowest time is when you're watching the clock, waiting for something to happen. Don't let your reader feel like this about the middle of your book.

A Sense of Urgency

You suddenly realized that you have nothing to say until the end of the book. That's where the "big" scene is. The scene that ties everything together. The explosive finale that you'd been looking forward to writing since you got your idea. The reader feels like she's being herded into a windowless train and transported somewhere without her knowledge or consent.

Writing is always deferred gratification. It's not the time to eat your dessert first. If you can't wait to write that last fateful scene, stop and write it down. Now, look at the middle without any impatience. Your reader wants to see your glorious ending but not if she has to wear a blindfold to make it through the middle.

Do one of those problems look familiar? Or is your sagging middle caused by a different problem? The biggest culprit is pacing or lack of pacing. Just like a long-distance runner, you have to conserve your writing energy so that it maintains at a certain level throughout the book.

The End

Is there anything more satisfying for a writer than that moment when he or she writes those two little words? It's the sigh of relief. The feeling that you've done it. You've written a novel. Maybe it's not perfect, but it's pretty good. There are moments of greatness in it. You can finally think about other things like cleaning your house or walking your dog—all of those projects that you put on hold or avoided to make time to write.

But ending the book is really just the beginning. This is the place where you start thinking about what happens next. Will you publish your book or shove it in the closet? Have you learned enough about the process to go on and do it again?

For the person sitting in the armchair by the fire reading the book you've written, the ending is the promise that you gave him at the beginning. You promised to keep him entertained, to show him things he may never have seen before, and to give him a satisfying conclusion. Have you lived up to your promise?

Letting Your Reader Down

You've read through your text. Twice. Everything sounds good, but the ending doesn't seem to be just right. There's something missing, but you aren't sure what it is. It was so perfect when you first thought about the idea. The perfect ending for the perfect book. It had just the right amount of action and emotion, and it finished the story. What happened?

Sometimes writers get so caught up in telling the story, especially the exciting parts like the end, they forget to tell the story. You may have to go back and rewrite now that the passion and writer's trance have faded. Take your basic premise and revise with the idea that the reader has to be excited too. If she doesn't know what happened, she may be frantically looking back through the book trying to figure out where she lost the thread.

Letting your reader down gently is a fine art. When you finish a book, you want to feel satisfied with the conclusion. You want the story to have enough time to play itself out. If the characters seem rushed or the plot seems cut off, there's a sense of feeling cheated. That changes the whole meaning of letting your reader down.

Finishing the Story

Not every writer has a snappy finish in mind when she starts writing. Some writers even dread the last scene. It's just as hard for a writer to let go of a character she really loves as it is for the reader. It can make any ending seem unsatisfying. But you can't drag out the book to stay in that world. You may be able to write another book with the same characters. First, you have to finish this story.

If you're one of those writers staring at a blank final page where your manuscript should end, ask yourself: What would a reader like to see here? What would give the reader a sense of ending and completion? What would make her come back to read about this character again?

The answers to those questions should help you finish the story, even if you don't want to. Be objective. Yes, you love this book. No, you don't want it to end, so every ending seems bad. But if you think about it from an outside point of view, that blank paper might fill itself up with words. Set it aside for a few days, if you can. See how you feel about it later when you've had time to detach yourself.

ALERT!

So you've decided you want to write a surprise ending. You want to totally shock your readers and leave them amazed and befuddled. This may be a good idea, but consider how shocking your ending is. Too much shock can be disconcerting and might keep a reader from wanting to read another one of your books.

Problems with Characters

Speaking of being in love with your characters, are there any you closely identify with? Maybe you've written yourself into the book as the maiden aunt. Or maybe you're the dashing hero who saves a world from certain peril. Most writers find that they see themselves as at least one of their characters.

Maybe that's why it's so hard to give one up or revise one. It's like someone telling you that they don't like your hair or the way you dress.

Sometimes, it's even worse. A writer creates a character from the memory of a dead loved one or a sick child. That makes the advice of an editor or friend telling you to change the character a sword to the heart. How could they?

While writers should always be objective about their work, they never truly are. Characters are taken from a place inside the writer and endowed with familiar emotions, fears, and memories. But while all that may be true, as you sit down to change a character, remind yourself that they aren't real.

Realistic Visions

When you began to write your book, you had certain expectations or visions for the plot and characters. Have they lived up to your expectations? If the answer is no, maybe you should look at your expectations. Were they realistic within the context of your book? Did your characters fit within what the plot needed them to do?

For instance, let's say you've written a wonderful, quirky mystery. Your sleuth is a younger woman who is a good judge of character. She's married and has three children, each two years apart. The oldest one is six. She's pregnant with another. Taking care of her family is an important part of her identity. Yet she constantly prowls the city streets, questioning lowlifes and scumbags. She bakes cookies for the school between pushing drug addicts for information. By the middle of the book, this sleuth seems a little pressed for time. You want her to deal with two cases of chicken pox at home, while a killer is stalking her.

FACT

Robie MacAuley and George Lanning have written a useful book that includes information about pacing. *Technique in Fiction* is an older book but still very useful to contemporary writers. Pacing is an important subject that this book treats well. Heed its good advice.

As you can see, this is an extreme case of mismatched identity. A character can only be doing so much at one time. She can only be so many things to so many people. At some point, you may have to give up one part of her to allow her to grow in the other part. Is it impossible that she could live this life? No. But it would be unbelievable for most readers.

Characters That Don't Make It

Ben and Jerry's Ice Cream has a wonderful Web site (✍ *www.benand jerrys.com*) that includes the Flavor Graveyard. This is a list of all the flavors of ice cream that they don't make anymore. Each flavor's name is inscribed on a tiny tombstone. It's a fitting end for the departed flavors. They're gone but not forgotten.

Maybe writers should have something similar for the characters that don't make it—a tiny tombstone for every character that seemed so promising but had to be cut. Maybe the inscription could always read: "Cut down in his/her prime."

That may seem a little maudlin, but many writers mourn the loss of a character like a member of their own family. Sometimes this loss may come after years of being published. Publishers and readers can get tired of reading about the same character. But usually, the character gets taken out before they ever see the inside of a book. Either they're an extra unneeded voice, or they didn't accomplish what the writer needed them to do.

How do you know when to omit a character? Even if you really love this person, he or she serves no useful function in the story. The character doesn't help the main characters or move the plot forward. If you found a character like this in your story, it's time to press the delete key. Maybe you can resurrect this character in another book.

Problems with Dialogue

No writer wants a reader to overlook anything in his or her work. After all, you've spent a lot of time doing this. You've given up golf games on Saturday and PTA meetings on Thursdays (well, maybe that last one wasn't such a loss). But the point is, you've made sacrifices to write this book. You want your readers to appreciate that sacrifice.

And now what you dreaded has happened: your spouse, a trusted friend, or an editor tells you that your dialogue seems a little strange. Maybe that person doesn't know exactly what's wrong with it, but now that you look at it again, you can tell it'll need to be revised. Where do you start?

Most people don't speak in complete, formal sentences—they tend to ramble, switch in midsentence, and use lots of words like *umm* and *like.* While good dialogue needs to sound realistic, you don't really want to re-create normal speech patterns—it'll make for a tedious reading.

Check for Sloppiness

Movies are a good place to study effective dialogue. Good movies usually have good dialogue. Bad movies don't. Think about the last time you saw a movie that was dubbed in English. That's bad dialogue. It makes you cringe to hear it. Good movies are a useful place for this study because they rely so heavily on dialogue. Listen to the words bandied back and forth between the characters. What works and what falls flat?

Sloppy dialogue doesn't sound real. It doesn't have contractions. It doesn't pause for breath. It doesn't reflect the personality of the character that is speaking. The lines are too long, too formal. No one talks like that.

Sharp, crisp dialogue jumps off the page. It sparkles and makes the character shine. It's so good that it can be the hook that drags the reader into the story all by itself. It moves the story forward and keeps up the pace.

Once you've had a chance to get away from the manuscript, you should be able to spot bad dialogue by reading carefully through the text. Reread your dialogues out loud. Can you tell the differences between how your characters are speaking? Does it sound different from your narrative text?

Follow the Plot Line

Revising a plot or subplot is no piece of cake, but many writers face this challenge in their revision process. It may be that you have a subplot that doesn't work with the plot or your subplot overshadows your main plot. Whatever the reason, you're going to have to tune up the story line. Most writers make that decision only after gut-wrenching agony followed by a short depression.

Give yourself a break between creating and editing so you can clearly see the problem. Then bite the bullet and get out the legal pad and a pen. Don't work on the story again until you've figured out where the problem is. Then prune cautiously and look for new growth opportunities. Don't be afraid to cut dramatically if you need to. Sometimes it can be better to have a very simple plot that shines than a complex one that doesn't work.

Move Forward with Confidence

You're ready to cut out the dead weight in your plot. You have your pruning shears ready. But how do you decide what should go and what should stay? The best way to decide that the plot needs fixing is to look for inconsistencies. Are you finding loose ends that aren't tied up before the ending or characters that seem to be playing Twister in order to make the plot work? It could be the result of overplotting—writing in too much plot that makes the book seem crazy. Or maybe there isn't enough plot— you get to the middle of the book and there's nothing. Either one of these problems can be fixed with revision.

ALERT!

Gaining confidence in your writing can take time and effort. Learn everything you can about the profession. Practice daily. Then watch out for writers who are not willing to take the time and effort. They can make you doubt your abilities. Never join a critique group with a person like this.

In the case of crazy plotting, you'll have to simplify and streamline your plot. Maybe your main character doesn't have to work as a pearl diver *and* a lion tamer. Maybe your sleuth should recover only 1 clue in a chapter instead of 100 clues. You'll have to be very honest and look for those busy moments. In the case of too little plot, you'll have to find ways to add to the original. Then you can carry it through, enriching the text as you go.

When It's Time to Change Course

Your main character is a rodeo clown. He knows about a murder at the rodeo. But he's an illiterate deaf mute, so he can't tell anyone about it. As you're reading through your manuscript, you see that he heard a shot that was fired at him by the killer. No problem. He didn't hear the shot after all. He saw the gun pointed at him.

Then you realize that you made a fatal mistake earlier in the book. Your cowboy also heard the villain threatening the victim before he was killed. Hmmm. That may be more of a problem—particularly since everything that's happened since the murder has been based on that detail.

You could make your cowboy able to hear but not speak. That could work. But why wouldn't he find some way to communicate this information with the police? Or you could change how the clown knew who the killer was. Maybe he saw the murder. But if he saw the murder and he's the heroic guy you've created, why didn't he try to stop it?

Thousands of questions are all built on the answers to the questions that came before. It's not easy to change course in midstory. But sometimes you have to. Just watch out for the intertwined workings of the plot that have to make sense when you finish. Like anyone else's life, straightening out your character's problems is tough.

Making Big Changes

Some writers are asked by an editor to make dramatic changes to plot or characters without the guarantee of a contract. This can involve anything: A 10,000-word rewrite that takes out your lead character and replaces her with an engaging secondary character; a switch in time that changes the time period from the nineteenth century to the present day; even a drastic change in point of view in who's telling the story.

Would you agree to make those changes? Writers do every day. Just the possibility of a contract is enough to sit them down at their computers. Any of those projects might take weeks, even months to complete. Most of the time, they end up sending the results to another publisher anyway.

Do they learn anything from the experience? Always. If nothing else, they learn that their work is flexible. They can write in or take out anything. They concentrate harder on their writing than ever before and look at it more closely than when they were writing it. In short, they become better writers. The only way to become a better, more experienced writer is to write.

QUESTION?

Can I call an editor and ask for more information about the revision?
If an editor takes the time to critique your work, he'll probably take the time to talk to you about it. Don't be surprised if the editor isn't sure who you are or is very brief in his critique.

Cutting Major Characters or Scenes

You just received a letter from an agent who looked at your work. She had plenty of nice things to say about it. But she had a few suggestions too. The first one is to cut one of the major characters. In this case, there is a duo of sleuths who are solving a mystery together. The agent tells you that you don't need both of them. One of them is dead weight. You argue with yourself because you're too nervous to call and argue with her. This duo you created is great together. Readers are going to love reading their exploits.

Then after thinking about it, you have to agree. You don't need the retired Sumo wrestler turned sleuth who was helping the Sushi chef solve murders. You reluctantly cut the wrestler from the book, leaving gaping holes in your text.

The next suggestion from the agent is to cut a major scene between the chef and the bad guy, where the chef accidentally cuts off a part of the bad guy's finger and slices it on a tray like sushi. The agent just feels this scene is too graphic. Especially since this is a young adult book. So you cut the scene. Now you have another hole in your manuscript. What are you going to do to fill in those holes?

This is a hypothetical case but not so far out. You could be asked to do something similar. If you agree to do it, look for places to beef up the remaining characters. Maybe you could give another secondary character a bigger part without making him the chef's partner. As for the scene the agent didn't like, maybe you should try making it less graphic while retaining the basic setup. If that doesn't work, you'll have to write another scene that fits into the hole left behind.

When It's Time to Start Over

Sometimes no amount of revising can help. After twenty revisions and rejections, it may be time to start over. Don't despair. Your experience didn't go to waste. Lots of published authors still have unpublished novels that they wrote just when they were starting out.

You are now in a much better position to start your next book. If you started writing with the knowledge that your first book might never see the light of day, this can help you keep going and achieve greatness in writing.

QUESTION?

How many times should I rewrite or revise a book before I give up and start over?
There's no simple answer. Every writer has to learn from experience. You learn a lot from revision, but if you're hacking away at the same book for more than a year without any real progress, it may be time to throw in the towel.

Chapter 19

Format for Submission

If you never intend to submit your book to publishers, you may not want to bother with this chapter. On the other hand, it's always good to have the information. The format is the presentation of your novel. The book is written and edited. It's time to consider the next step. For most writers, that step is getting published. Many things change in the publishing world but format has stayed the same for a long time. Learning how to present your work is part of being a professional writer.

Make an Impression

When you send your manuscript to an editor, that manuscript becomes your representative. You can't impress an editor with your personal charm. But you can make a good impression with your attention to detail and your writing style. The last part of that will take years of practice and hard work. But the first part is something every writer should learn right away.

Attention to detail includes where you send your work, what kind of condition it's in, and the correct format. All you need is a basic understanding of who publishes what to ensure you send your manuscript to the appropriate publishers. And you also need to make sure that your manuscript is presentable enough to be mailed out. There are certain specific guidelines for submissions, but most of them follow common sense. Don't send manuscripts marred with coffee stains. Don't send handwritten work, especially if you wrote it with crayons. This may sound funny to you, but editors receive submissions like this every day, and these submissions never make it to publication.

QUESTION?

What type of envelopes work best for sending a large manuscript?
Tyvek envelopes are more durable than plain paper. With today's machine sorting, manuscripts need all the help they can get to arrive on the publisher's desk intact.

If you want to be taken seriously, show your pride in every part of your work. Show an editor that you're ready to be a professional writer. It may seem like a good idea to be noticed by doing something unusual or weird. But editors have seen too many unusual and weird things. To get noticed, do your best work and present it in a clean, properly formatted way.

Paper Stock

Use inexpensive, twenty-pound, plain white copy paper for your manuscript. The kind of paper you use is not a good way to distinguish yourself, so forget 25 percent cotton or linen, fancy colors, or scalloped edges. The manuscript should be on white paper with black text. Nothing unusual.

If you want to get colorful or interesting, do it with your cover letter. That's the letter you use to introduce yourself to the editor or publisher. You can use colored paper or fancy lettering there. Just remember that this is a business letter. You're a businessperson sending a letter to another businessperson. In other words, don't get too carried away. If you want to be subtle, just use a heavier stock paper for your letter. That separates it from the manuscript.

If all you can send is a query letter, this has to look like a manuscript page. White paper with standard black print. A synopsis, proposal, or outline should be presented in the same way.

Writing in the Margins

Once you print out your manuscript, avoid making corrections with a pen or pencil. Whiteout used to be a popular staple for writers. You could make a mistake with your typewriter, brush some whiteout on it, and type over it. The whiteout was supposed to look like paper. It never did. But many writers got by with more than the three-errors-per-page rule by using it.

Editors just aren't that understanding anymore. They're held to a certain degree of professionalism in their own work and they expect writers to be responsible for one as well. They don't want to see white blemishes all over your manuscript. If you print out your manuscript and notice mistakes, go back to your file, make necessary corrections, and print it again. It will certainly be worth the extra work.

Also avoid making notes in the margins. The only people allowed to write in the margins are editors. You can't use notes to explain your thought processes or defend your ideas. Either the writing supports it or it doesn't.

Document Setup

The directions for setting up a manuscript aren't too complex. The more you do it, the easier it gets. If you work with a computer, it will help you set up the pages by giving you options on how you need them to look.

Your first step is always to consult the publisher's submission guide-lines. Most of them are pretty much the same, so pay attention to the differences. The guidelines presented here cover the most frequently seen directions.

> **ALERT!**
>
> If you're interested in publishing electronic books, formatting is completely different. Check with the publisher for specific guidelines that explain how to format and provide detailed facts on font, type, and spacing.

Use the Right Font

Two hundred years ago, a font was a set of movable type that the typesetter used to print the book that the author brought in as a hand-written copy. Then the typewriter was invented and revolutionized the way writers wrote their novels. For the first time, a writer could see what his work looked like in print before taking it to the publisher. The font or type preferred by editors was pica, 10 pitch. Another guideline for writers was a demand not to have more than three errors per page. The ribbon was supposed to be new to create the darkest type without smudging.

The electric typewriter sped things up for writers and made the job even easier. But nothing compared to the advent of the word processor. Today's writer can produce a virtually flawless text in half the time it took her contemporaries fifty years ago, and she can submit it in the size and font of the publisher's choosing.

Your submission should be in 10- or 12-point font. If you submit a manuscript with less than a 10-point font, it will probably be shuffled from one envelope to another in record time. No one is going to take out a magnifying glass to see your brilliant text. More specifically, Courier 10 point and Times New Roman 12 point seem to be the industry standards.

Header and Pagination

At the top of each page, in the margins, insert a header that includes your last name, the title of your book, the chapter number, and the page number:

Smith—Manuscript Title—Chapter 1   15

Make sure the header is located 1½ inches from the top, and the text doesn't run into it.

While adding headers to the manuscript used to be a time-consuming process in the era of typewriters, today all you need to do is create a header in your document, and your computer will automatically run the header on each page and insert the correct page number for you.

Most books today don't have chapter titles. Instead, most authors just numer them: Chapter 1, Chapter 2, and so on. The same is true of scene breaks. Three asterisks is preferable to a scene break title.

Framework and Layout

Take the time to make sure your manuscript is presented in the best light by making sure it's easy to read. By adjusting the margins and tabs, and following correct page layout, you'll create a more accessible document that will give the impression that you know what the rules are and have no trouble following them.

Set the Margins

Margins are the narrow strips of blank space that frame the page. Make sure your margins are set at 1½ inches. This includes top, bottom, and both sides. At this width, your manuscript will have a uniform, clean look to it, with just enough empty space to make reading it easy on the reader's eyes.

Check the Tabs

Each paragraph begins with an indentation of about five spaces, which on the computer may be created by hitting Tab. If your Tab indents appear too large or small, you can change their size. The correct option is 0.3 inches.

Every paragraph, including all dialogue, should start this way. No sentence in a paragraph should extend into the margins. Sometimes, this may cut a sentence short because a word will drop down to the next line, but that's okay.

Page Layout

The first page of a novel manuscript starts about 1½ inches from the top. This is where you type the title of your novel. Drop down four to six lines or two to three double-spaced lines, then indent and start your text. End the page about 1½ inches from the bottom. Most pages will contain about 250 words. This can vary according to how much dialogue is on the page.

Chapter Openers

Setting up a chapter opener is almost the same as setting up a page. You'll have to repeat the process with each new chapter. It has to start on a new page, not immediately following the end of the previous chapter.

A new chapter page is dropped one-third of the way down from the top of the page. The title and/or chapter number is set in caps and centered on the page. Drop four to six lines or two to three double spaces, then indent to start the first paragraph. The page ends at the same place, 1½ inches from the bottom.

Opening Words

You may choose to open each chapter with one or more quotes, epitaphs, or short poems. This brief subject matter is related to the chapter, but is not a part of the story. It can be important to the story line or simply help set a certain mood.

Opening words should be single-spaced and set in the manuscript before the chapter title line. They don't need to be explained to the editor unless he or she asks about them. They should be self-explanatory to anyone who reads the text.

Spacing and Breaks

The first step in a professional presentation is spacing. Knowing how much to space and when to do it doesn't seem that difficult, but writers still make mistakes on it. Rules for spacing a manuscript include formatting paragraph indention, chapter headings, and scene breaks.

FACT

If you're looking for a concise, well-written book about manuscript format, you should try *The Writer's Digest Guide to Manuscript Formats* by Dian Buchman and Seli Groves. There's nothing frilly or cute about it but it gives good diagrams that anyone can understand.

If spacing seems unimportant to you, think again. You wouldn't go to a corporate job interview wearing jeans and sandals. You want to give your manuscript the same fighting chance to succeed. Spacing is part of your manuscript's personal appearance. Do the work now and collect the rewards later.

Single Space or Double Space?

In fiction, there aren't many places where you will single-space your text. The only opportunities occur when you present block quotations as indented text. These might be poems, letters, diary entries, or sections from a book. In that case, single-space the items then double-space between each item.

The rest of your manuscript should be submitted as a double-spaced document. What's the big deal? Manuscripts are formatted in a way that makes them easy to read. Editors wade through too many manuscripts to count in a year. The ones that they stop to read follow the guidelines. Double-spacing makes the text easier to read. There's also some room to write edits between the lines of print.

If you're using a word processor, set your line spacing for double. This will prevent any confusion later if you have to reformat for submission.

> Cover letters and query letters (these are part of your arsenal for submitting your work) are single-spaced as well. They follow a general format for letter writing, the same way that you would write to your business associate.

Scene Breaks

A scene break is a switch in what's happening to the characters or plot. It can be a change in point of view that takes the reader from one character's thoughts to another character's thoughts. It tells the reader that something is different. You've changed location, time, or voice.

An example of this would be when your sleuth gets banged in the back of the head and loses consciousness. A scene break will either change point of view to someone who finds the sleuth, or take the reader to the next morning when the sleuth wakes up.

Writers have different ways of creating scene breaks in their manuscripts. This seems to be okay since publishers have different ways of marking scene breaks in published novels. One way to get this effect is to use a symbol that's centered on the page, like a triple asterisk (***), single asterisk, triple pound sign (###), or single pound sign. Check with the publisher before you submit. The scene break is always on a line by itself, not immediately after a sentence or before another sentence.

Spacing Between Symbols

Everyone knows that there's no space between the last word and the period. But what about the other spacing rules? Here are two guidelines you need to follow:

- There is no space between a hyphen or dash and the words they join: one-half, see—over there.
- Insert one space between sentences. Inserting two spaces is no longer in vogue.

Additional Materials

There are a handful of parts that come with the manuscript but aren't a part of your story. Known in the publishing world as "front matter," they include the title page, acknowledgments, dedication, and other materials that say something about your submission. You might not include all of these components with every submission, but if you do, format them correctly so that an editor knows what they are.

Title Page

The title page or manuscript cover sheet is a single sheet of paper that holds specific information about your manuscript. This information isn't fully repeated again but parts of it are repeated in the header. The information is used to identify your manuscript and tell the editor a few key things about it.

The page should start with your name, address, phone number, and e-mail address, all placed in the upper left-hand corner of the page, flush left. In the upper right-hand corner, list the word count: 100,000 words. This should start eight to ten spaces from the top after the margin. In the center of the page, sixteen to eighteen lines down, enter your novel's title in caps. Two lines down, insert "a novel by," then drop two more spaces and put your name, not in caps.

QUESTION?

Should the title page be numbered?
No, the cover sheet is outside the manuscript pagination. Start numbering on the first page of your story and continue consecutively after that, even if there are only a few words on a page.

Dedication

The dedication is a freeform part of your book. It's where you have the opportunity to tell the world who or what inspired you to write this book. Some authors skip this part or use it to thank their agent or editor. Usually, the dedication is personal.

The dedication should be attached on a separate sheet of paper and clearly marked. The publisher will know what to do with it. Don't overextend yourself on this. Keep it short.

Acknowledgments

Acknowledgments are placed in the front of the book. They are a brief message from the author thanking people for their help with the book. Think about the things that actors say when they win an Academy Award. That's what the acknowledgments are.

Just as the dedication, the acknowledgments are optional. Including them is completely up to you. If you do include them, do so on a separate sheet of paper and clearly labeled.

References

References may encompass any number of things. You might want to include references for any quotes or poems you include in your novel, complete with copyright information. If you created special terminology or used words from a foreign language in your novel, you might wish to include a glossary that defines these terms.

You might choose to include a list of your characters and their specific roles in the book. You can also suggest further reading on historical, scientific, or other specific subjects covered briefly in the story. Maps and timelines also fall into this category.

Most of this information would be available to the reader after the story. It should be separate when you send your manuscript. Be sure to clearly label what each part is in the header so that the editor knows what they are.

FACT

A dictionary or glossary of words usually accompanies a science fiction or fantasy novel that uses words that readers won't understand. This is done alphabetically or by order of appearance in the text. Writers also use this for foreign phrases or words.

Formatting Errors

Formatting isn't part of the creative process. At least, not in a way that writers like it to be. There are no interesting characters or places. There are only rules and guidelines that have to be followed if you want someone to read your work.

No one likes rules. Writers and other artists are notoriously bad at following them. They don't fit in with their style. But they're a necessary part of beginning to understand the publishing world.

Don't Make It Too Hard

Don't expect to remember all the rules at once. Get a good book. Find a good Web site. Learn the rules as you go. You don't have to make it harder on yourself than necessary.

But don't make it hard on the editors either. Contrary to many writers' beliefs, editors are only human. The rules are set up to make their job of weeding through massive amounts of work easier and faster. They have to try and distinguish a good writer from a bad writer very quickly. The only way to do this is by making the base criteria of a good writer as someone who knows the rules and follows them.

It may not seem fair or pleasant, but publishing is a business like any other. Respect the publishers' needs and you can succeed. Ignore them and you'll never see anything more than rejection letters.

Fiction Writer's Connection, at ✍ *www.fictionwriters.com*, is a great online resource for helping writers with the tools of their trade, including formatting and other less-creative aspects of submitting your work to publishers.

Not Following the Rules

Writers know how hard it is to get published in today's market. Not that it's really any harder today than it was fifty years ago, there are just more people who want to be writers. Many people think they can get noticed by not following the rules. And, truthfully, some people have done outrageous things that got them published. But many more have failed with their stunts and ended up as the butt of a joke between editors at lunch.

Consider that before you put the confetti into your manuscript envelope. Maybe the editor you're sending it to has never seen confetti in an envelope before and she will be totally amazed and delighted. But, if she's not, is this how you want her to remember you in the future? Do you want to be that writer who ruined the editor's lunch and coffee that day when she opened your package? How eager is she going to be to work with you again?

Present yourself in a clear, professional manner and you'll get noticed. It may not be as exciting as sending a sheep to your editor, but it will do the job.

Chapter 20

Publishing and Marketing

Books, like everything else, require good marketing. That includes the initial sale to a publisher and subsequent sales to readers. You have to put on your marketing hat before the manuscript ever goes out the door. Knowing who to send it to and when to send it should be part of your marketing strategy. Everything else you've done to this point is getting ready for the big day when your book goes out the door to the first publisher or agent.

Making the Decision

Not every book is meant to be published. Not every writer wants to be a published author. How do you decide when and if you're ready to be published?

Making the decision to send your work out is a logical next step for many writers. Many more never take that step. Their books languish with dust bunnies in forgotten corners. Those writers start something new and when they finish that, it joins the first one on the heap. They're perfectly happy never sticking their neck out to find out what anyone else thinks of their work.

FACT

Marketing your book can be a tough sell. To better prepare yourself for the battle, read everything you can about the subject including *The Sell Your Novel Toolkit* by Elizabeth Lyon. This will help you understand this sometimes difficult aspect of being a writer.

On the other hand, thousands of writers take the plunge every year. They go to conferences and send their manuscripts to editors. They enter contests and hire professional editors. They want to be published. They want to share their work with readers. They won't be happy until they're either broke or published.

Which are you? If you're the former, don't worry about it. Writing can be personally fulfilling without being professionally exhausting. But if you're in the second group, you've already made the decision. You know you want to be published and you're satisfied that your book is ready to be viewed by an editor.

Realistic Expectations

If you're serious about getting published, you've already entertained visions of limousines and Nobel prizes, movie right sales and guest spots on late-night television. You've followed the careers of John

Grisham and Stephen King. You know you can make the *New York Times* bestseller list if someone will just read your book. Now that you've mastered the unrealistic expectations of getting published, what are the realistic expectations?

In the real world, very few fiction novel writers support themselves from their work. They either have another job to support their addiction or they have a spouse who works to support them. They will never have a publisher send a limo for them. They're lucky if their publisher has a marketing plan for their work. Their book is on a bookstore shelf with thousands of other books and nothing to set them apart. Readers who flock to have their books signed by a bestselling author will walk by the average writer's table and not even look at his or her book.

But, the good news is, Stephen King had the same problems. John Grisham self-published his first book and sold it out of the trunk of his car before it was picked up by a major publisher. Anything is possible. You have to be a dreamer to be a writer. You might as well dream big.

Maybe It's Not for You

Writing and marketing are hard work. Being a professional, paid writer is a different world from writing whatever you feel like writing, any way you want to write it. There are enough rules and regulations that publishing could become a government agency. Agents and editors don't like to return calls. The whole process of allowing another person to read and critique your work makes you feel queasy.

Maybe publishing isn't for you. It doesn't have to be. If you're just as happy not seeing your book published, you can save yourself a long, tough road. You don't ever have to worry about changing a character or making your plot stronger just to satisfy someone who probably can't even tell you the title of your book.

If it doesn't bother you that one other person in the world could read your work and sit back with that sigh of satisfaction, gazing adoringly at the cover, then don't do it. But if you are ready for the challenges that lie ahead and to do whatever it takes to succeed, take the chance. It can't hurt to try.

Knowing Your Market

What made you decide to write this book? Was it because you're a long-time romance reader? Have you always loved mysteries? Is your family saga like a novel you read as a teenager?

FACT

Most writers say they write for themselves, but every writer has to consider her readers if she wants to get published. You have to be able to balance the creative idea that you nurtured inside of yourself while you were writing and the real-life idea that if you don't sell any books, you won't get another contract.

There are as many reasons for writing as there are novels and writers. For writers who write the kind of fiction they like to read, knowing the market comes easily. You see the trends, know the competition, and are aware of what publisher is publishing what fiction. There's no real homework to be done because it's part of your life.

But you might not be very familiar with the genre that you chose for writing your novel. If you decided to write mystery, even though you don't read them, it's probably because you felt that your talent could fit into this field. You may not know much about the publishing houses that are well known for their mysteries, and maybe you can't tell a cozy from a thriller. If that's the case, knowing your market is going to be a learning experience.

There's nothing wrong with deciding to write a book you feel inclined to write even if you don't know a lot about the genre. Not all mystery readers have a talent for writing mystery. Not all romance writers read romance. It doesn't mean you can't find the information that you need to market your book.

Your Audience

Who are the people who will be buying and reading your book? Spend some time at a local bookstore. Watch how people choose their books. Most readers buy books because they recognize the author's name. They've read Patricia Cornwell or Danielle Steele before and like the way they write. They've never been disappointed enough with one of their books to stop buying them.

If the author's name doesn't ring a bell, the bookstore customer might look at the cover and then read the back of the book. If what she sees intrigues her, she moves on to the inside. She flips through the book, and maybe reads the first page. Some might also read the last paragraph.

If you're a writer, the chances are that you're a reader. How do you choose what you read? What do you like to see in a story? What makes you angry about a book? Is there something that makes you feel cheated?

Knowing who your audience is and what they like helps you market your work. You know your target readers. You know what they like to read.

Slant Your Writing

The slant of your writing is affected by the publisher you hope to sell to and the audience you hope to attract. For example: You've written an inspirational romance with a strong Christian theme. You know there are a handful of publishers who will be interested in this book. Your audience is made up of readers like you who enjoy romance but want strong moral values with it. Your book is slanted for this audience. There's no swearing, no heavy sex scenes. The heroine not only keeps her clothes on, she inspires the people around her to lead better lives.

ALERT!

You have to consider what it is that sells a book. What is the particular thing your readers are looking for? That thing can be your hook or slant. Once you understand what your slant is, you understand how to market your book. You'll know what the publisher's guidelines should say for them to be interested in your work.

To market a novel, every writer has to realize what his or her target audience is looking for. That's what the publisher is looking for too. The editor will only buy your work if she believes it will appeal to the publishing house's audience. No one buys work that they feel is unmarketable. But half of the battle is getting your work into the hands of the people who will want it.

Marketing Tools

The tools that you'll use to market your work are specific to the writing field. But like tools for any other job, there's a right way and a wrong way to use them. The better you understand how to use these tools, the more effective they'll be.

Everyone wants to be published, but very few people worry about learning the craft of marketing. Imagine a car mechanic who wanted to fix cars but wasn't willing to learn anything about them. It's the same way with writing. Natural talent can go a long way, until it's time to find a publisher. Then you either learn what you need to know or you flail uselessly, hoping someone will look at your work.

Take the time now to learn everything you can about publishing and marketing. Join some marketing groups for writers online. There are many supportive communities on the Internet for writers just like you. They can help you learn about the industry, what you can expect, and what you should know.

ESSENTIAL

Marketing for Writers (✍ *www.marketingforwriters.com*) is a good online resource for ideas that will make you a top marketer. Look around the Internet and you'll find many other good sites. Another good resource is authors. Many published authors will be glad to talk to you about their efforts at marketing.

Synopsis: Your Story, Summarized

The word *synopsis* strikes more fear into the hearts of fiction writers than rejection. What is the dreaded synopsis? It's a short (five to ten pages) description of your novel.

Gasp! How can you possibly describe your book for an editor in so few words? Maybe you could do it for the blurb on the cover if they bought your book. But how can an editor appreciate the complexities of your novel unless they read at least three chapters?

Editors don't always have time to read sample chapters. Instead, they read the synopsis and either put everything back in the envelope or go on to read the sample chapters. If the editor likes the idea put forth in the synopsis and the sample chapters seem to be written in a way that supports the idea, then the editor will ask to see the rest of the manuscript. That's the way it works.

Writing a synopsis isn't so hard if you've written a good outline. Use the basic points of the outline to summarize your novel. Never withhold the ending or say something cute like, "You'll have to request the rest of the manuscript if you want to know what happened." Editors have seen it all before. Keep in mind that this is professional reading for them—they're looking for good material, not personal favorites.

QUESTION?

How long should a synopsis be?
The length of a synopsis will vary according to the length of the book. A novel of 50,000 to 70,000 words requires a two- to five-page synopsis. A longer novel may need a summary of about ten pages. Check with publishers for more specific guidelines.

Query Letter

If writers dread a synopsis, they despise the query letter—the short and polite introduction, book description, and bio make normal writers gnash their teeth and wail. Why would an editor want to read a query letter?

Editors like them because they are an efficient way of expressing very basic, fundamental information about a book and its writer. To begin with, it says how well you follow directions. But it also says how well you know your book and what's important about it.

A query letter should fit on one page. It can be divided into four paragraphs. The first one is the greeting. The second one tells the editor what the book is about. The third tells the editor a little about you (information that relates to the book). And the fourth mentions a little something about marketing the book. That's it!

The tricky thing is that you don't have much space. Think of it as a $100 piece of candy. It's small but tantalizing. It may only be good for a few seconds, but that's all you need to get in the door. A query letter can be your best friend if you take the time and learn to write a great one.

Cover Letters

Cover letters are not to be confused with cover pages. A cover page is the first page of a manuscript that has the title and your name. A cover letter is what you send with a synopsis or outline. It is a brief, polite note of introduction for yourself and your synopsis.

You have more room to play around with a cover letter and synopsis than you do with a query letter. But they both accomplish the same task. It's like knocking on the editor's door.

You can use your computer to create your own inexpensive stationary to use when sending cover letters to editors. A simple header that includes your name, address, phone number, and e-mail can be very effective.

The cover letter should be on stationary paper, slightly better weight than your synopsis. It has to have the company name, editor's name with his/her title, and address. It also must contain your name, address, phone number, and e-mail address somewhere on the sheet. A cover letter is never longer than one page.

Following Guidelines

Were you one of those kids in school who always got praised for following directions well? The chances are that most writers were too busy looking out the window to hear the directions. If you were that child, you'll have to pay close attention now.

Following guidelines is important for a couple of reasons. Number one, the editor knows you can read. Number two, he or she knows you're really interested in getting published. Number three, the editor knows you're a team player.

Guidelines are easier to get than ever before. They don't even cost a stamp since you can get them online. But you do have to put the effort into it. Because it says so many good things about you, it's certainly worth your time.

Word Count

You've got a great novel. You've never taken it out for critique but you just know it's good. You follow all the guidelines and get it together to send to the publisher. Three weeks after you send it in, it comes back to you. On the rejection sheet, the editor has indicated the reason for rejection: insufficient word length. In the margin, she writes, "Loved the characters but we never publish books this short."

This experience comes with a price tag. It cost you money to print up the manuscript and send it. It cost you all you had in pride to let someone else look at it. It cost you six months to a year writing it. Was the experience worth it?

Not enough words or too many words means you didn't look at the publisher's guidelines. Or worse, that you arrogantly thought you could ignore them. Either way, it cost you plenty. Now you're faced with the decision of whether or not to send out again. You may have to revise to add or subtract words. Then you'll have to go through the process all over again. Have you ever heard the old axiom, "What's worth doing is worth doing well"?

Appropriate Format

Despite the fact that you know how to send a manuscript to a publisher, a friend of yours suggests that you go beyond the ordinary and really make an impression. She suggests that you send your romance novel along with a fresh-cut rose. To do this, you'll have to put it into a box and ship it overnight so it gets there quickly. But when the editor opens the box, it will all be worth it. The smell of the rose will be sensational. If that won't get you a read, nothing will.

Unfortunately, no one at the publisher's office would sign for the package. So it was left with a receptionist who forgot about it for a few days. When she found it and saw that it was addressed to an editor, she sent it to the editorial department. It sat on a shelf for a month before it got to the associate editor's desk. When she finally opened it, the rose was dry, but it had left an impression on the paper. The stem was stuck to the paper, so when she tried to move it, the paper ripped. Rather than passing it on or giving it a read, the associate editor sent the whole thing back.

The moral of the story is simple: Formatting is not the place to be creative. Stick with the guidelines and don't try to distinguish yourself from the pack. Let your novel do it for you.

FACT

Sample chapters are usually the first three chapters of the book. Sometimes the publisher will ask for around fifty pages of sample text. Send complete chapters, even if it takes fifty-nine pages. Only send the first few consecutive chapters, not random ones. Always include a SASE (self-addressed stamped envelope).

Submissions to Agents and Editors

Deciding where to send your manuscript is the most important marketing decision you'll make. Getting a response from an agent or publisher can take as much as a year. That's why it's important to make sure that you send the right manuscript to the right person. Don't waste your time or theirs.

You've got two options for sending out submissions. You may choose to send your work to agents, asking them to take you on as their client, or you may prefer to send your work directly to publishing houses. Weigh your options carefully. If an agent agrees to market your work, he or she may have better luck with it than you will. And some publishers work exclusively with agents. But going directly to the source has its own benefits as well. Do what feels right to you.

Working with an Agent

A literary agent is part of a marketing plan. Some writers won't bother sending to publishers at all. They're convinced they can only sell a book with an agent.

That's not true, of course. Manuscripts written by unknown authors are bought by editors every day. An agent can give you a better chance at a sale, but they basically do exactly what you can do: send the manuscript to an editor.

An agent might know an editor personally from working with him and that would increase your chances of selling a manuscript to that editor. But they don't know every editor at every publishing house. They aren't miracle workers and they can't sell every manuscript. Just because you get an agent for your book doesn't guarantee a sale.

It's hard to get an agent when you don't have a track record. Even worse, it's hard to get a good agent when you've never had a sale. The bigger the agency, the less likely it is that you're going to get much attention from the agent.

Publishers

Publishers get a bad rap from writers. The idea that there aren't editors out there looking to buy good manuscripts is ridiculous. That's what editors do. A publisher pays them to sift through manuscripts from unknown authors, help authors already signed with the house, and edit books. Most editors are thrilled when they find a talent hidden in the slush pile (unsolicited manuscripts). They are still in the business of creating the superstar writers of tomorrow.

ALERT!

Publicists are promotional experts who help writers set up marketing strategies for their books. Not every writer has a publicist. Be sure you understand what a publicist can do for you and what they charge before you sign any contracts.

Sending your work to a publisher cuts out the middleman (agent). You may or may not get a better deal for your book with an agent. Some publishers offer a boilerplate (standard) contract whether you have an agent or not. The agent can look through the paperwork and tell you if the contract is sound, but so can a lawyer. And a lawyer will only charge you one time to do it. An agent will charge you at least 15 percent every time you make any money on the book.

Which to Choose?

The final choice comes down to you. Can you handle talking to an editor about a contract? Are you worried about not understanding what's going on? An agent can answer those questions. But they can't always sell a book to an editor any better than you can.

Multiple Submissions

Should you send multiple submissions? Whether you choose to contact agents or editors, the answer is a definite yes. Because the response time is so long, you'd be waiting years just for a rejection or request for a partial manuscript. Include in your cover or query letter that your submission has gone out to more than one publisher or agent. Don't worry about being rejected because of it. Agents and editors know the reality of publishing today.

Making Contact

Editors and agents have horror stories of being accosted by excited writers who are determined to make an impression. These writers make an impression, but it's not a good one.

Imagine being at a conference and going to the bathroom. While you're in the stall, a writer's head pops over the wall and the writer cheerfully starts telling you all about her book. That's only one of the hundreds of stories editors and agents tell. And it's not even one of the worst.

Even though you really want to sell your book and you have complete faith in it, give these people a break. No one likes to be badgered in his or her professional or personal life. Think about how you'd feel if the positions were reversed. Is what you're doing something that would influence you to buy a book? Or is it something that would make you run the other way?

Like everything else, there's a right way and a wrong way to approach an editor or agent. Be considerate in making your decision. If the editor hates you for invading her privacy, she's not going to read your book.

The Right Way

A good way to approach editors or agents is to meet them at a conference or party. You can introduce yourself to them and, if they're receptive, you can tell them about your book. At a conference, you should make sure they're wearing their name tag. This tells you that they're working and not on their personal time. If you know someone who's talking to an agent or editor, there's nothing wrong with joining them. Just make sure the agent or editor is ready to talk shop.

Another good way is to make an editor or agent appointment at a conference. These are times you've signed up for (and maybe even paid for) to discuss your book. This is the time to lay on the charm and be able to describe your book quickly and enthusiastically. This isn't the time to talk about the editor's personal life or your own. This is the opportunity to show him or her how professional you are.

Of course, if you don't plan on attending a conference or party where editors and agents will be, you can still go the old-fashioned route. You can send in a great query letter or cover letter with a synopsis. Use the opportunity to your advantage. It might be short but you can show them what a great writer you are. And that's what this is all about anyway.

The Wrong Way

Now that you have an idea about the right ways to approach any professional who can help you with your writing, you should have an idea about the wrong ways. Sometimes a good idea might not be the best idea. And before you think you have an original approach that someone has never seen, guess again. Follow something from the previous section and nothing from this list:

- If you see an editor at a bar, don't offer to buy him a drink if he'll agree to talk about your book.
- Don't try to pay a hotel clerk to tell you what the editor's room number is so you can knock at the door and tell her about your book.
- Unless you know the agent or editor, or you've had some contact with him, don't call him on the phone. He won't listen to you talk about your book.

- Never send an agent or editor a gift with a copy of your book to read.
- Never corner an agent or editor in an elevator, taxi, or airport limo and start talking about your book.
- Most importantly, never look up an editor's home address and wait outside to tell her about your book. This could be considered stalking.

QUESTION?

Is it easier to get an agent or a publisher?
Writers are split according to how many started with agents and how many started with publishers. Send to both. That way you'll have all your bases covered.

Dealing with Rejection

If you send out work, you're going to get rejections. Print out this sentence and paste it on your wall or your computer monitor. You're trying to sell a product. Every salesperson will tell you that it takes some no's before you get a yes.

That doesn't mean that your work is terrible. It doesn't mean that you'll never get published. All writers, even the famous and successful ones, get rejected. You'll probably get rejected too. It's nothing personal. It can mean your work isn't right for the publisher or agent. Or it can mean the publisher or agent was having a bad day and didn't want to look at anything. It's impossible for you to know.

Maybe you'll be lucky and your book will never get rejected. It will get picked up by the first agent you send it to and the agent will spark a bidding war between publishers who will fight for the right to publish it. You'll sell the movie rights within a few weeks and never look back.

That's the dream. It happens to some people. But the majority of writers aren't that lucky. Their books are hard to sell and it takes years for them to build up a following of readers. Only then can they reach bestseller status. Some writers will never reach that point. But you never know until you send your manuscript out and take that chance.

Coping with It

Rejection is like any other disappointment in life. The missed promotion, the anniversary trip that's bad from the beginning. Every person has his or her own way of dealing with disappointment. The same thing is true for rejection. Every writer finds his or her own way of dealing with it.

Some people are better at it than others. People who are already involved in sales know that it's a matter of the odds being in your favor. The more you send out, the more rejections you get. On the other hand, the more rejections, the better your chances for a sale.

Writers have boxes and files full of rejections. Some spend years without a single acceptance. How do they keep going? Maybe they make it into a game. How many rejections can I get this month? Or they just throw them away and don't think about it. Others search every rejection letter for any sign that they might be coming closer. A real signature. A hastily scribbled note from the editor. Anything that will help them keep going.

Should You Change Your Work

It's possible that some rejections will come with a note from the editor, who suggests that you rework your novel and then resubmit it for publication. There's a certain amount of hope implied in that request. Not that changing your manuscript is any easier. It just makes the idea of doing it easier to swallow.

If you find that several rejections all point to the same flaws in need of revision, the editors may be on to something. These editors or agents aren't out there ganging up on you. These are individual opinions from a group of unbiased professionals. If you're fortunate enough to get them to offer you free advice, you might want to take it.

Should you resubmit to those editors who offered suggestions? Yes! Write them back and thank them for their help. Tell them about the revisions you did and cross your fingers. At least they'll know that you're willing to work to make your manuscript better. Who knows? You might even beat the odds and make a sale.

After the Sale

The telephone rings. You juggle a bag of groceries, your son's soccer ball, and your purse. The dog is hungry and barking at you for food. Your son is cranky and wants to know what's for dinner. Your neighbor came over again as soon as he saw you come home. He wants to complain about your cat scratching his fence. You grab the phone, put off the neighbor, the kid, and the dog. On the other end of the line, a voice says, "This is Suzie Smith, managing editor for Runway Books. I'd like to talk to you about your novel. We'd like to make an offer for it."

ALERT!

Review copies are a costly part of marketing for writers. Be sure yours are getting into the hands of people who are actually reviewers. Ask for credentials—who they are and who they work for—before you send anything.

You did it! You sold that book after only three rewrites and fifteen rejections. Everything falls into place. The world changes. You're a published writer. You're an author.

After you call all your living relatives, friends, coworkers, and some people you know from church, you sit down and the enormity of it hits you. You're published. You're really published. Now what?

No Time to Rest

While this may seem a great time to go on a vacation and celebrate, keep it short. Having a novel accepted is no time to rest. There are contracts to be signed, details to be worked out. When will the book come out? How many books will be printed? Does the publisher do any promotional work?

It's time to look for an agent if you don't have one already. If an agent didn't broker this deal, don't expect him to step in at the last minute and close it. That probably won't happen. But this event does make you a more attractive client. This might be a good time to find the agent of your dreams.

If you don't have another novel, now's the time to start one. Send a query letter about it to the agent you're trying to attract. Also talk to your new editor about it. The quicker you sell your second book, the quicker you get over first-book syndrome (only selling one book).

Plan on Doing More Marketing

Unless your publisher has a massive promotional staff with plenty of money, expect to do most of your own marketing. Talk to your editor and find out what the publisher is willing to do for you.

ESSENTIAL

> It's difficult to write a good press release. What appeals to newspaper editors who are looking for news? Interesting and helpful answers to your questions can be found at Press Release.com's Web site (*www.pressrelease.com).*

The chances are you'll have to set up your own book signings, send out copies for reviews, and send press releases to local newspapers and bookstores. Book signings are a long way off at this point. They can wait until a couple of months before your book is released. But reviews are slow. Some print reviewers expect copies of books as much as a year in advance. Even small, online review sites need from three to six months.

Plan on sending out ARCs (advance reader's copies) of your manuscript anywhere from six months to a year before publication. These are copies of your final manuscript (minus the publisher's edits). Be sure to include your name, where they can send the review, and any other pertinent information. If you have bound galleys (copies of the book in paperback form with a plain cover) distributed by the publisher, that's even better.

Press releases should go out as soon as you find out about your book. Don't be afraid to release information about the book as the publication date comes nearer. Any publicity you can get will help with sales. Ⓔ

Appendix A

Additional Resources

The listings provided here are good sources of information about particular aspects of writing, editing, and marketing a novel.

Bibliography

Bickham, Jack M. *Scene and Structure.* (Cincinnati, OH: F&W Publications, 1999).

Bradbury, Ray. *Zen in the Art of Writing.* (Santa Barbara, CA: Joshua Odell Editions, 1994).

Buckman, Dian Dincin and Seli Groves. *The Writer's Digest Guide to Manuscript Formats.* (Cincinnati, OH: Writer's Digest Books, 1987).

Burack, Sylvia K. *The Writer's Handbook.* (Boston, MA: The Writer, Inc., 1990).

Chiarella, Tom. *Writing Dialogue.* (Cincinnati, OH: Writer's Digest Books, 1998).

Cook, Claire Kehrwald. *Line by Line: How to Edit Your Own Writing.* (New York: Houghton Mifflin, 1986).

Dixon, Debra. *Goal, Motivation and Conflict: The Building Blocks of Good Fiction.* (Memphis, TN: Gryphon Books for Writers, 1999).

Edgerton, Les. *Finding Your Voice: How to Put Personality in Your Writing.* (Cincinnati, OH: Writer's Digest Books, 2003).

Fulton, Robert, Jr., Ph.D. *"But . . . You Know What I Mean!" An Editor's Point of View.* (Port Orchard, WA: Tillie Ink, 2002).

Funk and Wagnalls Standard Dictionary. (New York: New American Library, 1980).

Kipfer, Barbara Ann, Ph.D., ed. *The Original Roget's International Thesaurus.* 6th ed. (New York: HarperCollins, 2002).

Lukeman, Noah T. *The Plot Thickens: 8 Ways to Bring Fiction to Life.* (New York: St. Martin's Press, 2003).

Lyon, Elizabeth. *Sell Your Novel Toolkit*. (New York: Perigee Trade, 2002).

MacAuley, Robie and George Lanning. *Technique in Fiction*. (New York: St. Martins Press, 2001).

Madden, David. *Revising Fiction: A Handbook for Writers*. (New York: New American Library, 1995).

Metter, Ellen. *Facts in a Flash: A Research Guide for Writers*. (Cincinnati, OH: Writer's Digest Books, 1999).

Morris, William. *Morris Dictionary of Word and Phrase Origins*. (New York: HarperCollins, 1998).

Oates, Joyce Carol, ed. *Telling Stories: An Anthology for Writers*. (New York: W.W. Norton & Co., 1998).

Plotnik, Arthur. *The Elements of Editing*. (New York: MacMillan Publishing Co., 1982).

Rico, Gabriele Lusser, Ph.D. *Writing the Natural Way*. Revised edition. (Los Angeles, CA: J. P. Tarcher, 2000).

Roman, Kenneth and Joel Raphaelson. *Writing That Works*. (New York: Harper and Row, 1981).

Shertzer, Margaret D. *The Elements of Grammar*. (New York: Longman Publishing Co., Inc., 1996).

Strunk, William, Jr. and E. B. White. *The Elements of Style*. 4th ed. (New York: MacMillan Publishing Co., Inc., 2000).

Szeman, Sherri. *Mastering Point of View*. (Cincinnati, OH: F&W Publications, 2001).

von Oech, Roger. *A Whack on the Side of the Head*. (New York: Time Warner Books, 1998).

Wallace, Carol McD. *20,001 Names for Baby*. (New York: Avon Books, 1992)

Resources on the Web

Aspiring Writer's Magazine

A good place for beginner writers to visit ✍ *www.aspiringwriters.net*

Association of Authors' Representatives

This site offers lists of literary agents and their contact information
✍ *www.aar-online.org*

BookWire

An industry resource that keeps writers up to date on happenings in
publishing ✍ *www.bookwire.com/bookwire*

Bulwer-Lytton's Guide

A guide to the worst beginning contest ✍ *www.bulwer-lytton.com*

Coffeehouse for Writers

The place to learn the craft, get motivated, and even test your grammar
✍ *www.coffeehouseforwriters.com*

Daily Grammar

A dose of daily grammar usage delivered to your e-mail box
✍ *www.dailygrammar.com*

Fiction Writer's Connection

One of the best resource guides on the Internet ✍ *www.fictionwriters.com*

Forwriters.com

A writer's forum and resource site ✍ *www.forwriters.com*

Gila Queen's Guide to Markets

A free online guide for selling your work ✍ *http://gilaqueen.us*

Literary Marketplace

Offers lists of publishers and agents for your work; you can subscribe online
or purchase the book ✍ *www.literarymarketplace.com*

Manuscript Editing

Lynda Lotman has been serving writers since 1976 with lists of agents, copyright information, sample contracts, and editing advice ✍ *www.manuscriptediting.com*

Marketing for Writers

Visit this site for useful marketing information and tools ✍ *www.marketing forwriters.com*

The NCES Students' Classroom

All the information you'll ever need about how to graph ✍ *www.nces.ed.gov/nceskids*

The Oxford Dictionary Online

A resource every writer will find useful ✍ *www.askoxford.com*

Poets and Writers

Includes the magazine and resources for creative writers ✍ *www.pw.org*

PressRelease.com

An excellent site for learning to write press releases that offers a free newsletter ✍ *www.pressrelease.com*

Punctuation Made Simple

A good place to find useful information about punctuation ✍ *www.stpt.usf.edu/pms*

Ultralingua

This site offers tons of information on words and language usage ✍ *www.ultralingua.net*

UsingEnglish.com

A serious grammar resource for writers ✍ *www.usingenglish.com*

Vocab Vitamins

Word a day for writers who want to improve their vocabulary ✍ *www.vocabvitamins.com*

World Wide Virtual Library of History

A wonderful place to look up anything you want to know about historical events ✍ *www.ku.edu/history/VL*

Writer's Digest

One of the biggest sources of information for writers, including their award-winning magazine ✍ *www.writersdigest.com*

The Writer's Hood

A virtual neighborhood of genres in support of beginning and professional writers ✍ *www.writershood.com*

Writers' Journal

Writer's magazine dealing with the psychology and practical aspects of writing ✍ *www.writersjournal.com*

Writers Manual

The bragging zone for writers—go there and tell the world about your writing accomplishments ✍ *www.writersmanual.com*

WritersMarket.com

The most trusted source of information about markets for writing now available in an updated online site or in book form ✍ *www.writers market.com*

The Writers' Portal

Offers help finding a critique group near your home ✍ *www.smotu.org*

Writer's Software SuperCenter

One-stop-shopping for all your writing software needs ✍ *www.writers supercenter.com*

The Writers' Well

An interesting and unusual assortment of references for writers ✍ *www.hellskitchen.com/well.htm*

Writers Write—the Internet Writing Journal

A great resource for books, writing, and publishing ✍ *www.writerswrite.com*

Writer Groups

American Crime Writers League
✍ *www.acwl.org*

Erotica Readers and Writers Association
✍ *www.erotica-readers.com*

Horror Writers Association
✍ *www.horror.org*

Mystery Writers of America
✍ *www.mysterywriters.org*

National Writers Union (freelance writers working in U.S. markets)
✍ *www.nwu.org*

Romance Writers of America
✍ *www.rwanational.org*

Science Fiction and Fantasy Writers of America
✍ *www.sfwa.org*

Sisters in Crime (a mystery writer's group)
✍ *www.sistersincrime.org*

The Society for Creative Anachronism
✍ *www.sca.org*

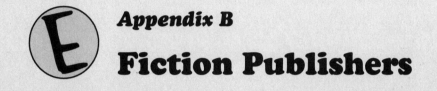

Appendix B

Fiction Publishers

Use the following listings to get submission guidelines and to submit your completed manuscript to the appropriate publishers.

Print Publisher (Large Press)

Dorchester Publishing

✉ 200 Madison Avenue, Suite 2000
New York, NY 10016

✍ *www.dorchesterpub.com*

Dorchester Publishing is an independent U.S. publisher of mass-market paperback books. They publish romance, mystery, horror, and Westerns under different imprints. Most of the lines are open to submission. Send an SASE for specific guidelines.

Harlequin Books

✉ 233 Broadway, Suite 1001
New York, NY 10279

✍ *www.eharlequin.com*

Harlequin Books is an independent publisher of romance books. They publish under different imprints. Most of the lines are open to submission. Send an SASE for specific guidelines.

Harper Collins

✉ 10 East 53rd Street
New York, NY 10022

✍ *www.harpercollins.com*

Harper Collins is an umbrella corporation for many different publishing houses. Together, they publish romance, mystery, science fiction, fantasy, and mainstream fiction. Most of the lines are "agented submission only." Send an SASE for specific guidelines available from each house.

Kensington Publishing Corp.

✉ 850 Third Avenue
New York, NY 10022

✍ *www.kensingtonbooks.com*

Kensington Books is the last remaining independent U.S. publisher of hardcover, trade, and mass-market paperback books. They publish romance, mystery, science fiction, fantasy, and mainstream fiction under different imprints. Most of the lines are "agented submission only." Send an SASE for specific guidelines available from each imprint.

Penguin Group

✉ 375 Hudson Street
New York, NY 10014

☞ *www.penguinputnam.com*

Penguin is an umbrella corporation for many different publishing houses. Together, they publish romance, mystery, science fiction, fantasy, and mainstream fiction. Most of the lines are "agented submission only." Send an SASE for specific guidelines available from each house.

Random House, Inc.

✉ 1745 Broadway
New York, NY 10019

☞ *www.randomhouse.com*

Random House is an umbrella corporation for many different publishing houses. Together, they publish romance, mystery, science fiction, fantasy, and mainstream fiction. Most of the lines are "agented submission only." Send an SASE for specific guidelines available from each house.

Simon and Schuster

✉ 1230 Avenue of the Americas
New York, NY 10020

☞ *www.simonsays.com*

Simon and Schuster is an umbrella corporation for many different publishing houses. Together, they publish romance, mystery, science fiction, fantasy, and mainstream fiction. Most of the lines are "agented submission only." Send an SASE for specific guidelines available from each house.

St. Martin's Press

✉ 175 Fifth Avenue
New York, NY 10010

☞ *www.stmartins.com*

St. Martin's Press is an umbrella corporation for many different publishing houses. Together, they publish romance, mystery, science fiction, fantasy, and mainstream fiction. Most of the lines are "agented submission only." Send an SASE for specific guidelines available from each house.

Time Warner Books

✉ 1271 Avenue of the Americas
New York, NY 10020

✐ *www.twbookmark.com*

Time Warner is an umbrella corporation for many different publishing houses. Together, they publish romance, mystery, science fiction, fantasy, and mainstream fiction. Most of the lines are "agented submission only." Send an SASE for specific guidelines available from each house.

Print Publisher (Small Press)

Avalon Books

✉ 160 Madison Avenue
New York, NY 10016

✐ *www.avalonbooks.com*

Avalon Books is a small press publisher of romance, mystery, and Westerns in hardback. Their imprints are open to submission. Send an SASE for specific guidelines.

Barbour Books

✉ 1810 Barbour Drive
Uhrichsville, OH 44683

✐ *www.barbourbooks.com*

Barbour Books is a small press publisher of contemporary Christian romance and fiction. Their imprints are open to submission. Send an SASE for specific guidelines.

Gardenia Press

✉ P.O. Box 18601
Milwaukee, WI 53218

✐ *www.gardeniapress.com*

Gardenia Press is a small press publisher of fantasy, horror, mainstream, mystery, romance, science fiction, Westerns, and young adult fiction. They are open to submission. Send an SASE for specific guidelines.

HAWK Publishing Group

✉ 7107 S. Yale Avenue, # 345
   Tulsa, OK 74136

✍ *www.hawkpub.com*

HAWK Publishing Group is a small publisher of adventure, fantasy, horror, mainstream, mystery, suspense, and science fiction. They are open to submission. Do not send SASE for information; use the guidelines page at their Web site.

ImaJinn Books

✉ P.O. Box 545
   Canon City, CO 81215-0545

✍ *www.imajinnbooks.com/for_writers.htm*

ImaJinn Books only publishes paranormal romance. They are open to submission. Send an SASE for guidelines.

Poisoned Pen Press

✉ 6962 E. First Avenue, Suite 103
   Scottsdale, AZ 85251

✍ *www.poisonedpenpress.com*

Poisoned Pen Press only publishes mystery. They are open to submission. Send an SASE for guidelines; submission guidelines are also available at their Web site.

Silver Dagger Mysteries

✉ P.O. Box 1261
   Johnson City, TN 37605

✍ *www.silverdaggermysteries.com*

Silver Dagger only publishes mystery. They are open to submission. Send an SASE for guidelines.

Willowgate Press

✉ P.O. Box 6529
Holliston, MA 01746

✍ *www.willowgatepress.com*

Willowgate Press is a small publisher of erotica, fantasy, horror, mainstream, mystery, romance, and science fiction. They are open to submission. Send an SASE for specific guidelines; submission guidelines are also available at their Web site.

E-Book Publishers

Atlantic Bridge Publishing

✍ *www.atlanticbridge.net*

Atlantic Bridge publishes fantasy, horror, mystery, romance, and science fiction. Check their guidelines carefully for online submission.

Awe-Struck E-Books

✍ *www.awe-struck.net*

Awe-Struck E-Books publishes fantasy, romance, and science fiction. Check their guidelines carefully for online submission.

C & M Online Media (Boson Books)

✍ *www.cmonline.com*

Boson Books publishes fantasy, horror, mystery, science fiction, and Westerns. Check their guidelines carefully for online submission.

Ellora's Cave Romantica E-Publishing

✍ *www.ellorascave.com*

Ellora's Cave publishes erotic romance in various subgenres. Check their guidelines carefully for online submission.

Fictionwise, Inc.

✍ *www.fictionwise.com*

Fictionwise publishes fantasy, horror, mystery, romance, and science fiction. Check their guidelines carefully for online submission.

Hard Shell Word Factory

✑ *www.hardshell.com*

Hard Shell Word Factory publishes fantasy, horror, mystery, romance, and science fiction. Check their guidelines carefully for online submission.

LTDBooks

✑ *www.ltdbooks.com*

LTDBooks publishes fantasy, horror, mystery, romance, and science fiction. Check their guidelines carefully for online submission.

New Concepts Publishing

✑ *www.newconceptspublishing.com*

New Concepts publishes fantasy, horror, mystery, romance, and science fiction. Check their guidelines carefully for online submission.

Wings ePress, Inc.

✑ *www.wings-press.com*

Wings ePress publishes fantasy, horror, mystery, romance, and science fiction. Check their guidelines carefully for online submission.

Writer's Exchange E-Publishing

✑ *http://ebooks.writers-exchange.com*

Writer's Exchange publishes fantasy, horror, mystery, romance, and science fiction. Check their guidelines carefully for online submission.

Index

The EVERYTHING Series!

BUSINESS & PERSONAL FINANCE

Everything® Accounting Book
Everything® Budgeting Book, 2nd Ed.
Everything® Business Planning Book
Everything® Coaching and Mentoring Book, 2nd Ed.
Everything® Fundraising Book
Everything® Get Out of Debt Book
Everything® Grant Writing Book, 2nd Ed.
Everything® Guide to Buying Foreclosures
Everything® Guide to Fundraising, $15.95
Everything® Guide to Mortgages
Everything® Guide to Personal Finance for Single Mothers
Everything® Home-Based Business Book, 2nd Ed.
Everything® Homebuying Book, 3rd Ed., $15.95
Everything® Homeselling Book, 2nd Ed.
Everything® Human Resource Management Book
Everything® Improve Your Credit Book
Everything® Investing Book, 2nd Ed.
Everything® Landlording Book
Everything® Leadership Book, 2nd Ed.
Everything® Managing People Book, 2nd Ed.
Everything® Negotiating Book
Everything® Online Auctions Book
Everything® Online Business Book
Everything® Personal Finance Book
Everything® Personal Finance in Your 20s & 30s Book, 2nd Ed.
Everything® Personal Finance in Your 40s & 50s Book, $15.95
Everything® Project Management Book, 2nd Ed.
Everything® Real Estate Investing Book
Everything® Retirement Planning Book
Everything® Robert's Rules Book, $7.95
Everything® Selling Book
Everything® Start Your Own Business Book, 2nd Ed.
Everything® Wills & Estate Planning Book

COOKING

Everything® Barbecue Cookbook
Everything® Bartender's Book, 2nd Ed., $9.95
Everything® Calorie Counting Cookbook
Everything® Cheese Book
Everything® Chinese Cookbook
Everything® Classic Recipes Book
Everything® Cocktail Parties & Drinks Book
Everything® College Cookbook
Everything® Cooking for Baby and Toddler Book
Everything® Diabetes Cookbook
Everything® Easy Gourmet Cookbook
Everything® Fondue Cookbook
Everything® Food Allergy Cookbook, $15.95
Everything® Fondue Party Book
Everything® Gluten-Free Cookbook
Everything® Glycemic Index Cookbook
Everything® Grilling Cookbook
Everything® Healthy Cooking for Parties Book, $15.95
Everything® Holiday Cookbook
Everything® Indian Cookbook
Everything® Lactose-Free Cookbook
Everything® Low-Cholesterol Cookbook

Everything® **Low-Fat High-Flavor Cookbook, 2nd Ed., $15.95**
Everything® Low-Salt Cookbook
Everything® Meals for a Month Cookbook
Everything® Meals on a Budget Cookbook
Everything® Mediterranean Cookbook
Everything® Mexican Cookbook
Everything® No Trans Fat Cookbook
Everything® One-Pot Cookbook, 2nd Ed., $15.95
Everything® Organic Cooking for Baby & Toddler Book, $15.95
Everything® Pizza Cookbook
Everything® Quick Meals Cookbook, 2nd Ed., $15.95
Everything® Slow Cooker Cookbook
Everything® Slow Cooking for a Crowd Cookbook
Everything® Soup Cookbook
Everything® Stir-Fry Cookbook
Everything® Sugar-Free Cookbook
Everything® Tapas and Small Plates Cookbook
Everything® Tex-Mex Cookbook
Everything® Thai Cookbook
Everything® Vegetarian Cookbook
Everything® Whole-Grain, High-Fiber Cookbook
Everything® Wild Game Cookbook
Everything® Wine Book, 2nd Ed.

GAMES

Everything® 15-Minute Sudoku Book, $9.95
Everything® 30-Minute Sudoku Book, $9.95
Everything® Bible Crosswords Book, $9.95
Everything® Blackjack Strategy Book
Everything® Brain Strain Book, $9.95
Everything® Bridge Book
Everything® Card Games Book
Everything® Card Tricks Book, $9.95
Everything® Casino Gambling Book, 2nd Ed.
Everything® Chess Basics Book
Everything® Christmas Crosswords Book, $9.95
Everything® Craps Strategy Book
Everything® Crossword and Puzzle Book
Everything® Crosswords and Puzzles for Quote Lovers Book, $9.95
Everything® Crossword Challenge Book
Everything® Crosswords for the Beach Book, $9.95
Everything® Cryptic Crosswords Book, $9.95
Everything® Cryptograms Book, $9.95
Everything® Easy Crosswords Book
Everything® Easy Kakuro Book, $9.95
Everything® Easy Large-Print Crosswords Book
Everything® Games Book, 2nd Ed.
Everything® Giant Book of Crosswords
Everything® Giant Sudoku Book, $9.95
Everything® Giant Word Search Book
Everything® Kakuro Challenge Book, $9.95
Everything® Large-Print Crossword Challenge Book
Everything® Large-Print Crosswords Book
Everything® Large-Print Travel Crosswords Book
Everything® Lateral Thinking Puzzles Book, $9.95
Everything® Literary Crosswords Book, $9.95
Everything® Mazes Book
Everything® Memory Booster Puzzles Book, $9.95

Everything® Movie Crosswords Book, $9.95
Everything® Music Crosswords Book, $9.95
Everything® Online Poker Book
Everything® Pencil Puzzles Book, $9.95
Everything® Poker Strategy Book
Everything® Pool & Billiards Book
Everything® Puzzles for Commuters Book, $9.95
Everything® Puzzles for Dog Lovers Book, $9.95
Everything® Sports Crosswords Book, $9.95
Everything® Test Your IQ Book, $9.95
Everything® Texas Hold 'Em Book, $9.95
Everything® Travel Crosswords Book, $9.95
Everything® Travel Mazes Book, $9.95
Everything® Travel Word Search Book, $9.95
Everything® TV Crosswords Book, $9.95
Everything® Word Games Challenge Book
Everything® Word Scramble Book
Everything® Word Search Book

HEALTH

Everything® Alzheimer's Book
Everything® Diabetes Book
Everything® First Aid Book, $9.95
Everything® Green Living Book
Everything® Health Guide to Addiction and Recovery
Everything® Health Guide to Adult Bipolar Disorder
Everything® Health Guide to Arthritis
Everything® Health Guide to Controlling Anxiety
Everything® Health Guide to Depression
Everything® Health Guide to Diabetes, 2nd Ed.
Everything® Health Guide to Fibromyalgia
Everything® Health Guide to Menopause, 2nd Ed.
Everything® Health Guide to Migraines
Everything® Health Guide to Multiple Sclerosis
Everything® Health Guide to OCD
Everything® Health Guide to PMS
Everything® Health Guide to Postpartum Care
Everything® Health Guide to Thyroid Disease
Everything® Hypnosis Book
Everything® Low Cholesterol Book
Everything® Menopause Book
Everything® Nutrition Book
Everything® Reflexology Book
Everything® Stress Management Book
Everything® Superfoods Book, $15.95

HISTORY

Everything® American Government Book
Everything® American History Book, 2nd Ed.
Everything® American Revolution Book, $15.95
Everything® Civil War Book
Everything® Freemasons Book
Everything® Irish History & Heritage Book
Everything® World War II Book, 2nd Ed.

HOBBIES

Everything® Candlemaking Book
Everything® Cartooning Book
Everything® Coin Collecting Book
Everything® Digital Photography Book, 2nd Ed.

Everything® Drawing Book
Everything® Family Tree Book, 2nd Ed.
Everything® Guide to Online Genealogy, $15.95
Everything® Knitting Book
Everything® Knots Book
Everything® Photography Book
Everything® Quilting Book
Everything® Sewing Book
Everything® Soapmaking Book, 2nd Ed.
Everything® Woodworking Book

HOME IMPROVEMENT

Everything® Feng Shui Book
Everything® Feng Shui Decluttering Book, $9.95
Everything® Fix-It Book
Everything® Green Living Book
Everything® Home Decorating Book
Everything® Home Storage Solutions Book
Everything® Homebuilding Book
Everything® Organize Your Home Book, 2nd Ed.

KIDS' BOOKS

All titles are $7.95
Everything® Fairy Tales Book, $14.95
Everything® Kids' Animal Puzzle & Activity Book
Everything® Kids' Astronomy Book
Everything® Kids' Baseball Book, 5th Ed.
Everything® Kids' Bible Trivia Book
Everything® Kids' Bugs Book
Everything® Kids' Cars and Trucks Puzzle and Activity Book
Everything® Kids' Christmas Puzzle & Activity Book
Everything® Kids' Connect the Dots
      Puzzle and Activity Book
Everything® Kids' Cookbook, 2nd Ed.
Everything® Kids' Crazy Puzzles Book
Everything® Kids' Dinosaurs Book
Everything® Kids' Dragons Puzzle and Activity Book
Everything® Kids' Environment Book $7.95
Everything® Kids' Fairies Puzzle and Activity Book
Everything® Kids' First Spanish Puzzle and Activity Book
Everything® Kids' Football Book
Everything® Kids' Geography Book
Everything® Kids' Gross Cookbook
Everything® Kids' Gross Hidden Pictures Book
Everything® Kids' Gross Jokes Book
Everything® Kids' Gross Mazes Book
Everything® Kids' Gross Puzzle & Activity Book
Everything® Kids' Halloween Puzzle & Activity Book
Everything® Kids' Hanukkah Puzzle and Activity Book
Everything® Kids' Hidden Pictures Book
Everything® Kids' Horses Book
Everything® Kids' Joke Book
Everything® Kids' Knock Knock Book
Everything® Kids' Learning French Book
Everything® Kids' Learning Spanish Book
Everything® Kids' Magical Science Experiments Book
Everything® Kids' Math Puzzles Book
Everything® Kids' Mazes Book
Everything® Kids' Money Book, 2nd Ed.
**Everything® Kids' Mummies, Pharaoh's, and Pyramids
      Puzzle and Activity Book**
Everything® Kids' Nature Book
Everything® Kids' Pirates Puzzle and Activity Book
Everything® Kids' Presidents Book
Everything® Kids' Princess Puzzle and Activity Book
Everything® Kids' Puzzle Book

Everything® Kids' Racecars Puzzle and Activity Book
Everything® Kids' Riddles & Brain Teasers Book
Everything® Kids' Science Experiments Book
Everything® Kids' Sharks Book
Everything® Kids' Soccer Book
Everything® Kids' Spelling Book
Everything® Kids' Spies Puzzle and Activity Book
Everything® Kids' States Book
Everything® Kids' Travel Activity Book
Everything® Kids' Word Search Puzzle and Activity Book

LANGUAGE

Everything® Conversational Japanese Book with CD, $19.95
Everything® French Grammar Book
Everything® French Phrase Book, $9.95
Everything® French Verb Book, $9.95
Everything® German Phrase Book, $9.95
Everything® German Practice Book with CD, $19.95
Everything® Inglés Book
Everything® Intermediate Spanish Book with CD, $19.95
Everything® Italian Phrase Book, $9.95
Everything® Italian Practice Book with CD, $19.95
Everything® Learning Brazilian Portuguese Book with CD, $19.95
Everything® Learning French Book with CD, 2nd Ed., $19.95
Everything® Learning German Book
Everything® Learning Italian Book
Everything® Learning Latin Book
Everything® Learning Russian Book with CD, $19.95
Everything® Learning Spanish Book
Everything® Learning Spanish Book with CD, 2nd Ed., $19.95
Everything® Russian Practice Book with CD, $19.95
Everything® Sign Language Book, $15.95
Everything® Spanish Grammar Book
Everything® Spanish Phrase Book, $9.95
Everything® Spanish Practice Book with CD, $19.95
Everything® Spanish Verb Book, $9.95
Everything® Speaking Mandarin Chinese Book with CD, $19.95

MUSIC

Everything® Bass Guitar Book with CD, $19.95
Everything® Drums Book with CD, $19.95
Everything® Guitar Book with CD, 2nd Ed., $19.95
Everything® Guitar Chords Book with CD, $19.95
Everything® Guitar Scales Book with CD, $19.95
Everything® Harmonica Book with CD, $15.95
Everything® Home Recording Book
Everything® Music Theory Book with CD, $19.95
Everything® Reading Music Book with CD, $19.95
Everything® Rock & Blues Guitar Book with CD, $19.95
Everything® Rock & Blues Piano Book with CD, $19.95
Everything® Rock Drums Book with CD, $19.95
Everything® Singing Book with CD, $19.95
Everything® Songwriting Book

NEW AGE

Everything® Astrology Book, 2nd Ed.
Everything® Birthday Personology Book
Everything® Celtic Wisdom Book, $15.95
Everything® Dreams Book, 2nd Ed.
Everything® Law of Attraction Book, $15.95
Everything® Love Signs Book, $9.95
Everything® Love Spells Book, $9.95
Everything® Palmistry Book
Everything® Psychic Book
Everything® Reiki Book

Everything® Sex Signs Book, $9.95
Everything® Spells & Charms Book, 2nd Ed.
Everything® Tarot Book, 2nd Ed.
Everything® Toltec Wisdom Book
Everything® Wicca & Witchcraft Book, 2nd Ed.

PARENTING

Everything® Baby Names Book, 2nd Ed.
Everything® Baby Shower Book, 2nd Ed.
Everything® Baby Sign Language Book with DVD
Everything® Baby's First Year Book
Everything® Birthing Book
Everything® Breastfeeding Book
Everything® Father-to-Be Book
Everything® Father's First Year Book
Everything® Get Ready for Baby Book, 2nd Ed.
Everything® Get Your Baby to Sleep Book, $9.95
Everything® Getting Pregnant Book
Everything® Guide to Pregnancy Over 35
Everything® Guide to Raising a One-Year-Old
Everything® Guide to Raising a Two-Year-Old
Everything® Guide to Raising Adolescent Boys
Everything® Guide to Raising Adolescent Girls
Everything® Mother's First Year Book
Everything® Parent's Guide to Childhood Illnesses
Everything® Parent's Guide to Children and Divorce
Everything® Parent's Guide to Children with ADD/ADHD
Everything® Parent's Guide to Children with Asperger's
      Syndrome
Everything® Parent's Guide to Children with Anxiety
Everything® Parent's Guide to Children with Asthma
Everything® Parent's Guide to Children with Autism
Everything® Parent's Guide to Children with Bipolar Disorder
Everything® Parent's Guide to Children with Depression
Everything® Parent's Guide to Children with Dyslexia
Everything® Parent's Guide to Children with Juvenile Diabetes
Everything® Parent's Guide to Children with OCD
Everything® Parent's Guide to Positive Discipline
Everything® Parent's Guide to Raising Boys
Everything® Parent's Guide to Raising Girls
Everything® Parent's Guide to Raising Siblings
**Everything® Parent's Guide to Raising Your
      Adopted Child**
Everything® Parent's Guide to Sensory Integration Disorder
Everything® Parent's Guide to Tantrums
Everything® Parent's Guide to the Strong-Willed Child
Everything® Parenting a Teenager Book
Everything® Potty Training Book, $9.95
Everything® Pregnancy Book, 3rd Ed.
Everything® Pregnancy Fitness Book
Everything® Pregnancy Nutrition Book
Everything® Pregnancy Organizer, 2nd Ed., $16.95
Everything® Toddler Activities Book
Everything® Toddler Book
Everything® Tween Book
Everything® Twins, Triplets, and More Book

PETS

Everything® Aquarium Book
Everything® Boxer Book
Everything® Cat Book, 2nd Ed.
Everything® Chihuahua Book
Everything® Cooking for Dogs Book
Everything® Dachshund Book
Everything® Dog Book, 2nd Ed.
Everything® Dog Grooming Book

Everything® Dog Obedience Book
Everything® Dog Owner's Organizer, $16.95
Everything® Dog Training and Tricks Book
Everything® German Shepherd Book
Everything® Golden Retriever Book
Everything® Horse Book, 2nd Ed., $15.95
Everything® Horse Care Book
Everything® Horseback Riding Book
Everything® Labrador Retriever Book
Everything® Poodle Book
Everything® Pug Book
Everything® Puppy Book
Everything® Small Dogs Book
Everything® Tropical Fish Book
Everything® Yorkshire Terrier Book

REFERENCE

Everything® American Presidents Book
Everything® Blogging Book
Everything® Build Your Vocabulary Book, $9.95
Everything® Car Care Book
Everything® Classical Mythology Book
Everything® Da Vinci Book
Everything® Einstein Book
Everything® Enneagram Book
Everything® Etiquette Book, 2nd Ed.
Everything® Family Christmas Book, $15.95
Everything® Guide to C. S. Lewis & Narnia
Everything® Guide to Divorce, 2nd Ed., $15.95
Everything® Guide to Edgar Allan Poe
Everything® Guide to Understanding Philosophy
Everything® Inventions and Patents Book
Everything® Jacqueline Kennedy Onassis Book
Everything® John F. Kennedy Book
Everything® Mafia Book
Everything® Martin Luther King Jr. Book
Everything® Pirates Book
Everything® Private Investigation Book
Everything® Psychology Book
Everything® Public Speaking Book, $9.95
Everything® Shakespeare Book, 2nd Ed.

RELIGION

Everything® Angels Book
Everything® Bible Book
Everything® Bible Study Book with CD, $19.95
Everything® Buddhism Book
Everything® Catholicism Book
Everything® Christianity Book
Everything® Gnostic Gospels Book
Everything® Hinduism Book, $15.95
Everything® History of the Bible Book
Everything® Jesus Book
Everything® Jewish History & Heritage Book
Everything® Judaism Book
Everything® Kabbalah Book
Everything® Koran Book
Everything® Mary Book
Everything® Mary Magdalene Book
Everything® Prayer Book

Everything® Saints Book, 2nd Ed.
Everything® Torah Book
Everything® Understanding Islam Book
Everything® Women of the Bible Book
Everything® World's Religions Book

SCHOOL & CAREERS

Everything® Career Tests Book
Everything® College Major Test Book
Everything® College Survival Book, 2nd Ed.
Everything® Cover Letter Book, 2nd Ed.
Everything® Filmmaking Book
Everything® Get-a-Job Book, 2nd Ed.
Everything® Guide to Being a Paralegal
Everything® Guide to Being a Personal Trainer
Everything® Guide to Being a Real Estate Agent
Everything® Guide to Being a Sales Rep
Everything® Guide to Being an Event Planner
Everything® Guide to Careers in Health Care
Everything® Guide to Careers in Law Enforcement
Everything® Guide to Government Jobs
Everything® Guide to Starting and Running a Catering
    Business
Everything® Guide to Starting and Running a Restaurant
**Everything® Guide to Starting and Running
    a Retail Store**
Everything® Job Interview Book, 2nd Ed.
Everything® New Nurse Book
Everything® New Teacher Book
Everything® Paying for College Book
Everything® Practice Interview Book
Everything® Resume Book, 3rd Ed.
Everything® Study Book

SELF-HELP

Everything® Body Language Book
Everything® Dating Book, 2nd Ed.
Everything® Great Sex Book
**Everything® Guide to Caring for Aging Parents,
    $15.95**
Everything® Self-Esteem Book
Everything® Self-Hypnosis Book, $9.95
Everything® Tantric Sex Book

SPORTS & FITNESS

Everything® Easy Fitness Book
Everything® Fishing Book
Everything® Guide to Weight Training, $15.95
Everything® Krav Maga for Fitness Book
Everything® Running Book, 2nd Ed.
Everything® Triathlon Training Book, $15.95

TRAVEL

Everything® Family Guide to Coastal Florida
Everything® Family Guide to Cruise Vacations
Everything® Family Guide to Hawaii
Everything® Family Guide to Las Vegas, 2nd Ed.
Everything® Family Guide to Mexico
Everything® Family Guide to New England, 2nd Ed.

Everything® Family Guide to New York City, 3rd Ed.
**Everything® Family Guide to Northern California
    and Lake Tahoe**
Everything® Family Guide to RV Travel & Campgrounds
Everything® Family Guide to the Caribbean
Everything® Family Guide to the Disneyland® Resort, California
    Adventure®, Universal Studios®, and the Anaheim
    Area, 2nd Ed.
Everything® Family Guide to the Walt Disney World Resort®,
    Universal Studios®, and Greater Orlando, 5th Ed.
Everything® Family Guide to Timeshares
Everything® Family Guide to Washington D.C., 2nd Ed.

WEDDINGS

Everything® Bachelorette Party Book, $9.95
Everything® Bridesmaid Book, $9.95
Everything® Destination Wedding Book
Everything® Father of the Bride Book, $9.95
Everything® Green Wedding Book, $15.95
Everything® Groom Book, $9.95
Everything® Jewish Wedding Book, 2nd Ed., $15.95
Everything® Mother of the Bride Book, $9.95
Everything® Outdoor Wedding Book
Everything® Wedding Book, 3rd Ed.
Everything® Wedding Checklist, $9.95
Everything® Wedding Etiquette Book, $9.95
Everything® Wedding Organizer, 2nd Ed., $16.95
Everything® Wedding Shower Book, $9.95
Everything® Wedding Vows Book, 3rd Ed., $9.95
Everything® Wedding Workout Book
Everything® Weddings on a Budget Book, 2nd Ed., $9.95

WRITING

Everything® Creative Writing Book
Everything® Get Published Book, 2nd Ed.
Everything® Grammar and Style Book, 2nd Ed.
Everything® Guide to Magazine Writing
Everything® Guide to Writing a Book Proposal
Everything® Guide to Writing a Novel
Everything® Guide to Writing Children's Books
Everything® Guide to Writing Copy
Everything® Guide to Writing Graphic Novels
Everything® Guide to Writing Research Papers
Everything® Guide to Writing a Romance Novel, $15.95
Everything® Improve Your Writing Book, 2nd Ed.
Everything® Writing Poetry Book